THE STORY
OF A SOLDIER

1940-1971

**THE AIRBORNE SPIRIT AND RECOLLECTIONS
OF COLONEL EDWARD S. MEHOSKY (RET.)
U.S. ARMY, INFANTRY**

To Ray,
Best regards,
Edward Mehosky

Ed Mehosky
717-766-5659

THE STORY OF A SOLDIER

1940–1971

THE AIRBORNE SPIRIT AND RECOLLECTIONS
OF COLONEL EDWARD S. MEHOSKY (RET.)
U.S. ARMY, INFANTRY

IVAN PAUL MEHOSKY

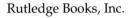

Rutledge Books, Inc.   Danbury, CT

Rutledge Books, Inc.
107 Mill Plain Road, Danbury, CT 06811
1-800-278-8533
www.rutledgebooks.com

Manufactured in the United States of America

Cataloging in Publication Data
Mehosky, Ivan Paul
    The Story Of A Soldier

    ISBN: 1-58244-124-3

    1. Memoir -- Soldier -- U.S. Army -- Twentieth Century. 2. World
War II. 3. Korean War. 4. Vietnam War.

Library of Congress Card Number: 00-109915

DEDICATION

I thank God, Father, Son and the Holy Spirit for giving me the second chance in this life to complete this story.

I dedicate this book to my hero, my wonderful and loving father, Edward Stanley Mehosky. His life, and hence this story, I hope, will be an inspiration to those who read its contents as it has been to me.

Ivan Paul Mehosky
24 July, 2000
North East, MD

TABLE OF CONTENTS

PART I

IT SEEMS SO LONG AGO, SO FAR AWAY, YESTERDAY,
WHEN WE JUMPED INTO NORMANDY.

Edward S. Mehosky
St. Leonard, Maryland
December, 1999

CHAPTER 1

NOT ACCORDING TO PLAN

Normandy, France, the Cotetin Peninsula, the low lying hedgerow country above the town of Carentan. It is after one in the morning, June 6, 1944. We are the first wave of the allied invasion of German-held France, paratroopers of the U.S. 101st and 82nd Divisions. I am from the 3rd Battalion, 506th Parachute Infantry Regiment of the 101st Airborne Division. Having made it down safely through heavy anti-aircraft fire, I land in a field bound by earthen mounds of hedgerows. I'm alone—no one from my platoon, those eighteen guys that I jumped with, are anywhere around. I thought they were right behind me when I jumped. I wonder what happened to them? Were we scattered that much? We were supposed to drop over a place called Drop Zone 'D', but intensive enemy ground fire disrupted the flight plan and our pilot took immediate evasive action and missed the intended drop zone. I wonder how the rest of the battalion fared? I have got to get my bearings. The best I can figure is that my position is a couple of miles north of the town of Carentan, because I could see the haze of lights in the distance as I was descending—probably a mile or so west of where I'm supposed to be.

Two paratroopers clunk down near me. They are from the 501st. Machine gun fire erupts off to my left front and we scramble on all fours to the only bit of cover available, which is only a cluster of tree saplings in the middle of the field. All I've got is my M-1 and a couple of hand grenades; everything else was lost during the jump. We are in a prone position behind those skinny saplings that provide a little cover, but our legs are exposed. As I prepare to throw a grenade, I hear a clicking sound that reminds me of my machine gun crew, and hesitate. Now German voices can be heard from that direction. I hand the grenade to the soldier on my right to throw while I pump a couple of rounds into the nest. In the next instance, the Germans swing their fire in our direction. A burst of lead rakes our position as chunks of earth are chewed up before my eyes. We are vulnerable. The soldier on my left is hit and killed. A second burst hits me in the thigh and right foot. Luckily these wounds are not debilitating, although my foot is completely numb. The other soldier has thrown his grenade and silences the enemy fire. This fire has delayed my getting to the objective area, which I believe to be east of my present location. I know we have to move away from the enemy, fast!

I had seen what I thought was a break in the hedgerow behind me. We crawl in that direction. On approach, we hear the 'click-clack' cricket sound used for identification by American paratroopers. There in the hedgerow are twelve paratroopers, also from the 501st Regiment. I don't know anyone, but I'm the only officer here and quickly take charge. A plan is formulated. One of the soldiers tells me that he scouted around and found a gate that opens to a dirt road. To our front, in the distance, can be heard sporadic small arms fire. That's the direction I know we must go. With scouts forward, we cross the road and re-form on the other side. Light is just breaking on the horizon. We are just below the road embankment and I make my observations. Over to my left are a farmhouse and a barn. To my front the land rolls downhill, and to my immediate left is a line of evenly spaced trees that gradually taper into a vast, inundated, area-flooded field. It is about 150 yards to the water's edge. Off in the distance in front of us I see signs of activity, troops of the 501st, I believe. Way off to my right, I can see a guard walking back and forth. The only thing open to us is to traverse the water and get to that road on the other side. We move out and follow the tree line to the edge of the water. I take my position in the middle of the column. From the tree line we move steadily through knee-deep water in a left diagonal direction toward the road embankment in front of us.

We are not long in the water when we are hit by automatic fire somewhere from the left! "Get down!" I yell as I drop to the water. Those who try to run are cut down. Bullets are ripping through the water like angry hornets around me! I zigzag like a madman under the water, clutching, pulling, kicking, and propelling myself in every direction until, mercifully, I come upon a sand spit covered by a fallen tree. I take cover. Half my body is on the spit, half in the water. Machine gun fire is being poured on us from up on the road that we crossed earlier. One of the men has come up alongside of me, but he doesn't want to stay. He says he wants to get to his buddies. Against my advice, he suddenly makes a run for it and is shot down. I can't see any of the men, but I hear moans of those wounded out in the water. The German fire doesn't let up. I'm mad and fire off a couple of rounds. The enemy answers with a severe peppering that ravages my position. I'm pinned down and can't move. All I can do is wait. I'll take my chances when it gets dark. My day will be spent in the water, wet, cold, and hungry. It's been eighteen hours since I ate and all I've got is a chocolate bar. I want to do something, but I can't, not now.

Toward the middle of the day, I hear the rush of what sounds like a freight train, then the terrific concussion of sixteen-inch shells raining all around my position out in the water. The earth around me shakes and trembles. I am sweating, because I think the next one might be my number; that's how close it is. Not only are my ears ringing, but my whole body also shakes as each explosion sends a fountain of water and mud high in the air and right down on top of me! Then, as I raise my head, I watch those shells stair-step right up to the road from where the enemy is firing and blow the hell out of everything that is up there! This heavy stuff must be fire from one of the invasion ships offshore, and probably one of their forward observers with the 501st is directing it.

It's not too much longer before dark. That was close! I might get picked off if I try to move out. No, I'll wait until dark, then move in the direction of the road we were trying to get to this morning. I think some of the men from the front of the column made it to a depression out there.

As the afternoon fades, thoughts cloud my head. My mind wanders and for a fleeting moment, I see a small boy, safe and secure. I know him. Then I hear the sound of the streets and the voices of my pals, the guys I grew up with. Now I see a young man turning into a soldier who becomes a leader. All that has happened in five short years seems like a blur. I seem to be a little warmer now, but everything seems so far away and so long ago.

PART II

JEDZ TWOJE KAPUSTE I PIEROGI A BEDZIESZ
MAIL DUZE NOGI

CHAPTER 2

BEGINNINGS

The south side of Reading, Pennsylvania lies below Never Sink Mountain and along the Schuylkill River. It was on the south side of Reading, in my grandfather's grocery store on the corner of Willow and Minor Streets where I was born to Mary and Stanley Mehosky on November 16, 1921.

Our family name of origin was Mechowski. My grandparents, Bernard and Anna, and their children, Ida and baby Frank, arrived in this country from Silesia in 1890, and settled in the mining town of Shenandoah, Pennsylvania. By 1920, my grandparents and my parents relocated to Reading.

Reading was known as a working man's town in those days. In my neighborhood, the south side, lived people who had resettled from Europe years ago.

My grandparents were Jadeck and Babka to me. Everybody in our house spoke Polish. It wasn't until I entered the second grade that I learned to speak English. If the grownups didn't want us kids to hear something, they'd speak in German(since the Germans where in control of Silesia in those years, they required everyone to speak German). Dad told me how Jadek used to talk to me in Polish when I was a child about his home in the old country, Silesia, what is now the western part of Poland. Bernard worked in the coal mines. He would tell me how, during one of the large migrations of those years, he walked to the German port of Hamburg in 1890, leading a small horse drawn cart that carried his wife, Anna, and their two children. Jadeck told me the story again and again, but I was too young to remember.

The store went bankrupt after Jadeck died, but my parents tried to make a go of it by using part of the house to sell ice cream and penny candy.

My dad was known as "Stiney" up in Shenandoah, but he was best known around the coal regions as an amateur fighter who fought under the name, "Kid Jackson." When he moved to Reading, he used to work out on the heavy punching bag and on the side, trained amateur fighters. One of those guys was a promising featherweight named Joe Suski. It was guys like Joe, Indian and Butch, friends of my dad who were always around the house and kept an eye on me.

During the summer of 1928, my sister, Augusta, "Gussie" as she was called, came to live with us in Reading. She and I did not get along at first. We were always fighting over something, mostly when doing the dishes. Dad settled our fights by putting boxing gloves on us and letting us go at it until we had enough and apologized to each other. That was Dad's way of settling disputes. He never hit us for fear of hurting us.

When you live through a time like the Great Depression of the 1930's, you never forget. Those were hard, tough years when there wasn't much money or many jobs, and everyone did whatever it took to survive. Like hundreds of other men, Dad went to work for the Works Progress Administration, the WPA as it was known, digging ditches for a nickel an hour. In the evenings and on weekends, he was cutting grass on the sides of hills up at the city park. Mom scrubbed floors. When I got a little older and Dad was running for city alderman, I helped pass out leaflets in the neighborhoods.

Nothing came easy but people were always finding ways to sustain themselves. There was a man a couple of houses over who had all kinds of cats around his house and was always taking in cats that no one wanted. Everyone thought of him as a kind man. Over time, the neighborhood cats began to disappear and people got suspicious. They found out later that this guy had been living very nicely on boiled cat! Then there was the man in the next neighborhood who had pigeons on his roof, only to find out he was eating them. I can remember eating lard on bread. My favorites were cabbage, dumplings, potatoes, pretzels and day-old bread. We didn't have much, but we got by, and we always had enough to eat.

Everybody had a small garden out back. You'd see fruit trees, grapevines, tomatoes, cabbage, and pole beans all over the place, and it was never a problem getting something to eat. Sometimes you had to run like mad, though. Then there were the industrious folks, like my dad and his friends, who did things on the side for extra cash. They had a home-made distillery unit they made from scratch and set up in the backyard where they brewed all kinds of drinks from potatoes, corn or apples, or whatever was more plentiful at the time. The way I heard it was that the stuff they made was strictly for indigestion. What they didn't drink, they sold. They stored the still in the outhouse so no one would find it.

Babush was my mom's mother. She was from Lithuania. She came to live with us at the hotel, on the corner of Wunder and Muhlenberg Streets. I remember Babush always asking me in Polish, because she spoke no English, to bring her beer. Then she'd hand me this large metal pail that had a lid and I'd go and fill it with beer. It was Babush who used to sing to me at dinner time: "Jedz twoje kapuste i pierogi a bedziesz mial duze nogi," which translates to, "Eat your cabbage and dumplings and you'll get big legs." What this really meant was you'd grow up big and strong if you ate your cabbage and dumplings. Having big legs was a sign of strength.

Once I was out playing when I cut my knee on a rusted tin can and ran home bleeding profusely. The knee got infected and started to swell. Babush washed it out, went to the backyard and picked two leaves from a wild broad-leafed plant they called "bapka liefche," or "grandmother's leaf," wrapped them around my knee, and in no time the infection was gone and the wound healed perfectly. I never had to have stitches. There were lots of things the grandmothers from the old country knew that died with them.

When summer came and school was finished for another year, my pals and I went swimming in the dam located about three miles from where I lived. Our lunch consisted of whatever fruits and vegetables we could carry after cutting through the farmers' fields. There used to be a baseball diamond there. The area near the baseball field was where we used to get cashmere root and where the sumac grew. We'd clear out all the sumac, then dig up enough cashmere roots so every guy had his own pile. Those roots were yellowish-white in color and smelled like a carrot when you cut off the top. Once peeled, you could eat the tasty, white, sweet meat all day. All I know is that these things grew wild and we ate a ton of them. Who knows, maybe they were of great benefit to the body.

The kids of my day were outside all the time. It seemed that we played from morning until night up on South Street and the hill above. Everything revolved around the cemetery wall and the light post, which served as home base, a meeting place or a rally point. Chase was one of our favorite games and the one we played the most. We marked the boundaries by streets, usually starting at South Street and winding up with an area that was comprised of about ten city blocks. Once sides were chosen, one team moved out to hide while the other team remained at the cemetery wall to start their count to 200 before pursuing. The skill was in finding good hiding places while trying to avoid being captured, all the while steadily advancing to reach home base. The other team had their lookouts posted and would try to flush out players in hiding and funnel them to areas where other pursuing players were set up. From that point, it was usually a foot race to see who would reach the wall first. The object was for the pursuing team to capture as many opposing players without letting them get back to the cemetery wall. We'd play for hours and hours, sometimes not going home until it was time to eat, or the ultimate, playing at night! There was a heck of a lot of running and hiding, short cuts, and quick dashes. It was sort of like playing war.

CHAPTER 3

THE DIAMOND BOYS

When I was ten and lived on Maple Street, all my friends called me Eddie. All of us guys used to greet each other with a "yo" in front of the name, like "Yo Bowlie, can you come out yet?" They'd come to the house and yell up to the window, "Yooo Ed-die! Yooo Ed-die," over and over until someone made an appearance. Even strangers, people you didn't know, addressed someone that way: "Yo, what'd you say? Yo, yous guys, I'm talking to yous guys!"

Playing baseball became the dominant activity, whether pick-up games or organized ball. It seemed that we were always playing baseball. Every playground around the city sponsored teams. Depending on which part of town the playground was located in determined how much money was provided for that team. I started organized ball in the midget leagues. We didn't have uniforms, new gloves, shoes or anything like that, and we really didn't care. Our equipment was used, handed down stuff. It never dawned on us we were without; we were just happy to be playing ball for the fun of it. That year the city championship came down to us, the south side champs, versus the champs from 11th and Pike in the north side of the city. The game became a contest for bragging rights among the adults, something like the poor people from the southern neighborhoods versus the rich from the north side. The game was played at Lauer's Park. I remember a big crowd of people rooting for our team, holding up big slabs of bacon on sticks, and chanting, "Bring home the bacon, boys!" That team from 11th and Pike looked like a bunch of professionals with their brand new uniforms and gloves, and there we were in our everyday clothes and pipe mill sneakers. What a contrast! We won the game and were the talk of the town.

During my teenage years, it seemed like everyone was playing "Nipsy." To play, you'd take a broom, cut the end off so you just had a long stick handle, then take the leftover part and cut off a six-inch piece and taper it at both ends. This piece was called the nipsy. You'd strike the nipsy so it would fly up in the air and then hit it with the stick handle, like in baseball, driving it as far as you could. Then you'd call out the distance from where you hit the nipsy to where it landed and the other fellow would measure it. If it was not close to what you called, he would take a turn and the sequence would repeat. Nipsy helped me develop a keen sense of range estimation which would help me later on.

Junior High passed quickly. By the time I was in high school, I was walking eight to ten miles every day to practice. During those summers, 1936-1938, I played baseball for Gregg Post American Legion Keystone Juniors. Doc Silva was my coach. At Reading High, I played varsity football and baseball under Coach Harold Rock. I played guard on the football squad, and shortstop, catcher, and first base during the baseball seasons. After graduation, I played organized football for the North End Collegians. I played against a lot of tough opponents, but none quite like "Fat Pepe." Pepe was a tough, rough, brawler who got into fights all the time. Most of the time he'd start a fight just to get the edge on his opponent. The first time I played against him, he threw some dirt in my face and leveled me. But that was the only time, because after that, I more than held my own against him. I knew what to expect. We developed a common respect for each other and soon became good friends.

I began to seriously entertain the idea of trying to play professional baseball. I played for Doc Silva's American Legion Post # 40, and got a lot of encouragement; the caliber of play was one step below the professional minor leagues. Doc Silva was a well-known former International League player and current sports editor for the *Reading Eagle* newspaper.

In those years we were all caught up with what we were going to do when we graduated. The world was changing faster than we knew, and who could see what was in store for us?

CHAPTER 4

A WORKING EDUCATION

Having graduated from high school in June 1939, at seventeen, I either had to do something with baseball or find a job. There had been scouts from the professional minor leagues and some college coaches interested in me. I was offered two baseball scholarships, one from Villanova and the other from St. Peters. At the same time, Congressman Guy Moser, a close friend of my dad, wanted to get me appointed to West Point. All he needed was my parents' consent. My parents had the wrong concept. I guess my mom and dad thought it was going to cost them a lot of money and since we didn't have much money in those days, well, they said I'd have to first work for a year, then we could talk about college.

When November 1939 rolled in and I turned eighteen, I got a job at Parrish Pressed Steel, over on the northwest part of town, working on the automobile frame assembly line. There the automobile frames hung vertically on hooks on a conveyor. The automobile frames moved on the conveyor from station to station. At one such station, welders attached cross brackets, then the frames moved down to the end of the conveyor to the jig station where the Dutchman and I worked. This Dutchman had to be one of the strongest men I ever saw. He was tall, muscular and wiry, not an ounce of fat anywhere, had a face like a boxer who had been in one too many fights, and he had these big hands, as big as toilet seats, I'd guess.

Everybody there was an old-timer, except me. Once those big, heavy, 800 to 900 pound frames arrived at our station, the big Dutchman would release the hooks and we'd have to physically manhandle each frame, first lowering it down to our waist so the frame held in a horizontal position, then carrying that heavy frame about thirty feet to another station called the jig. The trick was to swing that frame, in one motion, onto this platform a foot higher than our waist and onto the jig. There an inspector checked the fit, and if anything was off balance, he'd make a chalk mark and we'd pound out that defect with sledgehammers until the inspector was satisfied. From the jig we moved the frame to the ramp, which required the same thing: two men giving the old "heave ho" to these heavy, steel automobile frames, in unison, from the height of our waists to the height of our shoulders.

Many times that first week, I dropped my end before getting to that stage. Once we got the frame up on the ramp, I was required to push the damn thing down to the waiting repair crew forty feet away. My first effort resulted in the frame traveling only halfway. So in the face of whistles, hoots, and swearing from the crew at the end of the ramp, who, by the way, didn't lift a finger to help, I had to run down and strong arm the thing to the end of the ramp. By this time, the frames on the conveyor had stacked up at our station, so I was getting it good from the Dutchman and the inspector, too.

The assembly line process was interrupted, more frames were stacking up, and now the welders started hollering. They were all hollering and swearing oaths because down time meant money! The foreman had a scoreboard on the wall where he'd mark every frame completed against the daily quota, and every frame completed above that resulted in a bonus. That's why I was catching hell from everyone. Not wanting to make the same mistake, I gave the next frame on the ramp an extra hard push, and wham! Right off the far end of the ramp it sailed, scattering the repair crew like bowling pins! I got cussed out again. Every time I dropped my end of the frame, which happened a lot during that first day, the big Dutchman would swear at me in German and make these wild gestures with his hands. He was letting me know the frames were heavy enough without having to apply extra muscle trying to pick them up off the floor!

By lunch break we had caught up. I was so hungry I devoured five ham and onion sandwiches, a couple of apples, and a quart of milk. By afternoon I was beginning to get the knack of all this lifting and pushing, working in unison when we got the word from the foreman: "The next ten are convertibles." Convertible frames were heavier than regular automobile frames because they put all the weight in the frame. Heavier? I was starting to hate this job. My first day was a total nightmare! I was never so sore, and never so completely exhausted and beat in my life. Every muscle in my body ached. I could barely move. By the time I left the job six months later however, I was strong and muscular, muscle-bound like a bull.

In the spring of 1940, Mobil Gas Company sponsored a baseball team and had advertised for tryouts at Lauer's Park in Reading. I tried out as a catcher, but made the team as a first baseman. I was too old for American Legion ball and this was another level up. They entered us in a tournament where our first stop was in New York, and after beating a couple of teams from the Reading area, we went out to Pittsburgh's Forbes Field, but got eliminated in a close one, 5-4. I had hit a home run in that game to tie the score.

I was still thinking of a baseball career during that long ride home. I went back to sandlot baseball and hooked up with one of the local traveling teams in the area: Epherta. Mr. Weaver, a shop teacher from the high school, coached the team. His two sons also played on the team. We were paid meal money plus gas money if we had a car. In a game later that summer, I was taking a lead off first base when the pitcher made a pick-off move. I attempted to slide back to first, but my cleat caught a rock and turned my ankle as the full force of the slide hit the corner of the bag. I fractured my right leg just above the anklebone and had to be taken to the hospital. They put a cast on my leg, but it was so tight that the leg began to swell and hurt like heck. Finally they put on a walking cast.

As July rolled into August, I was mostly just hanging around the neighborhood at 11th and Muhlenberg. The cast had come off, but the ankle still swelled, especially when I tried to put weight on it. I was beginning to realize that my baseball days were over.

One of the men who hung around my house was "Indian", a short, hatchet-faced, rough and tumble fellow, who had black hair combed straight back, a hawk nose, and small, penetrating eyes. He reminded me of a bird. He was a friend of my dad's and always seemed to be there. Indian was one of those guys who had a great admiration for the state police, mostly because they wore the old campaign hat like they wore in the war, which he thought looked so sharp. "Hey Eddie, look at that," he said, pointing to the state police officers across the street. "That's what you ought to do, Eddie. Go join the army so you can wear one of them hats."

I didn't say anything, just looked in that direction and starting giving it some thought. "The army, huh?" I thought. "At least it would be better than what I'm doing now, which is nothing! Too late to get into college, don't have a job, can't play baseball anymore, so why not the army?" I guess that must have made a strong impression on me. I mean, the image of being a soldier in uniform with a sharp-looking hat and all, appealed to me; and, of course, there was the situation with my leg. Maybe this was the best thing I could do. I did not deliberate long in reaching my decision.

Having made some initial inquiries, but not telling anyone, not even my mom and dad, I was told to go down to the army recruiting office located in the post office building at 5th and Washington. I was to report there at 0700 on Monday for my initial physical examination and tests. Once that was completed, I would have to get my parents to sign the papers, then make arrangements to go to Philadelphia for the swearing in ceremony. There was just one small problem. How was I going to pass my physical with my leg the way it was, when putting weight on it would make my ankle swell? I got a good ankle brace, tightened it around the ankle, tried putting more weight on it, and started walking as long as I could, stopping only when the pain and swelling became too great. I'd rest a little, put some ice on it, and then try to walk a little more. I kept tabs on when my ankle swelled. Maybe I could get through the physical if I could get down there when it wasn't so swollen, just do what was needed, try to act natural, and get through it. "Yeah, that's what I'll do," I thought. "No sweat!"

Bright and early the next morning, Stanley Godeck took me by car to the recruiting station. He let me off at the side entrance so as not to attract attention, and I hopped up to the door on my left foot and went inside. In the same manner, I negotiated two flights of stairs up to the second floor, then hopped down the hall to the enlistment office, where I took a seat with my high school buddies, Edward Melerski, Clayton Shaeffer, and Phil Wessner. We had all decided to enlist together. When my name was called, I walked into the office without even a hint of a limp. I passed the physical, even the requirement to hop vigorously on my right foot, then the left. With papers in hand, I walked down to the end of the hall, found a chair and took off my shoe; my ankle had swelled to twice its normal size.

When I got home and broke the news, Mom cried and Dad just shook his head, and Gussie was hugging me, tears in her eyes, not wanting to let go. It seemed the whole neighborhood knew because there were well wishers coming around all afternoon.

PART III

BROWN SHOES AND LEGGINS, SPRINGFIELD RIFLE, CAMPAIGN HAT, AND HALF-DAY DUTY. I CAME IN AT THE TWILIGHT YEARS OF THE OLD PEACETIME ARMY.

Corporal Eddie Mehosky

CHAPTER 5

THE 12ᵀᴴ INFANTRY REGIMENT

On August 14, 1940, the three of us, Melerski, Shaeffer and I, got on a bus for Philadelphia to be sworn into the army. There we were administered the Oath of Allegiance..."and defend the Constitution of the United States, so help you God."

"I do."

"Congratulation men, you are now in the United States Army. You will report to the 12th Infantry Regiment at Arlington Cantonement, Virginia. Sergeant Sheppard here will escort you to the train for Washington, D.C. Good luck, men."

It was early afternoon when our train pulled into Union Station in Washington, D.C. during a hot, muggy, typical August day, 1940. Corporal Daniel B. Campbell introduced himself and had us recruits get to the trucks for our ride over to Ft. Myer, Virginia, to the in-processing building, where we would draw our basic gear. Each man was issued two pair of soft brown, over-the-ankle shoes, one pair for drill, the other for dress; blue denim fatigues and shirt; and a round, floppy hat. That was the fatigue uniform of the day. The other gear would be issued at our new home on the south side of Ft. Myer, known as Arlington Cantonement. Today, that area is the north parking lot of the Pentagon. We were taken over to our barracks and down to the orderly room for further assignment. I was a buck private assigned to K Company, First Platoon, under the command of Captain J.M. Churchill.

Corporal Campbell put us in formation and then proceeded to read us the riot act, "...and when I say lights out, no talking, I mean lights out, no f——— talking, and no f——— whispering, period! Is that understood?" The corporal was a tough, old army soldier with a lot of power and authority, as all corporals were in that army, and if we ever talked after lights out, as we did once or twice until we learned better, why, he'd throw a big, old brown shoe down the length of the barracks hall where it would slam into one of the metal wall lockers. "Damn it all, when I say no f——— talking, I mean keep it the f— quiet!" After that you could hear only the crickets and the soft Virginia breeze.

During those days weapons were stored right there in our barracks in a weapons rack, under lock and key. The sturdy Springfields were carefully issued and controlled by the CQ (charge of quarters). Every morning at 0600 we'd fall out for reveille, march to the mess hall for breakfast, then back to the barracks where the CQ would open the rack and issue weapons. One of the first things you were required to do was memorize the serial number of the rifle issued to you, and you had better have known it at the next formation. Then we'd break into small groups where we were taught close order drill (the Manual of Arms), how to properly salute, whom to salute, how to stand at attention, and all the facing movements.

Most of basic training was taught right there in the unit under the watchful eye of the sergeant. As you progressed, you were taught how to read a compass, then elementary map reading, and more drilling. Then they would take us behind the barracks, each man with his rifle, where we'd get into the prone position and take aim at the panoramic view over Arlington Cemetery. Here we practiced the dry run principles of marksmanship. Our instructors made sure you held the rifle properly, and that you held your breath and squeezed the trigger with no jerky movements. It was the basis for fire discipline: you fire exactly the way you practice, and that's how we became proficient. If a soldier followed the principles of dry run, breathing, knowing what a good sighting on a target looked like holding his breath and squeezing the trigger, he could consistently hit the bull's eye. We did a lot of sighting our weapons by what was known as "triangulation" (a method of simulating firing three shots, using correct breathing and squeezing techniques, and having a partner with a bull's eye target in front of you to mark center, left, right, and connect the three points). A good, clean, steady shot, fire as you practice, was always emphasized.

We were a spit and polish unit, the "President's Own," there for duty at Arlington Cemetery and the Tomb of the Unknown Soldier. We didn't have the dress uniform they wear today. We wore the regular khaki duty uniform, spit-polished brown shoes, shirt and tie, and the army campaign hat of World War I. We learned all the precision movements of the Manual of Arms through constant drill. If we weren't drilling, we were sighting our weapons and practicing the trigger squeeze. Back at the barracks, we learned how to spit polish shoes: strip 'em, dye 'em, spit polish 'em, always army brown. You learned to keep them that way all the time or catch it from the corporal or sergeant. You learned how to keep your uniform neat and pressed and how to keep your wall locker to standard, always ready for inspection. Making your bunk was an exact science in and of itself. I mean, it had to be right and tight, just like a drum, so that the corporal conducting morning inspection could bounce a quarter off it. That's the way the army wanted it. At the end of each bunk was a footlocker where you stored your personal items. Personal items had to be rolled a certain way, and the same with socks, towels, and belts. There was space enough for your toilet kit, shoe polish and brush, and they had to be placed in the same spot every time.

There were several occasions when we found our footlockers on the lawn in front of the barracks, ransacked, all our stuff thrown everywhere. After careful check, the only item missing was shoe polish! The army has always had its share of heavy drinkers, even then. They'd get so desperate for a drink that they would actually steal shoe polish, boil it down, strain it, and drink it!

A sergeant and his assistant, a corporal, were in charge of the day room. They had a little racket going where you had to pay them just to drop off your laundry. This was a choice assignment a lot of guys tried to get, because all you had to do was keep the area clean and functioning, and the floors polished. The old army seemed to have a gimmick for everyone. The sergeant in charge of the day room also had a little something going on the side. Soldiers who ran out of money before pay day would borrow money from the good sergeant, with a small interest fee, of course. At the end of the month, no sooner did the soldier receive his pay in his hand, then he turned around and handed what he owed over to the sergeant. These guys were always broke.

Those were the twilight years of the old peacetime army and the half-day work concept. A soldier's day started with reveille at 0600, and ended at 1100. That's when I first heard the Wabash Cannonball via the barracks orderly whose job was to make sure we were up and ready to go every morning. No sooner did the reveille bugle call finish, then out blared the Wabash Cannonball, the barracks' door flung open and lights were flicked on. It was Corporal Campbell who had come to awaken his boys: "All right now soldiers, out of those bunks. Rise and shine; let go of your cocks and grab your socks." We'd tumble on out of the barracks for formation and roll call. It was at this time I was contemplating becoming a company bugler.

Soldiers sat by squads at long picnic tables in the mess hall. The food was brought out family style. Each entree was placed at the head of the table where the corporal in charge sat. Each man, in turn, passed the food to the soldier on his right. Food was asked for in a certain manner, starting with "please." As the food was passed down the line, if any soldier dared short-stop a dish, or reached across the table, the corporal was up in a flash and delivered a quick, hard rap across the knuckles with the end of his knife, or poked the offending party in the hand with his fork.

From the mess hall we went back to formation to receive the schedule of training for the day. We finished by 1100 and got cleaned up for lunch with enough time to go look at the bulletin board. If your name was not on the bulletin board for detail, the afternoon was yours. You then had the rest of the day for "bunk fatigue," because a detail was called "fatigue duty." Bunk fatigue meant you were free to do anything you wanted in camp. If you wanted to sleep all afternoon, that was up to you; if you wanted to play volleyball or just walk around or sit and talk with the fellows, that was your business, too. Most of us used the time to get ahead, doing things like shining our shoes, polishing our belt buckles, or practicing the things we screwed up that morning so we could get it right the next day.

CHAPTER 6

THE PRESIDENT'S OWN

The 12th Infantry and the Third Cavalry rotated duty in providing the honor guard at the Tomb of the Unknown Soldier and for duty at military funerals. Of course, we always pulled guard duty at camp. Every day there was a change of guard and if you were detailed, you would fall out in spotless uniform, spit-shined shoes, a rigid campaign hat (we had to soak them to get them stiff-rigid), and your rifle at your side. The sergeant of the guard would then march us up to the guardhouse, report in, and prepare the first relief of our detail to relieve the guards on duty at various posts around camp. One relief slept while the other pulled guard duty. At the appointed time we were awakened and got prepared to relieve those coming off duty. The sergeant in charge marched us to each post as one by one, we replaced each guard. Whether you were assigned to the main gate post, the motor pool, or the ammo dump, guard duty was serious business. You could expect to be inspected at any time, and you had better know your general and special orders. Most importantly, you challenged anything and everything that moved in your area, alertly calling out, "Halt! Who goes there?"

Looking back to that period in the army, I still say one of the hardest things we had to overcome during basic training was learning the Manual of Arms. We all wore the fatigue hat when we drilled, so you could really snap the rifle around while going through the motions. But come the day when you had to fall out in uniform and perform the Manual of Arms wearing a rigid campaign hat, well, that was a different matter altogether. The brim of the hat stuck out several inches from your head, and every time you nicked it or creased it as you went through the motions with your rifle, you'd catch hell. So you had to learn the Manual of Arms without the campaign hat, and in such a way that you'd compensate several inches further from your body and go through all the moves at this same interval, moving the rifle in this way, keeping the exact distance your hat stuck out from your head. Then when you wore the campaign hat during close order drill you wouldn't even nick it. To get to that stage took long hours of practice. I got to where I was one of the best in the company.

All that hard work paid off. I learned my basics the right way, at Arlington, where you had to do it just right. Every motion was done with spit and polish, and a lot of effort and enthusiasm. That's what the army expected of recruits, and that's what they taught. There is a constant theme I held to all those years that still holds true today: you fight like you practice; you fight like you train. It all comes down to that and always will. That was something I always tried to instill. It all starts with that first critical part of the young soldier's training, simply, the "School of the Soldier."

How to look like a soldier, and how to act like a soldier were constantly practiced: Look sharp and be sharp, and let your military bearing show. You don't have to be an elite unit to have these values. What it really comes down to is leadership! Drill until you get it right, by the book, by the numbers, and do it with a lot of enthusiasm. That was the standard I learned, and that was my standard with the men I commanded, and I'm convinced they became better soldiers because of it.

On January 24, 1941, I was promoted to corporal, serial number 13005159, special orders numbers 16, by order of Colonel Saunders, Regimental Commander, and Robert H. Soule, Major, Adjutant. That spring had been the tenth month for us at Arlington. We not only looked like soldiers, now we acted like soldiers. We were sharp, full of pride and enthusiasm. Things were falling into place. I saw a notice on our bulletin board announcing tryouts for the post baseball team. We had some pretty good players in the regiment from all parts of the country. I made the team as the first string shortstop and batted third. We played teams in and around the D.C. area, even some college teams, and made a pretty good showing of ourselves. By then, my leg had healed nicely and it didn't swell anymore. The last organized baseball I ever played was that spring at Arlington.

Company K shaped up like this in 1941: the commanding officer was Captain J. M. Churchill, Jr.; his subordinates were First Lieutenant John A. Katalinas, and Second Lieutenants Frank P. Burke, James M. Kelly, Fred J. Corson, and Ralph W. Payne. The First Sergeant was Raymond L. Andrews, and the staff sergeant was Ralph W. Gilliland. Company K also had one mess sergeant, a supply sergeant, a clerk, one mechanic, four cooks, and three buglers. Six men had the rank of sergeant; at corporal, thirteen. We had twenty-six privates first class, and seventy-one privates.

Every unit has its history and the commander wanted all soldiers to know something about the 12th Infantry and instill some pride. We were expected to know by memory our unit crest and history:

Headquarters, Arlington Cantonment, Virginia, May 27, 1941.
Memorandum To: All Organizations, 12th Infantry. The Secretary of War on
June 27, 1921, having approved a Coat of Arms for the 12th Infantry,
the following blazer and description of this Coat of Arms is furnished for
the information of all concerned:

BLAZORY

SHIELD: Azure, in fess two crosses moline agent, in base of wigwam of thee like garnished gules with five poles of the last; on a chief embattled on a sea lion of the third holding in dexter paw a sword of the field.

CREST: On a wreath of the colors an armored arm embowed proper, grasping in the naked hand a broken flag staff gules, to which is attached a pennant.

MOTTO: "Ducti Amore Patriae," which means, "Having Been Led By Love Of Country."

DESCRIPTION: The field in blue is for infantry. This regiment took part in the Civil War. Its great achievement was its first engagement at Gains Mill, Virginia, June 27 and 28, 1862, where its losses were almost 50%. This is shown by the Moline crosses, which represent the iron fastening of a millstone and the pair recall the crushing losses sustained. The wigwam with its five poles is for the five Indian campaigns in which portions of the regiment took part. The chief is for the Spanish and Philippine Wars, yellow and red being the Spanish colors; red and blue the Katipunan colors. The embattled partition line is for the capture of the blockhouse at El Caney, Cuba, 1898, and the sea lion is from the arms of the Philippine Islands. The crest in the Spanish colors is to commemorate the capture of a Spanish flag at El Caney.

It is generally expected of the regular army, and it is its pride, to maintain the highest standards of training and discipline. The maintenance of these highest standards in the 12th U.S. Infantry Regiment depends on every man now in the regiment, and those who will join us in the near future. The maintenance of these highest standards is not a mere matter of the words "regular army," but rests on the actual superior performance of duties and on excellent conduct at all times. Then the words "regular army" have a real meaning in which all members of the regiment can feel a justified pride.

Colonel C. A. Bagby, Commander, 12th Infantry
Regiment, 1941

A WAR-LIKE MARCH

One of the dumbest things I ever came across in the army occurred in the 12th Infantry at Arlington Cantonement. It was mid- September, still hot and humid as hell, upper 90's, when the colonel decided to do a twenty-five mile forced march: full combat gear, shoes and leggings, helmet (we still wore the doughboy helmet of World War I), backpack, rifle, and heavy overcoat. Those of you who have ever been in the Washington, D.C. area in late summer will know what I'm talking about. Just walking a third of that distance in that climate in shorts and shirt would make you sweat, but full gear and overcoat? Nevertheless, we stepped out smartly and marched in those conditions through Arlington and the surrounding area and back to the post, twenty-five hot, grueling, sweaty, miles. Throughout the march the commander was heard to say, "Warlike, men, warlike! You've got to experience warlike conditions!" That, sadly, was the thinking of the peacetime army, commanders who were between wars. We came back soaking wet, dehydrated, and disgusted. It's a wonder nobody got heat exhaustion or died; not one man fell out. That night, as exhausted as we were, we rallied down at the canteen, better known as the "Lion's Den," for some cold beer and hard-boiled egg sandwiches, and some of the best wind I ever heard! To a man, K Company rose to the occasion.

That was my introduction to the tail end of the peacetime army, for swift new changes were on the way that would modernize the army in preparation for the war overseas. I believe that the garrison mentality of that army: the barracks soldier, the non-tactical thinking and the focus on the half-day duty was the pervading attitude that contributed to a lack of preparedness and caught us with our guard down.

CHAPTER 7

THE 4ᵀᴴ MOTORIZED INFANTRY

In July 1941, our regiment got orders to move to Fort Dix, New Jersey, for deployment to Aruba, an island off the coast of South America. The mission had something to do with guarding a submarine base against German naval forces in the area. We were ready to deploy, but for some reason the mission was cancelled. During this time we had frequent live fire exercises down at the firing range where we were able to use everything we learned at Arlington. Here, for the first time since our arrival at basic training, we got to know just how good the new army issue rifle, the M-1 Garand, was. A semi-automatic .30 caliber, weighing a little over nine pounds and forty-three inches long, it was accurate, reliable, easy to maintain and carry, and packed a wallop. I was always very comfortable with it and scored consistently high during firing exercises. I even qualified as an expert marksman. After a couple of months at Dix, the regiment received orders to move to Camp Gordon, Georgia, where we would become part of the newly organized 4th Motorized Infantry Division.

The 4th Motorized Infantry was designed specifically for large scale armored operations and had trained in conjunction with the 2nd Armored Division at Ft. Benning earlier that year. It possessed two fully motorized infantry regiments, a mechanized infantry regiment and enough trucks to move the entire division without shuttling.

The mood of the soldiers at this time was one of anticipation and eagerness. We were getting into a brand new organization, a motorized infantry outfit we knew nothing about. As a matter of fact, no one really knew how motorized infantry was supposed to work, or how to use the equipment we were supposed to receive, so most officers just improvised as they went along. Instead of marching into battle, we would now use motorized vehicles to haul us. The primary vehicle authorized for this purpose was the armored half-track personnel carrier, a heavily armored vehicle with two wheels up front and two half-tracks in back, capable of transporting a squad of men into battle.

One of the first big problems we faced was the seats in the half-track. They were made of hard canvas and had a zipper on the side, but no padding or cushion. In order to prevent butt bruise during a jarring ride, higher authority determined that every soldier would use his blanket as a cushion. Improvisation thus became a valuable lesson. The idea was to fold your blanket to the size of the small seat in the half-track, stuff it in, and zip it . Easier said than done. You never heard such cussing! Those stubby metal zippers were hard enough to work, but when you got that seat bigger, puffed out more because of the blanket, why, it took some kind of strength in your fingers and hands to zip it. I always said they made those seats in the half-track strong enough to take a direct hit. Even before the half-tracks arrived, all we had were trucks. For training purposes, our trucks were converted to personnel carriers and tanks by simply painting the words, "personnel carrier" or "tank" on the sides of the vehicles, or hanging a sign. For guns we used cut tree limbs as 75mm canons or .50 caliber machine guns. That's what our mechanized infantry trained with up to and during the 1941 Carolina Maneuvers.

Nobody knew how to tactically deploy a motorized unit. Company commanders went by the Basic Infantry Manual, since it was thought you'd deploy the same way infantry units deploy. Well, we practiced with our trucks, pretend half-tracks, lined up side by side, out in wide-open fields. On the signal from the company commander standing in the lead jeep (he would suddenly cross his arms over his head), we would go into the old flying wedge football formation, simulating moving into the attack. Down the field we went, looking mighty fierce and determined, dust kicking up dust everywhere, shouting and yelling in the charge. Then we'd get another signal from the lead vehicle (this time his arms straight out from his sides) and we'd go into another formation, now abreast of each other. I was stationed in the passenger part of the half-track, responsible for helping transmit the signal. We roared to a designated drop-off point, each squad jumping off and taking up their positions. You should have seen those fellows of the .37 mm anti-tank crew!

There they were, simulating going into battle, sitting in a truck with the gun being pulled behind, the gun crew sitting ramrod straight, their arms folded and out from their chests, the old, steel pot helmet strapped tightly around their chins, nodding and smiling as they passed by. Those guys were in their element.

Around this time I was promoted to buck sergeant and assigned as weapons platoon sergeant, 4th Platoon. We were always doing some kind of training with heavy weapons, and it was now my responsibility to learn all about the heavy stuff and become an expert.

During those years all soldiers took their basic training with the unit to which they were assigned at the time of enlistment. Starting at Camp Gordon, we had more personnel assigned to bring the division up to strength, so basic training and proficiency were continual requirements. The first new equipment to arrive was helmets and canteen covers. Now, owing to the weight of the new helmet, wearing the thing without a liner was pretty rough, so we put the canteen cover on top of our heads, then strapped the helmet on top of the canteen cover and went about our business. Like I said, we improvised.

Just prior to the Carolina Maneuvers we had new half-tracks come in, but no one told us or taught us what to do with them. Then came the maneuvers. Now there we were, my crew and I, way out in the deep woods in the middle of nowhere, completely quiet except for occasional enemy patrols passing in the distance. We were in our half-track, but we should have been outside the vehicle, on the ground. That's when I learned another valuable lesson: if you're going to go out there, don't be enclosed. You're helpless. Always plan to be outside of the vehicle and set up your perimeter and your listening posts so no one can sneak up on you like a sitting duck.

On December 7, 1941, we went on full alert in the wake of the Japanese attack on Pearl Harbor. Sirens were wailing all over the place. Our regimental commander ordered machine guns mounted on top of the roofs of the barracks in case of attack. We stayed on alert all that day and the next.

During this time new weapons started arriving. One day the company executive officer approached. "Sergeant, I want you to conduct a weapons briefing for the company tomorrow morning at 0700 on the water-cooled .30 caliber machine gun. Go over to supply and draw out the weapon and the instructional charts. Any questions?" Up to that time I had not seen that much of the .30 caliber machine gun, let alone handled one, but we were to get acquainted real fast. I'd do the briefing and Sergeants LaValle and Miller would assist. We stayed up all night looking at the charts, taking the gun apart, learning all the parts and pieces, reassembling the gun, and rehearsing our roles. We became experts overnight. The briefing demonstration went off without a hitch.

A week later, during my Thompson submachine gun briefing, I needed an assistant to hold up the charts, but my buddy, Corporal Melerski, wasn't up for it. For some reason he was angry with me, but I never knew why. I tried to get Eddie to go with me to officer's candidate school. Instead, he said he would rather stay there with the boys. Other than a couple of letters we exchanged, I didn't see him for years, not until after the war in Reading, and then only from a distance. In the letters I got from Eddie, he always said how he and the guys were rooting for me.

In January 1942, I was still in charge of the weapons platoon, a twenty-one-year-old buck sergeant, making $70 a month. Most of the men in the company were much older than I. We had a lot of older soldiers who had been around the army a long time and had been overseas several times. Some of these men had been up and down in rank because of their drinking habits and getting into trouble.

Here's the way the old organization of Company K, Weapons Platoon looked: the machine gun section leader was Sergeant LaValle. He was an older man who looked something like Senator Arlen Spector, articulate, educated, and outgoing, very capable, and extremely dependable. Corporal Christoff was first squad leader, with PFC Perry and Hagemann, and Private Robeski filling out that section. Christoff was a squat, heavyset fellow. Sergeant Corr was in charge of the second squad, with PFC Bielen, Privates Mileski and Pipino attached. Private Mileski was another old soldier, pushing forty, who had numerous tours in Panama, too many, some said, and had been the rank of sergeant a couple of times, but drinking kept him down. This guy knew everything and anything about the army. If you wanted to know something, you asked

Mileski. Privates Purcell and Whiting, and PFC Sefcovic were the messengers. Eisenhuer, Jonas, and Raczynski were half-track drivers. Sergeant Miller was in charge of the mortar section. Miller was a young, quiet type of a guy. Corporal Kennedy was first squad leader, followed by Diereck, Dudas, Pyral, and Nipper. "Moon" Mullins, a country boy from Mullins, West Virginia, was in charge of second squad, with Soffa, Alioto, Smith, and Gresh rounding out that group. The leader of the third squad was Corporal O'Donnell with Amos, Franciosa, Weisenborn, and Scully attached. That's the way my platoon stacked up with thirty soldiers in all.

Saturday, January 24, 1942, my Weapons Platoon, K Company, won the distinction of being the best looking platoon during inspection. In February, I was ordered over to E Company as weapons platoon sergeant. On the 21st, this platoon was the best appearing platoon during inspection. I felt pretty good about my men and receiving recognition two months in a row.

The Army Maneuvers of '41, the Carolina Maneuvers as they were known, should be touched on before leaving this part of the story. I remember it rained a lot that November when we were in the reserve area, and since we didn't have any tents, our biggest problem was trying to stay dry. This was to be America's last peacetime training exercise.

The 12th Infantry Regiment was a part of the 4th Motorized Division of the Red Army located on the west bank of the Catawba-Wateree River, South Carolina. On November 16, at 0630, the Red Army was put in motion with the 4th Motorized Division on the north flank, the 1st Armored in the center, and the 2nd Armored on the southern wing. The plan was to quickly reach the Pee Dee River in North Carolina and push into Blue Army territory seventy-five miles to the northwest.

By nightfall, the 4th was fighting a fragile delaying action against overwhelming enemy forces and retreated across the Rocky River to set up a defensive position. By morning, the Blue 1st and 26th Divisions continued their punishment of the overmatched 4th Motorized, driving it further back and threatening the defenders with envelopment.

The way it was determined that a tank, or what was supposed to be a tank, was knocked out, was a direct hit with a sack of flour thrown by the soldiers. With that distinct marking on the attacking vehicle, a nearby umpire could easily declare the vehicle out of the contest.

Phase one of the maneuvers ended with the 4th Infantry again in the attack, but we got flanked, mauled, and lost one of our regiments. It was on the 20th or 21st of November that our division went into reserve, and it rained the whole time.

The Second Carolinas Maneuvers kicked-off early on the 25th of November on a cold, clear day. Aggressiveness again marked this phase as the 4th Motorized assaulted Monroe and by nightfall held half the town. Retreat soon gave way to Blue pressure and a head-on collision with the 29th Division coming in from the southwest. The maneuvers ended with the Red Army in a strong defensive position around the Camden area.

By late February, I was on my way to officer's candidate school at Ft. Benning, Georgia. Here was yet another turn in the road of my new vocation. With all self-doubt behind me, I was excited and eager about the prospects of becoming an officer; a brand new, hard charging second lieutenant was within reach.

It rained from November, 1941 to February, 1942. Those were wet, soggy days, but allowed for some good training opportunities.

February 10, 1942: "Dear Mom and Dad, A rainy day. A rainy day which didn't have any rain. It only drizzled. We had a hike in the morning; it took but three hours, which equaled seven and a half miles, for infantry troops travel at the rate of two and a half miles per hour. I read in the paper where a fromer French ship called the "Normandie" caught fire; forty people were killed. Sabotage is feared. I'll bet that there will be an invasion of France. A.E.F. will be the landing party in the vicinity of Bordeaux. Love, Edward."

PART IV

A NEWLY COMMISSIONED SECOND LIEUTENANT

CHAPTER 8

OFFICER CANDIDATE

"HONORABLE DISCHARGE from THE UNITED STATES ARMY. TO ALL WHOM IT MAY CONCERN: This is to certify, that EDWARD S. MEHOSKY, 13005159, Sergeant, 22nd Company, 2nd Student Training Regiment, ISSC, Fort Benning, Georgia, THE ARMY OF THE UNITED STATES, as a TESTIMONIAL OF HONEST AND FAITHFUL SERVICE, is hereby HONORABLY DISCHARGED from the military service of the UNITED STATES by reason of convenience of the government to accept appointment as 2nd Lieutenant, Army of the U.S., and active duty. Said Edward S. Mehosky was born in Reading, in the State of Pennsylvania. When enlisted he was 18 8/12 years of age and by occupation a laborer. He had blue eyes, brown hair, ruddy complexion, and was five feet 8 3/4 inches in height. Given under my hand at Fort Benning, Georgia, this 28th day of May, one thousand nine hundred and forty-two.

M.G. Stubbs, Colonel, Infantry, Commanding.

At a hotel in Augusta, Georgia, ten of us, all enlisted soldiers from the 12th Infantry Regiment, 4th Motorized Infantry Division, sat around a table for a big, home-cooked meal in enroute to Fort Benning. It was a small farewell celebration, very enjoyable, although we were anxious to get started in our new assignment. Our spirits were high. We arrived by train in Columbus, Georgia, on Saturday, February 28, 1942. From there a bus took us to the post where we signed in and got situated in our new home. Our schooling would start at daybreak on Monday morning.

Here I met Frank Reis and his wife, Betty from Reading, Pennsylvania. Frank and I would be assigned to the same camp after graduation, the 85th Infantry, and, still later, would serve together in the 506th. We'd remain the best of friends after the war. Frank was as fine an officer as I ever knew. He was in his thirties when we met.

OCS

At the officer's candidate school at Ft. Benning, I was a member of Officers Candidate Class #16, The 22nd Company, 2nd Student Training Regiment. I was one of 120 student candidates.

During the twelve-week course each man was assigned a specific job in the company: guidon bearer, platoon sergeant, platoon leader, and company commander. Only twelve of us would be designated to serve as company commander for a week. I was one of the twelve picked. As acting company commander during my designated week, I was responsible for all company formations, meeting all phases of the training schedule, and making sure the company got from one area to another on time. Reveille came first. At 0600 every morning I had to make sure every man was present and accounted for at formation, so I had to be up and ready hours before any of them. At formation I annotated the morning attendance report, then hustled the report to Lieutenant Rowe, the faculty company commander. This was followed by marching the company to the training area. Most of the day focused on a field exercise involving the rifle company in the attack.

Weapons demonstrations were scheduled practically every day and were a favorite among the men. To see those demonstration teams in action was something to behold, like the time we saw them demonstrate firing a water-cooled .50 caliber machine gun. I mean, those guys were slick in the way they set up so efficiently. Then we'd get a demonstration on lighter automatic weapons, weapons we would use in the individual platoons like the .30 caliber machine gun. My notes on this exercise: "Interlocking fire is devastating!"

I remember those three months at OCS as a blur. The course was such a fast-paced affair with a heck of a lot of information and work crammed into a short period of time. We had classroom work, tests, field work and live demonstrations, then more tests, lectures, films, a ton of manuals and other materials to read, map and compass work, terrain walks, more tests, M-1 instruction and live fire at the range. Every morning we were off and running with our physical training program. After breakfast we started with classroom lecture followed by a live fire demonstration over on the range. You got to know everything there was to know about the M-1 rifle: you fired it, cleaned it, took it apart and put it back together, and you learned to blend every technique and principle of firing. We learned how to do efficiency reports and how to read a map and aerial photographs. They taught us to build hasty field fortifications and we saw just about every weapons fire demonstration in the army arsenal. However, the primary emphasis was the M-1 Garand rifle, the dependable mainstay of our infantry and a weapon that would achieve acclaim as one of the finest small arms weapons to come out of the war.

First Lieutenant Rowe rose to the lectern. "Now, when instructing marksmanship, men," he said with effect and to be heard, "use the triangulation box as a rainy day subject for the troops, as you can't always be outside. It's what I call preparation marksmanship: sighting and aiming, position, trigger squeeze. Sighting and aiming are done in three phases: use a sighting bar to set up the correct sight picture, use the rifle box and, of course, never underestimate the value of triangulation. Everyone must know all mechanical functions of his weapon. Use the time allotted for range instruction to your advantage. This is one of the most important things you'll ever do as a platoon leader or company commander."

The triangulation method was simply being able to line up the top of your rifle sight to the target in front of you. We paired off in teams; we primarily used the prone position for sighting and firing. This was a dry run, no ammunition, exercise. While I got into the ready position, my partner moved to a point about twenty-five feet in front of me, straddling a wooden box with a piece of paper affixed to it. In one hand was a pencil; in the other was what looked like a thin strip of wood with a three-inch disk attached. In the center of the disk was a small hole. As I adjusted my rifle sight on the center of the paper target, he slowly lowered the disk to the center. I aimed for the center and when the bottom of the disk was sitting on top of my rifle point sight, I called out, "Mark!" and he marked a dot with the pencil through the hole in the disk. This was repeated three times. The dots were then connected so as to form a triangle. The closer the dots, the more your shots were going to hit the center of the target in which you were aiming. If your dots were far apart, it

The Story of a Soldier • 43

meant you did something wrong and you corrected it. Getting the proper sight picture was the most important thing, the whole purpose of the exercise, and it always told on the firing range. You learned it right and practiced it right so you could teach it right, and those instructors were always there to make sure of that.

Map reading was a very important subject. It's something I picked up easily and something I felt I was always good at because I could visualize the map features and the contours in my mind. How do you know where you are at any time out there in the field? Being able to orient yourself with a compass and map, regardless of rank, knowing where you are and where you need to go, day or night, and being able to follow a map from one point to another are key. You must also know how to find prominent features, how to estimate distances, be able to visualize and understand contour features, know a good defensive position and know a good place where the enemy might hide. It's not just another course to be brushed over. What it's really all about is interpreting terrain, using it to your advantage, using it to get the job done, and surviving.

Each week you were given a detailed schedule of instruction for subject areas to be covered. For example, March 30, 1942: 0730-1145, company assembled at Range B for .30 caliber machine gun fire technique. Lieutenant Wolfe was the instructor in charge. The uniform was coveralls, leggings, and garrison cap. We ate lunch in the field. From 1300-1700 hours, more on machine gun fire, defilade and masked firing positions. On Tuesday it was back to the range with Lieutenant White for machine gun anti-aircraft firing followed by a training film. Next, we learned about the 81mm mortar in attack and defense, and anti-tank platoons in defense. We were given a little booklet to study on survival: size up the situation, undue haste makes waste, remember where you are, vanquish fear and panic, improvise, value living, act like the natives, and learn basic skills. That's how it went for that week.

I received a couple of letters from Eddie Malerski. He was now a staff sergeant, cadre, with Company K, 314th Infantry at Camp Pickett, Virginia. He said all the guys of the old company are rooting for me.

May 17, 1942, Dear Mom and Dad: The board has met and has decided on who will graduate and who will not. Well, I haven't been called before the board, so that's an interesting factor. Our class will graduate on May 29th, and from rumors I have been hearing, upon graduation the candidate gets ten days leave. I hope I'm one of the lucky ones. I have already made reservations on a train for D.C. It leaves Atlanta at 8:30 P.M. on the 29th. It's a fast train and only makes two stops, one in Washington, D.C., the other in New York. That's why I have to get off in D.C. I'll be there at 10:00 Saturday morning. I hope you can drive down. With much love, your son, Ed.

The big day came at last and I made it! We were now "shave tails," hard charging, brand new second lieutenants. Some called us "ninety-day wonders." Some of us were wonders, all right, and some just wondering, but we were bound for new infantry assignments at camps all over the country. I was assigned to the 85th Infantry Division at Camp Shelby, Mississippi.

CHAPTER 9

CAMP SHELBY

I arrived at Camp Shelby near Hattisburg, Mississippi in the swelter-
ing heat of June aboard a bus. I was further assigned to L Company, 339th
Infantry Regiment under the command of Lieutenant Colonel Paul Vivia.

Camp Shelby was a training camp. It was our job to provide the basic
training necessary for turning civilians into soldiers. I was a platoon
leader and didn't know too much yet as a second lieutenant, mostly
learning my role and trying to apply some of the things I learned at OCS.
A lot of things you just picked up on your own. You quickly found out
whom you could rely on. Things were pretty lax, but at the same time we
were always busy with a heck of a lot of work. It was a big responsibility training these men; most of them were right out of high school and had
never been on their own or away from home for that long. We were just
trying to make them good soldiers before they shipped out.

The one constant problem for everyone was getting accustomed to the
heat. To help, ice cold drinks were available everywhere around camp.
Those summer months went by pretty fast, as I recall. I suppose the most
eventful thing about this assignment was signing out of the regiment in
September for assignment to a newly formed airborne combat unit. The
antics of the regimental commander sparked this development.

Colonel Vivia had this quirk about mess hall garbage. The word
going around at that time was that he had a deal going with some of the
local pig farmers to sell them mess hall garbage as food for their pigs at a
price far cheaper than they could get anywhere else in those parts. So
Colonel Vivia made sure everyone in the regiment knew the difference
between edible and non-edible garbage. Whenever some soldier on mess
hall duty dumped something of an edible nature into non-edible garbage,
or something non-edible into edible garbage, look out, because we'd
catch hell that evening. If Colonel Vivia happened to be in one of the mess

halls that day, and found things to his unliking, by after duty hours, all officers of the regiment were assembled in the camp theater. There out on the stage were rows of folding tables containing heaps of foul, smelly garbage, each pile labeled either "EDIBLE" or "NON-EDIBLE." The good colonel would then proceed to reach deep into a pile of say, edible garbage, and pull out a tin can. Now the lecture began.

"Gentlemen," the colonel shouted, pointing to the sign above the steaming pile, "this is edible garbage! Non-edible garbage must never, I repeat, never be found in edible garbage." He continued, "This item," holding the can high over his head, "belongs in non-edible garbage!" Then Colonel Vivia went on to the next pile, and to the one after that, and so on down the line until he came to the last pile of garbage. "This is non-edible!" He'd reach down through the cans and what not and produce a wad of dripping mash potatoes and corn. "And this, gentlemen, belongs in edible garbage, do I make myself clear, gentlemen? Are there any questions?" There were never any questions, just thoughts of disgust. Then, after a pause, "if there are no questions, you are dismissed." We were fed up to say the least, and a lot of us were keeping an eye open for other possible assignments out of Camp Shelby.

July 26, 1942. Dear Mom and Dad: We are just getting to do some range work. The weather down here is so hot that my face is getting blacker and blacker every day. Time is flying so fast it's a shame. I guess it's because they have us doing some kind of work all the time. I saw Yeggs a few days ago and today he came to my hut and stayed for about an hour. Gee, I never expected to see anyone down here that I know, but he says there are quite a few of the fellows down in this part of the country. Oh yes, I saw Johnny Mish about two weeks ago. He's in the Medical Corps. Yeggs is here attending a cook and baker school. I am thinking about going into the parachute troops. If they accept me, I'll go, for I already put my application in. That's it for now. With love, your son, Ed.

July was coming to a close and it seemed hotter than the previous month. Could that be possible? By August, I had been accepted into the newly activated 506th Parachute Infantry Regiment at Toccoa, Georgia. Of my regiment, Ronald Spiers and David Hebert, were also accepted. It was June 8 when I reported to Camp Shelby, Mississippi, and now, a scant three months later, I was heading to a new assignment and the unknown. It would be the toughest, most rewarding and the most important thing, up to that point, I had ever done. As history would later prove, I was to become a member of one of the finest fighting units our country ever produced.

PART V

HE (COLONEL ROBERT SINK) FORMED AND LATER TOOK INTO COMBAT, ONE OF THE FINEST AND MOST PHYSICALLY RUGGED PARACHUTE REGIMENTS IN THE ARMY. IT WAS SINK'S REGIMENT THAT ALWAYS PASSED IN REVIEW AT THE DOUBLE AND BROKE ALL LONG STANDING RECORDS SET BY MILITARY UNITS AROUND THE WORLD FOR MARCHING GREAT DISTANCES IN SHORT PERIODS OF TIME.

From the book, "Paratrooper," by Gerald M. Devlin

CHAPTER 10

THE 506ᵀᴴ PARACHUTE REGIMENT

A steady rain soaked Hattisburg, Mississippi on a chilly September day, 1943. We cleared Camp Shelby early that morning, Second Lieutenants Ronald Spiers, David Hebert and I, having volunteered and been accepted into a parachute regiment. We were on our way to join the 506th Parachute Infantry, a brand new regiment being formed in northern Georgia at a place called Toccoa. By train, the first leg of our journey took us through Meridian, Mississippi, across Alabama by way of Birmingham and Anniston, and into the outskirts of Atlanta. There we changed trains and boarded the Northern Express, a slow moving train that stopped at every little town and hollow along the way. But it wasn't so bad because we had seats in the dining car. The conductor called, "all aboard," as the train began its northward route through a bunch of little towns with names like Chamblee, Doraville, Suwanee, Flowery Branch, and Chicopee, stopping at each just long enough for passengers to get on board or detrain. "Tickets please!" shouted the conductor. "There'll be a thirty-minute stop-over in Gainesville. We'll pass through New Holland and Lula, then Alto, Cornelia, Mt. Airy, and Toccoa. Good to have you soldiers aboard Southern Railroad Lines. I can remember when I was your age and going off to war. When I got back home I joined the railroad and have been with them ever since. Headin' up to Toccoa, huh? Thought so. We heard the army was doing something up there. You boys might be able to see some of the camp from the Ayersville area as we pass by. Well boys, best of luck to y'all."

Toccoa was a small southern town nestled in the foothills of the Appalachian Mountains, in the northeastern corner of Georgia.

As the train approached the Ayersville area near Camp Toccoa, I couldn't help notice, way off to the right, a prominence jutting high above both the woods and hills, and the corn fields and tobacco patches com-

The Story of a Soldier • 53

mon to this part of the country.

We disembarked at the train station, located in the center of town between Foreacre Street and Railroad Street. Spiers and Hebert went to get sandwiches and sodas while I looked for a taxicab. A cab driver was waving to me across the way, trying to get my attention. "Right here, sir! Right here! Yes, sir. Let me put those bags in the trunk. Two more of you fellows, you say? All right, then," he said, spitting a big, wet chew of tobacco on the sidewalk. He was a friendly sort of guy, had a full red beard, liked to chew tobacco, and was born and raised in Stephens County. He worked in town, was a mechanic, but drove the cab on weekends for a little extra to make ends meet. On his head was a dirty, grease-stained baseball cap, which he wore clear down to his ears. I asked him if that big rock I saw coming into Toccoa had a name. "Sure does. Folks in these parts call it Currahee Mountain," he said. "Going way back," he continued, "used to be Cherokee people living in this here region, but not no more, no sir! That there name of the mountain comes from the Cherokee language. It means 'stands alone.' Tell you the truth, it sort of looks that way, huh?"

I stood there trying to catch another glimpse of the mountain when Spiers and Hebert made their way toward us. The cab driver broke the silence. "Hell, Lieutenant, I hunt up there with my brothers all the time. Walked that area for years. Know it real good, I do. I reckon she's well over a thousand feet to the top. You hike on up to the top of that mountain, you'll know it all right. Some mighty rough country up there, Lieutenant. Not too many folks go up there, you know."

Little did I know in a day's time we'd be running that mountain practically every day for the duration of our training at Toccoa. From the train station we headed down West Currahee Street, past the Toccoa Casket Company, then about five miles on Georgia Highway 184 to a fork, bearing right on another road for two miles, and left on Ayersville Road. It was a half-mile to the camp entrance.

Camp Toccoa, formerly Camp Toombs, used to be a National Guard facility named after the Civil War general. The way I heard, the regimental commander didn't like the sound of the name, and owing to the close proximity to the casket factory, well, it got changed pretty quickly. As we pulled into camp we saw some tents, quadrangular types, but mostly rows of long, wooden buildings with tarpaper roofs, situated in a huge clearing and surrounded by thick pinewoods. The camp roads were hard-packed, red Georgia clay. At the camp entrance was a large painted sign, "Headquarters, 506th Parachute Infantry."Below was a distinctive insignia: a pair of dice, one showing five dots, the other six. They were connected by a ring. An eagle and a parachute completed the picture. This was the "506th Para - Dice" insignia that became our informal patch we were to wear on our jackets and shorts.

We signed in and processed the necessary paperwork at the head-quarters building, completed physicals at the dispensary, and reported to the adjutant's office for assignment. I was assigned to 3rd Battalion, H Company, as an assistant platoon leader. This was new to me, as most infantry units did not have assistant platoon leaders. Before going over to the company area, I made a courtesy call at battalion headquarters and there met Major Robert Wolverton, the battalion commander. Major Wolverton was of medium height, had a large, bull-like frame, and hailed from Elkins, West Virginia. He was mighty glad to meet me and happy to have me in the battalion; I felt the same way about him. "You're getting here at the right time, Lieutenant. You're on the ground floor with new officers arriving every day. I expect the troops will start arriving in about two weeks. We're going to get 3rd Battalion in top shape-lean and mean. It's going to take a lot of hard work with no let up. Captain Harwick is a good man to work for-steady, not loud, but firm. Well, good to have you here, Lieutenant Mehosky."

"Thank you, sir," I replied, saluted, and exited his office. There was something about the major that was genuine, something that told you that you'd go to hell and back for him and then some.

I reported to company headquarters but Captain Harwick was out and about, so I was directed to the supply section, and there was my gear and the uniform of the day: shorts, boots and socks! It was here that I first met Second Lieutenant Ken Christianson from California, who would become one of my best friends. We returned to the company commander's office and were enthusiastically greeted by the captain, who, in turn, intro-duced his platoon leaders. Captain Robert "Bob" Harwick was from

Philadelphia, Pennsylvania. He was about 5'10" in height, of stocky build, and soft spoken. He was well-educated and had been a chemical engineer before going into the army. Harwick hardly ever raised his voice, only had to say it once and it was done, or else he raised those bushy eyebrows and you'd know. Captain Harwick was a gentleman and was respected and well liked by everyone.

Captain Harwick got us together and began: "Men, I'd like to welcome you to the 506th. Our regiment was the sixth parachute regiment formed, activated in July of this year. You men are part of the officer cadre that's been arriving every day. Troops will start coming in by the end of the month. And we've got a small cadre of NCO's on hand, too. That's how we stand today. This regiment, the 506th, is an independent regiment. Lieutenant Colonel Robert F. Sink commands the 506th. Colonel Sink is from Lexington, North Carolina. Third Battalion is commanded by Major Robert Wolverton, whom some of you have already met. It is Colonel Sink's intention to forge an aggressive, tough, hard-hitting regiment capable of dropping behind enemy lines and accomplishing the mission wherever and whenever that might be. The colonel believes in moving fast and light. To do this everyone must be in prime shape! I want you to know this: we are an independent organization, we train alone, and we train hard. We must be capable of standing alone, together. That's what the colonel had in mind when he selected this lovely piece of real estate. Over the next couple of days you'll get to know the terrain first hand. Your uniform of the day, the only one you'll need for the next couple of weeks, is the gear you were issued today. So it is your sole duty, your responsibility, to get in the best physical and mental shape of your life. That, gentlemen, will be your duty for the time being. And you'll need to be in top condition to pass the 'Saturday Morning Olympics.' That's the first stage, the 'A' stage of parachute training here. You can't get to the next stage of training, which is parachute packing, until you pass the Olympics. Starting today, and from here on out, we will achieve and maintain the highest level of fitness second to none. You men have been hand picked and thoroughly screened and are the best. But don't be fooled. Any man not able to pass after three tries is out."

We all laughed at that, a little nervously perhaps, but that half-smile, half-grin on the captain's face invited it. "So, the sooner you men pass your PT, the sooner you'll make your five qualification jumps. Otherwise, you will have to take this training at Fort Benning with the rest of the troops and make your jumps there. And one more thing, men. Morning formation is 0600. Each company will pass in review on the run. From today on, we run all the time, everywhere, double time. All right men, that's about it for now. Are there any questions? Your platoon leaders will help you get acquainted with the camp layout and the daily schedule. We'll assemble back here at 1800 hours for officer's call."

I was assigned to the first platoon. First Lieutenant Butch Kendricks was my platoon leader. He was an all-conference football player out of Louisiana State University. Butch had already made his five jumps and was airborne qualified, but he suffered greatly every time he made a landing. His knees were so damaged from football injuries that they'd pop right out of joint when he hit the ground. Kendricks was one of those up and coming stars, an officer marked for higher duty. Within less than a month of my arrival, he got orders for Airborne Command Headquarters duty under General William Lee. When he left the organization, I was given first platoon.

CHAPTER 11

SATURDAY MORNING OLYMPICS

Captain Harwick had made it perfectly clear that our main function in life was to get into shape. The determining factor in all this was being able to pass the physical training which culminated at the end of each week in the Saturday Morning Olympics: calisthenics, the six-mile run up Mt. Currahee and back, and the obstacle course. Nothing was scheduled, training was left up to each individual. Ken and I worked out together, running, rope climbing, wrestling, and doing our sit-ups and push-ups, always in a competitive manner, against each other and the clock. Every day we'd run to the top of Mt. Currahee and back, three miles up and three miles down. It was tough, slow going at first. You swore you were breathing in the whole sky when you got to the summit. Then, just that fast, you got your second wind and started down, past the ranger tower and down that winding, rock-strewn road we would come to curse, and a mountain that would make or break us.

Our physical training program was a test of all the physical strength, stamina, and endurance you could muster. I mean, it took every ounce of the best you had, plus more. You had to be mentally tough as well as phys-ically tough, because you couldn't do one without the other, not in the air-borne. You'd either toughen or you'd be out. First thing Saturday morning you reported to the athletic field. First came one hour of exercise: jumping jacks, duck walk, sit-ups, push-ups, pull-ups, knee bends, and all sorts of log exercises you can imagine. After the muscles were nice and warm, you were timed in the 100-yard dash. This was followed by a one-mile run, timed, then a two-mile run, also timed. Now came the obstacle course, the best and toughest I ever experienced in my entire military career. It was built over a creek with most of the obstacles situated on the side of a very steep hill. You started the course going downhill with a sprint to a tower, climbed a rope to a platform fifteen feet high, then hung from a tower bar and dropped ten feet into a sawdust pit where you performed a shoulder tumble and crawled belly-flat under a fence. Next, you shinned up a twelve-foot pole to grasp the first rung of a hand-walk ladder, thirty-five rungs long. The next obstacle was a sixty yard sprint through a labyrinth of waist high poles set three feet apart. A log walk followed. To cross the creek you had to climb up to another platform ladder and hand walk across. Once across, you took a right turn to a ditch you had to jump over, only to land in a very deep pit. Then you scaled an eight-foot wall, then crawled under a low chicken-wire fence. You crossed back over the creek via a log bridge. Now came a large pipe on a steep incline that you had to snake your way through. Once you got through the pipe, there was a twelve-foot drop into a sawdust pit, and from there you grabbed a rope and swung back across the creek from whence you started! Here you climbed up a rope to a ten-foot platform for another jump and tumble and some more belly crawling. The end was now in sight. It was a sprint uphill and a jump over a four-foot ditch, a scramble over a log embankment, then straight up the hill to the next to last obstacle: the coffins. These delights were ten yards of smooth, solid wood and built, you guessed it, on the steepest part of the hill. Here you had to crawl on your hands and knees as fast as you could to get through, and once out, you ran another twenty to twenty-five yards to the finish line. Just before you got to the finish line, and believe me you were spent by this time, you had to throw yourself over a shoulder high embankment, then cross the finish line with whatever you had left. You crawled across it if you had to, but you finished. And that was what our obstacle course and the Saturday Morning Olympics were all about. It was Colonel Sink's intention to get all his officers airborne qualified before taking the troops down to Fort Benning's jump school. There would be a number of officers of the regiment who took their jump training at Benning. Either they had arrived at Toccoa later, or they had not yet passed the physical training stage.

I had kept myself in good shape to begin with, and with all that running up and down that mountain twice a day, finished the obstacle course with one of the highest scores in the battalion. Captain Harwick later told me that my score stacked up as one of the top five in the regiment.

Colonel Sink and Major Wolverton and the other battalion commanders were always on hand to see who passed and who did not, and also to see how officers did against officers of the other battalions. Everything was competitive and that's the way I liked it.

Toccoa was a weeding out process from start to finish, no doubt, but it was a necessary method in order to arrive at the kind of regiment Colonel Sink wanted. It was said that he personally screened and hand picked his men. To give you an idea of what I'm talking about, during the period August through November of 1942, more than 250 officers and 3200 enlisted men reported for duty. Of these, 1900 enlisted men and 160 officers were selected and retained for parachute training. There were a lot of rugged, muscular men running around Camp Toccoa in those days and somewhere along the line, someone coined the phrase, "Colonel Sink's Muscle College."

NORTH AND SOUTH

After duty hours, during the evening, all officers assembled at the officers club located in a remote area on the other side of camp. There to greet us was Colonel Sink with his staff and each of the battalion commanders. Now these get-together functions were something absolutely unique to a parachute regiment. The 506th had its share of characters and hell-raisers just like any other military organization. The officer's club was like any other, too, with dance floor, tables and chairs and all that, but there was a partition that separated the kitchen from the dance floor. There was a large opening in the partition from which food and drinks were served. What used to catch my eye as the evening wore on, was to see who would get punched when they poked their head in to order a drink. By that time everyone was pretty much gone, drinkers and servers alike, so when, for example, a wiseguy or loudmouth went to order a drink, whack! Someone in the kitchen slugged him and he'd go tumbling back across the dance floor. Then he would pick himself up and go back in line, wondering what happened. I used to watch guys come flying out of there all the time. Later in the evening amid the bantering and good-natured kidding that seemed to intensify everyone's combativeness (you kind of just got caught up in all the fun), there would be officers gravitating to one side of the room or the other, sort of like a North versus South kind of thing, where upon officers from northern states would wind up on one side of the room and officers from southern states opposite them. I don't really remember how it started, but there we were on different sides of the room, like a face-off as it were, hooting, hollering, and bantering back and forth, all in good fun. As the noise rose to a feverish pitch each side gravitated closer and closer to the middle of the floor until we converged in a wild melee! Why, you had people knocking each other down, pushing and shoving, and some piling on those engaged in some serious wrestling on the floor. I usually managed to stay on my feet, mostly throwing challengers back into the pile. Colonel Sink loved this kind of stuff, as did his staff, for they seemed to look on in great delight. Suddenly it ended as quickly as it began with everyone shaking hands and talking about what had just happened. Starting there at Toccoa, North and South became a tradition in the regiment, something that just happened whenever we had a regimental get-together. I think these planned "getting together" functions at the officer's club mirrored exactly what we were: a regiment that was coming together as one; a regiment that lived its actions, that trained hard, played hard, and fought hard. We were getting ready for war and knew soon we would be deployed somewhere overseas. I don't know if there was ever anything like it in the other airborne regiments, but then there was never anything like the 506th.

DERWOOD

Second Lieutenant Derwood Cann, a platoon leader in G Company, remembered how, up at the Saturday night "prop blasts" at the club, he always seemed to get into a fight with some officer, yet he always shook hands with the guy he just knocked off the porch (Derwood was an all-conference boxer from Louisiana State). Derwood never held a grudge and you usually saw the two of them drinking beer and laughing about it. One story has it that Derwood and some of his teammates in college would dress up as fancy-dans, go down to the local bar in town, start fights with the local toughs and clean house. He called that "just good, plain old physical fun." I saw him in action and even fought against him with gloves, and I can attest that he was one heck of a tough boxer!

Derwood went about six feet and was more on the slender side. He had a very youthful looking face, was quiet, mild-mannered, smooth in his actions, very capable, and very well-liked and respected. He certainly liked the ladies and the ladies liked him.

According to Derwood, the officers of the 506th were a rough bunch of men in excellent physical condition and damn tough men with high morale, men who knew how to lead men, and men who knew how to discipline soldiers to make them good fighters. He remembered how they drummed out an officer who had deserted, went AWOL, and was brought back. That was the only one and the last one in the regiment who ever did. He also recalled how it was tougher going down Currahee Mountain than up, and remembered all the other hell everyone went through. How many times had we heard that the colonel was going to make training so tough that combat would seem like a lark? "That's right," Derwood recounted, "the 506th was without doubt one of the toughest, tightly wound, most cohesive units of the war, all due to our one and only commander, Colonel Robert Sink, who led us and was with us the whole way. Colonel Sink knew his officers and cared deeply about each and every one of them, 'My boys,' he was always fond of saying." Somewhere along the line Colonel Sink took a liking to Lieutenant Cann and instead of calling him Derwood, called him Dagwood. "I remember a particular jump where I landed real hard," Derwood recalled. "I was stunned and sprawled on the ground in a heap when, I saw a cloud of dust and a jeep roaring straight for me! It was Colonel Sink!"

'Dagwood,' he yelled, 'you hurt?'

'No, sir,' I said.

'Well, damn it, get the hell up, then!' Colonel Sink yelled as he drove off. That was Colonel Sink's way."

Now Derwood had this mutt of a dog he called "Sergeant Extra." He was a variety mix, but more a bull terrier. Everywhere Derwood went, there was the mutt. This dog had a very peculiar habit, or, perhaps I should say, the dog was a bit confused. As sure as the sun set, whenever a group of us officers was standing around talking to Derwood, this mutt would come up to you and start humping your leg! You'd shout or cuss at the dog and kick him a little, enough to get him away. Derwood always smiled, acting as if nothing was happening, as that mutt would just find another leg of someone in our group. An officer once remarked that that dog would, "…hump the wind if he could." Well, his remark came true, because later I heard that Derwood made a parachute jump with his dog, so I guess that mutt got his chance.

CHAPTER 12

JUMP WINGS

The second phase of airborne training, known as the B stage, started at this point. Here you learned all about the T-7 parachute and watched the parachute riggers pack a chute. You had to pay strict attention because your first jump would be made with the parachute you packed. The first stage was training on a mock-up C-47 platform (it looked like the fuselage of a C-47 airplane). As in the fuselage of a C-47, the platform had two rows of benches, which faced each other, enough to seat nine men on each side, and an exit door called the jump door. The platform was about two to three feet high. This phase showed the men the proper technique for standing in the door and the proper technique for exiting the aircraft. The procedures inside the plane prior to exiting the aircraft were not emphasized during this time. An instructor critiqued each man on his position in the door and the exit jump into the sawdust pit.

Our instructor was Captain Jim Morton, known as "Jungle Jim." He ran W Company. Morton had been a newspaper reporter who covered the roller rink circuit in the New York city area. Anything having to do with public relations, Morton was the man.

The parachute landing fall or PLF was done from a five-foot high platform during the next phase of instruction. This training taught the proper method of landing. You would jump off the platform with feet together and the knees slightly bent. When you hit the ground you immediately fell to either the right or the left, absorbing the fall with the side of your body.

From the PLF you progressed to the fifty-foot high mock-up tower. Here you climbed up to the mock-up cabin where you were placed into a parachute harness that hooked to a cable above your head. Once hooked up, harness and cable properly secured and the leather football helmet snugly fastened, you stood in the door. On the signal, you jumped straight out into the sky, looking out over the horizon, your chin tucked into your chest, your hands holding the middle of the harness where your emergency chute and ripcord were located. As you fell the ten feet in mid-air, you counted out loud, "One thousand one, one thousand two, one thousand three." At one thousand three came the jolt, simulating the opening shock of the parachute canopy. Then you bounced and jiggled on that wire as your momentum carried you down the cable to the opposite side where you abruptly came to a stop. By the end of the second week, we had passed the second stage of parachute training.

To qualify as a parachutist you had to perform five parachute jumps from an aircraft at an altitude of 1200 to 1500 feet. This was the third stage of becoming airborne qualified, something that was usually accomplished within a relatively short period of time, say within a week and a half to two weeks. At Toccoa, a special dispensation was given to Colonel Sink whereby training and jump qualification to the officer cadre was expedited. Over fifty officers received training in parachute packing and landing techniques outside the parachute school at Fort Benning, which was a first, and a distinction which no other regiment could claim. Of this group, there were two classes of eight officers each, that I know of, who qualified by making five jumps in one day! I was one of the sixteen who completed that memorable event. I think it all came about because Airborne Command was having second thoughts about the whole idea of Colonel Sink wanting to qualify his officers at Toccoa rather than at Ft. Benning. As a result, everything was accelerated!

It was late in October 1943. I'll never forget that time as long as I live. On this particular day, at the crack of dawn, we went by truck to an airfield on the other side of Toccoa. There on the runway in front of us was the "Flagship Toccoa," an old C-47 aircraft that would carry us for our five jumps. The aircraft had only one door and could transport a stick of sixteen men or so. Each man put on the chute he packed the day before and boarded the aircraft according to his position on the jump manifest. Soon we were up at about 1200 feet and making a wide turn south over a cornfield north of the camp. On approach to the drop zone, a red light came on and the jumpmaster yelled out four commands: "Stand up! Hook up! Check your equipment! Sound off!"

From the back of the stick to the front came the reply in turn, "16, OK, 15, OK, 14, OK," and on down the line to the first jumper. The next command was "Stand in the door," as the first jumper now assumed the correct position in the door, looking straight out at the horizon while the rest of the stick shuffled forward to close the gap, tightly packed together. Now the green light came on and the command, "Go!" One by one, in rapid succession, our tight file jumped out into the cold, blue sky.

As you exited the door you counted, "1,000, 2,000, 3,000...," then immediately looked up to see if your chute had deployed. The opening shock of the T-7 parachute we used at that time felt something like getting hit by a two-by-four, heavy and hard. The rate of decent was pretty fast and even faster for a man of my weight. By pulling the risers apart moments before landing, as we were trained, you were able turn the chute, land forward and execute a correct landing. I landed in good shape in the cornfield, rolled up my chute, and ran to the assembly area where we got into the truck and roared back to the airfield. There we put on another chute and boarded the aircraft for our second jump. We followed this procedure until we had completed our five jumps in one day. It was quite a feat, and best of all, we were now airborne qualified. We had earned our jump wings. It is really something that not one man was hurt or injured in any way during those five jumps. It seems the Good Lord must have wanted us over there.

Not long after that there were two accidents where the C-47, Flagship Toccoa had gone off the runway, and Army Ground Forces Command put an immediate stop to any further jumping at Toccoa.

THE PROP BLAST

It is a tradition in the airborne that once an officer has successfully completed five parachute jumps, he is to be properly initiated and fraternally accepted into the regiment by "prop blast." At the next scheduled regimental party at the officer's club, the celebrated Prop Blast Committee, a mix of officers from the battalions, was responsible for the proceedings and the secret mix of beverages to be consumed that night. The committee had huddled to go over the list of officers who would be initiated. They decided who might be deserving of the "long count." Then, one at a time, each of the newly qualified jumpers was called forward by the Master of Ceremonies, none other than Major Charlie Chase, the executive officer. My turn was not long in coming. "Lieutenant Mehosky, Edward S., First Platoon, Company H, Third Battalion; front and center, Ivan! Lieutenant Mehosky is one of our 'young oaks' of the regiment as I think many will attest. Major Wolverton says you're fast and hit hard." There was a long pause. Major Chase continued, "Well, judging from the way you land on your jumps... yeah, you hit hard alright, like a ton of bricks! The medics always get excited, Lieutenant, when they see you coming down!" That brought on a chorus of laughter.

Then all eyes focused up front. Suspended from the ceiling by four parachute risers, two on each side and attached to handles on each side of what looked like a very large bowl, was the nose cone of a C-47, and which served as the drinking mug for all prop blast ceremonies. This clever contraption was filled with so many different kinds of alcoholic beverages that its exact contents were known only to the committee. As I shuffled forward toward the drinking station and got into position, hands behind my back, two officers began tilting the nose cone to my mouth while the master of ceremonies counted out loud, "One thousand one, one thousand two, one thousand three," the same time it would take a parachute to deploy. I gulped down everything that was being poured for fear if I stopped the count started over. Whatever was spilled was caught in a cup by another officer, who added the spilled contents to the bowl, and which also had to be drunk while the count continued. I was lucky, I guess, because I got the short count! I still I felt wobbly, dizzy, my head spinning; it was as if someone had knocked my feet out from under me. Those officers that got the long count, they were even worse, some making it just outside the club before passing out or throwing up. Feeling no pain, and happy and proud, I spent the night in my car along the side of the road at the officer's club, out like a light! I had just experienced my first prop blast.

TROOPS ARRIVE

The troops arrived the last week of September. All incoming troops reported to W Company, an acre or so of tents located about a mile from camp. W Company really meant "wash-out" company, because here every soldier reported in, and if they didn't make the grade, it was from here they left. There was no such thing as a W Company in the army, but the 506th had one. From W Company they were marched from area to area to take care of essential administrative paperwork, physicals and shots, and their gear. From there they were assigned to companies.

Once we got the troops settled it was time to get them in shape. We fit them into a unit and made sure they knew the basics of soldiering. They were introduced to weapons with which they would become proficient. The basic training phase would encompass about twelve weeks. They would receive preparatory parachute training, too.

Toccoa would get them ready for airborne qualification at Ft. Benning. Their first day in the company was an introduction of what was to come. For starters, they were introduced to the six-mile run up and down Mt. Currahee in combat boots. Within a week the run was instituted as a daily unit run every morning, six times a week! That was a real killer, the "separator," as it quickly became known. By platoons in company formation, we left camp on the Ayersville Road, turned right on to Lathan Road, then about a mile or so to the base of Currahee Mountain Road. There wasn't any time to get ready or think about it, and you had better not fall out! Up we ran, the whole regiment, battalion by battalion on that tough mountain road, three miles to the top. At the summit we turned around and started down as other companies were coming up. By the end of that week, the pace quickened and now it became a timed event with each company competing against the other. After the morning run, troops were taken to the obstacle course, which also became a regular part of their daily training: morning, run to the top of the mountain and back; afternoon, physical exercise and the obstacle course; squeezed into the rest of the day was everything else on the schedule. Wherever the troops went, whether to the battalion mess hall, firing range, or barracks, it was always double time. Our sergeants handed out push-ups with great frequency and which correctly added to unit discipline and to the development of the soldier. It was all part of the rigorous training required in getting those soldiers tough and ready for war. Come

Saturday morning the entire regiment passed in review at double time, dressed out in shorts and boots only, as Colonel Sink looked on. We were again on our way up to the top of Mt. Currahee and, the culmination of a seventy-hour week.

Long marches in full combat gear started at this time. These marches were "forced marches," meaning you fell out in full combat gear and equipment, with a specific goal, or in other words, to complete the designated distance in a specified amount of time as fast as our legs would carry us, and this meant even double timing it in order to meet the prescribed time. First came the ten-mile marches, then fifteen, and then twenty-five, in company formation. Many were up in the wilds of Black Mountain, north of camp. By dawn we were on the road. After a couple of miles we left the road and started cross-country. It was usually dark when we returned to camp.

On our first twenty-five mile regimental march we were given the task of completing it in four hours! We started out at 0800 sharp with the idea to be back in camp by noon, at regular chow time. Well, we just about did it. The entire regiment arrived back in camp at 1230, only thirty minutes off! We all thought that it was demanding, and at the same time, a good piece of soldiering. Of course, you know that nobody's going to make that kind of distance in that kind of time unless you double-timed a good portion of the way. Double time became the norm. The men became more confident because they had experienced the march first hand and knew what they could do.

On October 18, all qualified officers and cadre performed a low level jump near Clemson College, South Carolina, where the 3rd Battalion was firing on the rifle range. The following day we joined 3rd Battalion on a forty-five mile march back to Camp Toccoa. We arrived in camp thirteen hours later. We did a heck of a lot of forced marches during this span.

PLATOON TRAINING

Anytime we marched to a training area, I was always on the lookout for terrain which could be used to teach tactical deployment. I would halt the march and assemble my platoon sergeant and squad leaders and present them with the scenario. "I think this piece of terrain is an ideal location for teaching the platoon in the attack." I then followed troop-leading procedures and presented them with the situation. "That hill off to the right is held by the enemy. They control the road ahead. First platoon will attack at 0800, first squad on the left, second squad on the right, and third squad in support. Location of the support squad is the vicinity of the road junction behind us. The line of departure will be the road, there, that we were marching on." After the training exercise was completed, the platoon was assembled and I conducted a critique of the training.

To keep contact and communicate with my scouts up front, normally deployed 200-300 yards ahead of the platoon, we used sound powered phones and arm and hand signals. The sound power phone had a short wire with a clip at the end of the wire. This clip would be attached to a wire fence and we could initiate communication with a scout a short distance away. Otherwise, my commo man had to lay wire. I'll never forget Gordon Yeates, H Company's commo man, introducing the call words to our platoon. "Ham, this is Spam, over, do you read me?" "Spam, this is Ham, over. I read you loud and clear!"

During this time my troops got their first taste of map and compass reading. We studied terrain features and contours, and interpreted map features. This was always an area I stressed with my soldiers. I tried to also instill in them the idea that in repetition of a task, practice makes perfect. Acquiring the basic skills to where a soldier becomes proficient equals confidence, and confidence is one of the keys to performing effectively. I had my platoon out there at night to find their way back to camp, working in small teams, two to four men each, using only map and compass. There were those in the battalion that said that H Company, and especially Mehosky's 1st Platoon, did more night training than anyone in the entire regiment, especially those night compass marches. Maybe so. But I was determined that every one of my men could find his way in the dark in any terrain, under any condition.

LEADERSHIP

The atmosphere in the 506th was electrified! Every day was something different. There was always something going on, new learning situations, and because training was decentralized, a platoon leader could be innovative, try his ideas to accomplish the training objectives, and enhance leadership skills. One of the basic ideas instilled by Colonel Sink was: when we move, we move fast; when we stop, everyone is responsible for security, and we dig in, even if it's only ten minutes. It became one of the cornerstones of our training. Nothing here was overlooked. Our training was designed to produce the best possible soldiers, second to none. Down at my platoon, as with the other platoons in the regiment, "digging in" was conducted as a habit. We stop, dig in, we have our security out, and we're prepared. It's the same thing as when you have incoming rounds or a sniper shot in your area. The men become so accustomed to hitting the dirt that it becomes instinctive. You just react.

Unit level company commanders and platoon leaders in the 506th were a very creative and energetic lot, especially when it came to instilling hard lessons which would carry over to the battlefield. Where one company commander may have been criticized for using such a tactic as confiscating weapons while the soldiers slept to instill in his men the value of safeguarding their weapons at all times, others in the regiment were applauded for being imaginative and innovative. Everybody had their own techniques that either caught on or didn't. In H Company, and I think in the other companies as well, we were basically all doing the same thing, only with a little different twist. Enthusiasm, motivation, and attitude were words and actions pretty much ingrained in the men. You took care of your weapon, you avoided carelessness, and you went the extra five miles on every march. You made them tougher by demanding more. If the men liked you, they liked you. If they didn't like you, they didn't like you, period. That was the nature of the beast of the airborne soldier! Some officers were disliked because of the style they used in preparing their men for combat. Others ran their platoon or company by committee, while most followed the book.

Until the closing stages of the Holland Campaign, I was 3rd Battalion all the way, didn't know anyone in 1st Battalion, and only a couple of guys in 2nd. Third Battalion was a pretty close-knit group of people. We didn't have individual company mess halls, only battalion mess halls, so the men ate together and the officers from the companies got to know one another better. It didn't detract, but made us closer and helped create cohesiveness and camaraderie. I think all these things entered into the wonderful spirit we had.

It was always in the mess hall where you could get into some good discussions. Leaders of past battles and campaigns were always popular topics. One of my heroes was General Rogers, leader of the famed "Rogers Rangers" of the American Revolutionary War period. I liked the way he fought... hide-and-seek style. Another was Colonel William O. Darby and his Rangers and the famous raids they made during the early part of the war. A unit like that stirred my imagination, and that's exactly what Colonel Sink envisioned. Colonel Draza Mihailovic and his right-wing "Cetniks," Serbian patriots who fought against the Nazis, Tito's Communists, and Muslim factions in Yugoslavia during the years 1941 to 1943, were highly admired by officers of the battalion. That surprise British commando raid on the German-held town of Dieppe we heard so much about definitely stirred the fire of imagination in us as to what we could do to get at the enemy. We were training for that sort of thing, as our commander constantly reminded us.

Captain Harwick had a most positive influence on me at my young age. Does a man have to be loud, threatening, or boisterous to be demanding? Of course not. Or can a person be demanding by saying, simply, "Men, here's what I want, and if it's not done, proper action will be taken." He only had to say it once.

Whenever we marched, we carried everything. Sometimes we loaded the equipment on hand-pulled carts, a novelty we mostly used during training in England, but we never had vehicles to carry us or our equipment, not until Holland and Bastogne. We were not like regular infantry; we were not road-bound, and certainly not mechanized, two more key differences of the airborne organization and its training.

CHAPTER 13

THIRD BATTALION'S MARCH

By November 28, 1943, 1st Battalion had completed its basic training and moved to the "Frying Pan" area of Fort Benning, Georgia, for training at the parachute school, and to serve as the advance party to set up camp for the regiment. The 506th was one of the first parachute units to undergo basic and parachute training as a regiment.

When the 2nd Battalion completed its basic training and was ordered to the parachute school for jump training, the new battalion commander, Major Robert Strayer, decided to march his battalion the 110 miles to Atlanta. With full field equipment and crew-served weapons, including the heavy 81mm mortars, the men and officers marched the distance in three days. On December 2, the battalion marched down Peachtree Street to Five Points, and there was presented a streamer by Mayor Hartsfield on behalf of the city of Atlanta.

Major Wolverton, 3rd Battalion Commander, was determined to show that his battalion was in top shape for jump training, second to none, and he meant to prove it! Third Battalion, along with Regimental Headquarters Company, left Toccoa by train on December 3 and entrained north of Atlanta to start its historic 136-mile march to Ft. Benning. The uniforms we wore were our work uniforms-one-piece coveralls. This was to be a combat march in full combat gear: helmet, field pack, and weapons. Officers were distinguished by a dark brown, leather bomber jacket with the 506th patch worn on the upper left of the jacket. H Company was designated to lead with 1st Platoon at the point. The march was a spirited affair completed in good order in eighty-two hours and ten minutes, less than four days. Every single officer and soldier of 3rd Battalion and Regimental Headquarters Company completed the grueling, fast-paced march, arriving at Ft. Benning the evening of the third day. There were times we double-timed during the march! Blisters plagued us throughout, but our medics did a marvelous job patching us up. We had a big problem with our boots. They were hobnail boots and with the extreme heavy pounding they were taking, the nails began to tear through the leather into the foot. One of the first things I did early in the march was to remove the nails from my boots, as the nails were starting to break through the skin. The only time we stopped was to sleep, eat, or take a ten-minute break. Trucks brought in our meals. We slept on our bedrolls under the stars. When we arrived at Ft. Benning, the Airborne School Commander, Brig. Gen. Howell, and Colonel Sink and his staff enthusiastically greeted us. The other two battalions had also turned out to greet us. The mess hall was ready and awaiting our arrival, and once we got all the troops and officers in, 3rd Battalion set new records in food, coffee and ice cream consumption.

That march tested the toughness and preparedness of our battalion, hence the regiment as a whole, and it is an honor to say that upon completion of this great feat we shattered the world record for this distance then held by the Japanese Army. Perhaps the significance of what we accomplished was best captured by the newspaper account from the *Atlanta Constitution*, which gained national attention on Friday, December 4, 1942:

HIGH SPIRITED 'CHUTISTS SET RECORD IN 136 MILE MARCH...IT WAS TRAMP, TRAMP, TRAMP FOR THE THIRD BATTALION, 506TH...RECORD-SMASHING PARACHUTISTS SHAVE OFF HOURS FROM BUDDIES' SPEED...ARRIVE AT POST FROM ATLANTA IN FOUR DAYS...Foot weary, but filled with pride on their record, the Third Battalion of the 506th Parachute Infantry Regiment encamped at Fort Benning today, after marching 136 miles in eighty-four hours and ten minutes.

Trudging along the Georgia highways for four days and nights, the battalion of tough and rugged paratroop trainees accomplished a mission which is comparable to the forced march of 102 miles of the Second Battalion several days ago from Toccoa, Ga. to Atlanta, and matches records set by other U.S. Army units and other foreign armies.

The battalion ploughed along the highway from Atlanta through the outskirts of Columbus late yesterday singing chanting army ditties.

Major Robert L. Wolverton, of Elkins, West Virginia, commanding officer of the battalion, marched at the head of his husky troops, the full 136 miles to the frying pan area of Fort Benning, where the unit is located.

Major Wolverton exclaimed today that his troops comprised the "finest bunch of soldiers I ever saw." And Major Wolverton should know good soldiers when he sees them, for he graduated from the United States Military Academy in 1938.

"I didn't hear a grumble from one of my men," Major Wolverton related today, "even though we trudged along for the first three days in rain and nasty weather."

Col. Robert Sink, commanding officer of the 506th Parachute Infantry Regiment, lauded Major Wolverton and the members of the Third Battalion highly this morning. Colonel Sink said Major Wolverton "set a fine example for troops, leading them personally through the long forced march."

When the Third Battalion marched into Fort Benning at Outpost No. 1 last night, Brig. Gen. George P. Howell, commanding general of the parachute school, met the incoming troops with Colonel Sink.

The band of the 506th Parachute Infantry Regiment was at the outpost and rendered several numbers for the troops as they marched into the camp.

Shortly after arriving at their destination, the troops filed into their mess hall where they sat down to a meal of loin of pork, spinach, mashed potatoes and ice cream. At the meal, the soldiers consumed ninety gallons of hot coffee. "Far more coffee than I have ever seen as many men drink," the mess sergeant observed.

This morning, after a good night's sleep on army cots again, the soldiers got up at their leisure for an easy day and consumed scores of grapefruit, hundreds of pancakes with syrup, and about eighty gallons of coffee.

In the line of march with the Third Battalion on the hike was Regimental Headquarters Company of the regiment, commanded by Capt. Harold W. Hannah, of Urbanna, Ill. An agricultural lawyer in civilian life, Capt. Hannah is now a qualified paratrooper.

Cpl. George Sams, of Gastonia, N. C., observed this morning as he was going into the mess hall for his pancakes, that he would "sure love to fight under Major Wolverton. The thing I like about our C.O. is that he won't ask his men to do anything that he won't do himself."

"My men are enthusiastic as hell," Major Wolverton said today, as he recounted the long march and spirit of his men. "Those fellows are flowing over with morale and they're anxious to get along with their jump training."

CHAPTER 14

SINK'S CURRAHEE'S

Colonel Sink wanted to bring his regiment to Ft. Benning in the best physical and mental condition of any regiment to date, one that would have the lowest failure rates for parachute training completion. And he did! Our troops used to laugh when the school instructors called them to fall in for the daily run. After running Mt. Currahee at Toccoa, nothing came close. Nothing! The instructors at Benning, as they confided to us later, had never seen a more fit and enthusiastic bunch of soldiers.

Headquarters, 506th Parachute Infantry
Office of the Regimental Commander
December 18, 1942

Memorandum to Soldiers of the 506th Parachute Infantry:

You have now become qualified parachutists and wear the wings of the parachute soldier. You are a member of one of the finest regiments in the United States Army and, consequently, in the world.

You are about to go on furlough into the homes of relatives or friends. I feel that I should remind you of certain things that are expected of you, not only while on furlough, but also a creed by which you are expected to govern your life and your actions:

1. You must keep in mind that first you are a soldier in the Army of the United States; that you are a parachutist, the elite of this army; and finally, that you are a member of the 506th Parachute Infantry.

2. You must walk with pride and with military bearing.

3. You must be careful of your personal appearance, keeping your uniform neat at all times.

4. You must do nothing to bring discredit upon the army, parachute troops or this regiment.

5. Remember our battle cry and motto, "CURRAHEE," and its meaning: "Standing Alone." We Stand Alone Together!

The regimental commander desires that you convey to the members of your family his personal greetings.

R. F. SINK, Commanding Colonel,

506th Parachute Infantry

We were billeted in tents on the Alabama side of the post. We turned our troops over to the school for their parachute training, seeing very little of them except in the morning and evening. The troops went through landing and exiting techniques, platform jumping, and the high tower. Three weeks later, they had made their five qualification jumps. I roomed with Christianson. Most of the time we went over to Sam and Hattie's where the most incredible, absolutely delicious, fried chicken and ice cold milk was to be had. I was really starting to like this good southern cooking I had heard so much about. To this day I'm convinced that the secret to their chicken was that they let them run around free. Ken and I always got a couple of boxes of chicken to go and, back at our quarters in the two man tent, we'd start in on the extra chicken and talked into the early morning hours.

It was here that I met Bob Moon, the regimental signal officer who owned a big Harley Davidson. He let me ride his motorcycle to where I could handle the thing pretty darn well, and I even thought of buying one, but that passed, too. Bob Moon became another close friend. I would not see him again until the mid-fifties with the 11th Airborne at Ft. Campbell, Kentucky.

SOME THOUGHTS

Before I relate the next phase of my journey, I want to review a couple of points to provide a little more insight into the workings of the 506th. Everything was hard in the 506th, but we did the tasks over and over, with enthusiasm, always going the extra mile so that the hard things became easier and easier, and so over the long run, the soldiers gained confidence in their ability. In order to do this you had to inspire the men, not in a mechanical way, not by yelling in their faces or grumbling all the time, but in such a way that the men could see in their commander an officer who had the ability to accomplish whatever task, objective or mission that might arise. Confidence is all about inspiration. Each officer had his own technique and his own way of operating and leading, providing he was inspired to do that. If you have someone in a command position who's not inspired, he's not going to put forth the maximum effort; consequently, the men are going to reflect exactly his attitude. You have to set the parameters in training so the mission can be carried out in combat. If a leader is not going to do everything with the utmost feeling, when the time comes to deploy, the soldiers are going to do it in a half-assed manner. They're not going to try and accomplish the mission; they're not going to double-time or move in concert with others, because they are just going through the motions. How many times has this happened again and again and lives were lost because of it? And how many times did I see this coming into a new unit, before I got them moving in tune with what I was trying to do? In a nutshell, we trained the way we were going to fight!

On the 7th of January, 1943, the regiment had completed jump training at Ft. Benning with the lowest failure rate of any regiment to date. A month later the regiment moved across the Chattahoochee River into Alabama to begin the first stage of advanced training. We got in a lot of range firing with all the weapons that the platoon had at its disposal, including light mortar and machine guns. Scores of ten-mile marches and small unit tactical problems filled the bulk of our schedule, augmented by platoon parachute jumps. Every jump was different than the last. Sometimes you landed hard, sometimes easy, but always the elements and terrain played a big factor. During one platoon jump, our machine gunner, named Moose Walker, jumped while cradling the machine gun all the way down. I don't know if this had been duplicated in any of the other outfits or not, but Moose was one big, tough son of a gun, and one of the strongest men in my platoon.

CHAPTER 15

THE SWAMPS AT MACKALL

Headquarters, 506th Parachute Infantry Regiment, Camp Mackall, North Carolina, 1943. To the men of the 506th Parachute Infantry:

When this regiment was first organized at Camp Toccoa, Georgia, several months ago, I made you all a promise. Amid the privations, the lack of heat and hutments, the red mud, Currahee, and the obstacle course, I promised you that things would get a lot better before they got worse. You have been through the cycle several times. It was better before you left Toccoa and worse before you reached Benning. It was better before you left the frying pan and worse in Alabama, and it is better now. I can and do adhere to my statement. Things are going to be a lot better before they get worse.

This regiment is getting ready for combat. The combat you're going to enter is not a fair weather fight, nor is your opponent expected to use the Marquis of Queensbury rules. It is a fight for existence—yours, that of your comrades, and in the last analysis, that of your relatives and your country.

By application must you strive to learn the intricacies of war. By suffering must you learn to suffer. By doing must you learn to act.

R.F. Sink
Colonel, Commanding

By the end of February 1943, we moved to our new home at Camp Mackall, in Hoffman, North Carolina, to begin the second stage of advanced training. We were the first tactical unit to move to Camp Mackall, which was also the headquarters of the airborne command.

It was an advantage to have had different areas in which to train. Toccoa was the metal which forged our units into iron; Ft. Benning and Alabama made us a fully qualified parachute regiment; and North

Carolina would afford us new challenges for training in yet a different terrain. Here we would further solidify cohesiveness in steadily moving closer to our purpose in life, namely to leave this country, enter Europe or the Far East, and engage and annihilate the enemy where found. Although nobody said so, the fact that we would be training in the swamps had many believing that our next destination would be somewhere in the Pacific.

As part of our physical training regimen, everyone had to box twice a day. This part of the training came under the direction of Lt. Kelly, the 506th boxing coach. Kelly usually paired me with one of the officers who had boxed in college and most of the time Derwood Cann was my opponent. I always held my own in those three-round bouts. Lieutenant Kelly said afterward that I would have beaten him in a street fight. Derwood and I became pretty good friends after that. He used to tell the other officers that I was one of the strong, tough guys in the regiment, or as he was fond of saying, "A guy nobody in their right mind would ever want to cross swords with."

TACTICAL TRAINING

Once the company commander got the training schedule from battalion, it was up to us, the platoon leaders, to conduct the training objectives in the best way we knew to meet them. We always met or exceeded those objectives! I'm convinced that decentralized training was, and still is, the superior method of training infantry. You learned by doing, by mistakes and lessons learned; you were essentially on your own, limited only by your imagination and energy. This, in turn, spawned initiative and innovation, and you learned to overcome and adapt, and above all, to always improvise no matter where you were. What this did was foster strong confidence and a sense of "can do" that permeated all levels, all soldiers, and all ranks. There was never any shortage of imagination or innovation in any of the units. Enthusiasm? Let me tell you straight. There never was a more enthusiastic unit than the 506th, not before nor since, and the spirited 3rd Battalion led the way.

Officers were always highly visible in the regiment. You got around at all levels and you made corrections on things that needed correcting. You looked for it, saw it, and corrected it on the spot. You knew what was going on because you saw and heard for yourself. You knew someone was always watching, too. You had to be a step or two ahead of your superiors. As the regimental commander was always out there with his soldiers, the example was set and it flowed down to the battalion commander, the company commander, and the platoon leader. He knew if his policies were being instilled and carried out. It wasn't management from the office hoping nothing erupts.

We did a hell of a lot of tactical training at Mackall, and it seemed like we were in the swamps most of the time with the snakes, water and mud. It was good maneuvering terrain because of the concealment factors. Flanking movements were practiced every chance we got against companies G and I.

We lived off the land for days at a time. There were many, many times we would send out reconnaissance (recon) teams to scout local towns for food and beverage stores. Once this intelligence was known to me, we'd take up a collection, send out a recon team to the town and secure the proper food from local merchants in order to properly supplement our rations. We got items like bread, cheese, cold cuts, butter, crackers, beer, and doughnuts. The merchants and town people were amazed when we came into town, wondering where we came from and not realizing we were camped in their backyards.

Every man had bouillon cubes and crackers in his knapsack so that we could always boil a cup at any time. There was a standing joke among the officers of the battalion: first platoon would go out for days with practically nothing and come back ten pounds heavier to a man!

We became so adept at hiding that not only couldn't you see us, but you couldn't find us either. We made bedding roles out of shelter halves and carried them in our packs. We traveled light and fast. We were always on the lookout for snakes. It was impressed upon the men to take extra precautions as to where they would sit or sleep, and not to put hands under logs or rocks at any time, especially when looking for firewood. They were taught to probe the area with a stick and to be careful.

In all the time we spent training in those swamps, I never had one man bitten in my platoon. I can still remember Ken Christianson of 2nd Platoon saying words to the effect: "Damn! Just think. Fifty years from now our bones and joints will be so sore with aches and pains and rotting because of being in this stinking, filthy, swamp water muck so much."

When H Company was out there conducting day and night exercises in the swamp, each platoon was assigned a certain area for the purpose of setting up a base camp from which to conduct patrolling and reconnaissance training. We carried three days rations and intended to live off whatever was available in the swamp, even purifying swamp water so as to be fit to drink. We went so deep into the swamp that not even the company commander knew our whereabouts. There was a lot of reconnaissance and counter-reconnaissance going on. Companies G and I were out there also, but the trick was to find and not be found. Our base camp was not easily found, but we located their area because we had a pretty darn good intelligence system set up, and also because we usually outflanked them by going through the most difficult areas to achieve our objective. Next to combat, this was as real as you could get. We were in a tactical situation.

By April, we were involved in a series of ground forces exercises and tests which included competitive physical fitness, platoon and company problems, battalion twenty-five-mile forced marches, and attack problems against prepared and defended positions. Third Battalion did well in all phases of these exercises, but there were a lot of interruptions caused by brush and grass fires in our training areas. We became expert at fighting fires, too.

Perhaps a good summary of the regiment up to this point was the comment made by a high-ranking general officer who was inspecting the regiment at Camp Mackall one afternoon in 1943. As we passed in review formation on the double-time, the general made the comment to Colonel Sink and all those on the reviewing stand, and eventually it got down to the company level: "Colonel Sink, this regiment is the toughest, most rugged, and most unusual regiment I've seen!" Our conduct became a 506th trademark. The entire regiment passed in review on the run, dressed out in only shorts and combat boots!

CHAPTER 16

THIRD BATTALION OFFICERS

In trying to describe some of the officers I came to know in the 3rd Battalion, I will start first and foremost, with our battalion commander, Lieutenant Colonel Robert Wolverton, a West Point graduate from West Virginia. Colonel Wolverton was stocky and of medium height, an officer and gentleman in every sense of the word and highly regarded. He was the heart and soul of 3rd Battalion. He was athletic, tough and strong as an ox! He could certainly play the tackle position on a football field with the best of them. I know because I played right next to him. His down field blocks were vicious! Colonel Wolverton was the kind of man who would never ask anyone to do something he couldn't do. Sometimes he would sort of playfully wrestle with officers in his office, especially if someone was really feeling his oats, like, "Come on, Lieutenant, come on. Let's see what you got. Let's see how strong you are. Good move! Good move! What do you think of this one?" Wham!

He was very close to Colonel Sink, and, like Sink, he was physically tough, but more than anything else Wolverton was mentally tough, and that's what made the battalion so good.

Lieutenant Fred Anderson, a platoon leader in I Company, was the comic of 3rd Battalion. Fred was 5' 10", a stocky, round-faced fellow who hailed from Charlotte, North Carolina. He was well liked by Colonel Sink, so well in fact that the colonel valued his opinion. Fred was funny and always smiling. He was one of those guys that once he got a couple of drinks in him, the wit and one-liners just kept coming. Fred always took the worst situation and make it light and humorous, and always found good things in everybody. It was Anderson who gave the officers in the battalion their nicknames. For example, one of the officers with a broad back was named "The Back," while another who had a large hawk nose was simply known as "The Nose." Colonel Wolverton was "The

The Story of a Soldier • 87

Bull," but never to his face. James Walker, H Company, 3rd Platoon and later battalion mess hall officer, got the tag "Knothead," but everyone knew him as plain old Knot Walker. Knot was a 5' 7", wiry redhead who hailed from Alabama. Walker was quiet and very capable, another officer Colonel Sink took a liking to.

I got the nickname "Ivan" from Bob Harwick as he was always singing "Ivan, scavinski, scvar..." every morning when he shaved. Once Fred Anderson got hold of it, it stuck. From then on I was known as "Ivan."

There was Ken Christianson of 2nd Platoon, H Company. At 5'11", Ken was the strong, intelligent, quiet type of officer, extremely capable and well liked by everyone. To this day he has been one of my best friends. From the start, we competed against each other as if we were on opposite teams, fiercely pushing to the limit, neither of us wanting to give in; we made each other better. We learned from each other and that made our platoons better. Ken and I confided in each other about lots of things, especially platoon problems and training techniques. I have great memories and the greatest respect for Ken. Ken was without doubt a fine officer, one of the best our generation produced.

Dick Meason was the XO of H Company, Harwick's right arm. A lean 5' 11", Meason was a lawyer from Arizona, thoughtful, easy going, easy to talk to, and very capable. He would command A Company during the Bastogne Campaign. Bill Reid handled the Headquarters Companys' heavy weapons section, his specialty, the 81mm mortar. He was a New Englander and a fine officer and friend. Joe Doughty and I were roommates and friends in England. Affable and well liked, Joe was from the mid-west, fairly tall at 6' 1", extremely capable. The youngest of the bunch and one of the most energetic was the slender, wavy-haired Windish, whom Anderson nicknamed, "Blood and Guts."

If Colonel Wolverton was the heart and soul of the battalion, our commander, Captain Robert "Bob" Harwick was the heart and soul of H Company. Of medium height and frame, dark features and dark hair, Captain Harwick became one of the most stable influences in the battalion. He was more on the quiet side, a gentleman in every sense of the word, calm, steadfast, clear thinking, and decisive. He made H Company into the fighting unit it became and his influence was far reaching. Harwick later took command of 1st Battalion at one of the most critical junctures of the war, Bastogne, and did an admirable job. I cannot say enough about my old company and battalion commander.

CHAPTER 17

THE 101ˢᵀ "SCREAMING EAGLES"

By the middle of May we had reached the third stage of advanced training. On the 15th of that month the Gum Swamp Creek Operation was held, which was a regimental exercise designed to emphasize combined training. Among other things, we were resupplied with ammunition, food and bedrolls by parachute, as we were way out in the middle of nowhere. Four days later came the Sand Hills Operation where we were resupplied at night.

The beginning of the last stage of advanced training started with the Camden-Kershaw Operation in North Carolina on the 28th of May. This was the first large-scale airborne maneuver in which the 506th combined with other units of the 101st Airborne Division to prove the use of paratroops. Despite some miserable weather, we accomplished our mission in good shape.

Up to this time we had been an independent regiment. On June 1, 1943, the 506th was attached to the 101st Airborne Division under the command of Major General William C. Lee. The 101st Screaming Eagles now consisted of the 501st, the 502nd, and the 506th Parachute Infantry Regiments. The division was mighty glad to have us, and we were glad to be a part of a new, aggressive organization. No sooner had we caught our breath and sorted out our gear, then we were enroute with the division into the 2nd Army Tennessee Maneuvers. On the sixth of June 1943, we camped at an air base in Sturgis, Kentucky. I note the irony of this date, for one year later we would be the first to invade Hitler's Europe during the predawn hours of June 6, 1944! I think it was during the first phase of the maneuvers, the California Hollow Operation, where we jumped at so low an altitude that we had parachutes opening just before the men hit the trees. There had been some confusion and even some evasive action on the part of the pilots for some reason never known to us, but the similarity between this event and what happened over Normandy is too profound not to mention.

All things were pointing to deployment to Europe, something all us officers felt at the time. We next moved to Camp Breckenridge where defensive operations were conducted in the area around Springfield, Kentucky. The 506th made two jumps near Hartsville, Tennessee. Back at Camp Breckenridge we received our warning orders to prepare for shipment overseas!

It was late July when we moved to Ft. Bragg, North Carolina, for refitting. Company and platoon training concentrated on schooling in mines, booby traps, gas training, and weapons firing. Formation running still continued at a good clip every morning. Our last big function before heading out was a parade review of the entire division by the 2nd Army Commander.

It was during this time that final leave was requested. I managed to get a couple of days leave at home in Reading. After saying my good-byes to friends and family, I rejoined the regiment at Ft. Bragg.

PART VI

YOU DON'T KNOW WHAT'S IN STORE FOR YOU...YET IT WAS A ROMANTIC TIME, A DIFFERENT TIME, AND A SPECIAL FEELING.

Yvonne Joy Bevis, American Red Cross

CHAPTER 18

THE FORTY THIEVES

The 506th entrained for the New York port of embarkation on August 28, and arrived at Camp Shanks, Orangeburg, New York, a day later. Final processing and equipping was completed, and on September 5, we set sail for England on the H.M.S. Samaria as part of a large convoy.

On any troop transportation of any kind, officers are assigned certain duties. One of mine was to inspect the company mess area. I was assigned to check the mess on E deck, way down in the bottom of the ship. The day I was to make my rounds I never made it that far, because once I got to the stairs to go down, all those cooking smells from below, combined with the rocking motion of the ship, overwhelmed me! I had been a bit sick before that, but when those awful, sickening smells hit me, I got sick as a dog—green, nasty, and violently ill. I went on deck a couple of times, but threw up over the side of the ship. I tried breakfast, but that didn't work either. I just couldn't get that lousy, nauseating smell out of my system no matter what I tried. Everybody was so concerned about me that they took turns poking their heads in the cabin door and calling out, "Hey, Ivan, how about a hot bacon sandwich?" All I could do was moan. Moose Heyliger, one of those who frequently checked on me, nicknamed me "The Green Death."

After eleven days at sea, we docked at Liverpool, England on September 15, 1943, and boarded a troop train. We were all glad to be back on dry land and eager to get settled and back to our routine. It was on this train that I first got acquainted with watercress and cucumber sandwiches, always placed on nice, thinly-sliced white bread, and at every station stop the best cup of tea in the world-good old English tea with milk.

We detrained on the 16th at the Hungerford train station in Wiltshire, south central England, and boarded trucks for the six-mile ride over to

Ramsbury, where 3rd Battalion, Headquarters 1st Battalion, and C Company would make their new home. Regimental Headquarters and Regimental Headquarters Company were billeted at Littlecote Manor, while 2nd Battalion, A Company and B Company were housed in Aldbourne; Special Units and Service Company were at Chilton-Foliat and Froxfield.

RAMSBURY

How does one describe such a village as Ramsbury? You could say it was a typical English village with a history dating back a thousand years. It was situated astride the Kennet River, in a valley. Ramsbury to me was unlike anything I had ever seen before—a place right out of a picture book. The Ramsbury I came to know was quaint and charming. It was a quiet kind of place with a uniqueness all its own. There were butcher and baker shops, pubs, and a barbershop. Most of the cottages had thatched roofs. Two churches and two large, prominent manor homes caught your eye, and there were some hills not far beyond. There were two main roads which formed an oval around the village. They merged at the east end of the village at the village square and then branched off. In the village square was the Bell Hotel and Pub.

Most of the officers of Third Battalion were billeted in a large manor house called Parliament Piece, known also as the "Rookery" in former times, which was built between 1620-1650. As the story goes, Oliver Cromwell held a council in Black Lane at the house called the "Rookery," and sometime in the 1920's, the owner of the estate changed the name to Parliament Piece to commemorate the historic event. The current owner and resident of the house was the charming Lady Violet Wyndham, a gracious hostess who extended every kindness and courtesy to all the officers of the battalion. From then on we knew the place simply as Lady Wyndham's House.

I roomed with Joe Doughty from G Company. We'd often bounce ideas off one another to see how things were going, check what was going on in the company and the battalion, and share thoughts on the war and the role we would soon play. But the talk most of the time, however, centered on the English women we had seen and met ever since our arrival in Ramsbury.

Lieutenant Colonel Wolverton had one of the big rooms on the second floor. There was another fairly large room, which served as our club room. It was a comfortable place where we could get together after duty and let down a little bit. The battalion officer's mess was located in the great hall. Of all the things I remember about Parliament Piece, this room holds my fondest memories, and not just because of the great food. It was here, on a particular evening in the autumn of '43, that the American Red Cross touring show came for dinner, and it was here that I met my future wife.

From the side entrance of the house was a parking lot and a large hedge with a throughway, and on the other side was a big field lined with rows of Quonset huts where the soldiers of G, H, and I companies slept and fell out for morning formation. If you had to go over to regimental headquarters you'd take the shortcut through these hedges, through the woods, and across the fields to Chilton Foliet, a little over three miles away. That was always a nice little run. If something needed to get over to headquarters, we'd run it over.

Lieutenant Rudolf Bolte joined us in England as a replacement. Bolte was a married man, a quiet fellow with a lot of heart. He was assigned to me as my assistant platoon leader and Harwick said, "just follow Mehosky around." During platoon formation, just before the company commander took his place in front of the platoons, I would post to the front of my platoon to receive the report from my platoon sergeant, J.J. McCollough. He would then post to the rear of the platoon and I would pivot and make my "platoon all present and accounted for" report to the company commander. As I pivoted around to face my platoon, there was Bolte, right in my face, staring me right in the eye. He wasn't supposed to be there, but he was! I guess he took it to heart when the captain told him to "shadow Lieutenant Mehosky."

"Bolte," I said, "you need to get back to your position at the rear of the platoon," speaking so only he could hear me. He saluted, wheeled about, and moved off to the rear of the platoon.

Hank DiCarlo of 1st Platoon recalled Lieutenant Bolte as an "eager beaver," a college boy type who seemed somewhat of a green horn when he joined the platoon in England. "He was a good man and a fine officer, but had a tough time taking Lt. Mehosky's place with those of us who had served under his command. Lieutenant Mehosky had gone into the hospital and missed the Holland jump, so Lieutenant Bolte took over 1st Platoon."

DICARLO'S INSIGHTS

Every platoon in 3rd Battalion got nicknames in England. My guys, the "Forty Thieves" of 1st Platoon, were an energetic bunch who liked to let off steam. Mario (Hank) DiCarlo was one of my riflemen and a fine infantry soldier. He was from Philadelphia, Pennsylvania, and served in 1st Platoon, H Company starting at Toccoa, Georgia. It was DiCarlo who, in his correspondance, has provided some insights as to what made 1st Platoon tick.

DiCarlo: "the platoon was like a bunch of old women, rehashing and re-analyzing everything the officers told us to see if we could read any sinister implications into their pronouncements. Those were exciting times, especially when the "Forty Thieves" were operating at full throttle. I can state with no little pride that the 1st Platoon of H Company, in my opinion, had more expert scroungers, scavengers and liberators of material and equipment than any unit in the ETO. General Sherman would have loved us."

"As far as how 1st Platoon got the name 'Forty Thieves,'" DiCarlo continued, "we were inadvertently named after several months in England in what was known as the 'Silver Spoon Mystery.' It happened during a regimental night problem where we were located next to a YMCA. And since it was raining, an unlocked door was found and the next thing you know some silver spoons from a table were missing! The next day, the possessors of the spoons were so unhappy they let the chain of command know. Lt. Colonel Wolverton was not deaf and had to investigate. Suddenly, the Colonel and Captain Harwick are racing around the corner in search of Lt. Mehosky. Wolverton unwittingly named the platoon when he said to Lt. Mehosky, 'O.K., Ali Baba, let's run your forty thieves out here and get the score on this thing.' But Lt. Mehosky knew nothing of his men taking any spoons, and every one of us displayed a collective case of amnesia. So the thing was quickly dropped when the 'Affair of the Bell Hotel', another Forty Thieves enterprise, began to occupy the official mind."

"Now Lieutenant Mehosky," DiCarlo continued, "was the First Platoon leader in England and into the initial phases of the D-Day Invasion. Most of us were still teenagers and still wet behind the ears. By this time we had been under the command of Lt. Mehosky long enough to know that he was informed and fair but not to be messed with. One of the things that impressed us the most was his attitude that 'we are all in this together, men, so let's get it right.' Lieutenant Mehosky couldn't have been more than twenty-three at the time, but his brawn, his physical presence and that ubiquitous mustache adorning his upper lip gave him the appearance of solidity and a grasp of the soldierly qualities that everyone should expect to find in a leader. I will not say he was unconditionally loved by all those under his command, but he was certainly respected, which, at that time and place, was far more important than mere affection. The platoon, as a whole, felt we had lucked out in having an actual adult leading us. He was no older than we were as a group, but he seemed older and in command of his life in general. If he depended on us, he had no idea how much more we depended on him. Without being the martinet that many officers became in the field, his insistence that we learn the proper basics of survival in combat went a long way toward the success we enjoyed when put to the ultimate test. He always seemed to be thinking about some new way to get the message across to us, especially some of the dimmer bulbs. He was known to us as 'Moose Mehosky' and, unlike many other cases I could mention, not derisive in nature but a well-earned accolade. I can still remember him clear as day. There he was, in his dress uniform, looking right at us. He looked like a big, solid bear. He had physical stability and it carried over in everything he did. We were all impressed by his size, and my buddy, Joe Harris, was no exception. One day Harris said to me, 'you know, Hank, if you put a set of antlers on Mehosky, he would look like a moose.' And so the nickname stuck and Lt. Mehosky was forever known as the 'Moose.'"

"Lieutenant Mehosky prepared us very well for what we were going to run into. I can well remember our training in England, whereas some platoons didn't train the way we did and maybe took the easy way, he had us out there more than all the others, in nasty weather, night and day, simulating all kinds of problems. And he got us together and said that in combat there is no simulation! He prepared us. He was a very practical man. The impression he gave his men was the fact that he actually cared about getting us through any stuff we'd encounter."

1ˢᵀ PLATOON

England offered an ideal terrain for training, more on the line of what we would face when we got to the continent. I always tried to give my guys the best training possible, a lot of different situations, repetition of things so as to become proficient, getting them to think and function as a team, and what to do if they were on their own. We were always out there in the woods and hedgerows. I thrived in the field and I think it rubbed off on my men, too. I was in my element and never missed an opportunity to practice a combat scenario. I studied the lay of the land, noting what was immediately around me and to my front. I'd call my platoon sergeant and squad leaders in, tell them what we were going to do, and send them back to the platoon waiting in the assembly area. I would go through all the troop leading procedures to get them going into an attack formation: we'd conduct a reconnaissance, set up the machine gun, and check the fields of fire. We practiced a lot with fire and movement and cover, pointing out the little things, the important things that each soldier needed to stay alive. Things like ideal places to be ambushed, where would an enemy place a machine gun, and don't make yourself an easy target were stressed to the men frequently. I arranged bus tours and took the platoon out in the countryside to some prominent land features. Each man had a map and a compass. As I point-ed out various features and contours, they'd have to find it on the map. What you first have to do is know the parameters, the terrain you're in, and then make a reconnaissance of the terrain features you want to teach. Next you have to orient them on the ground; as they are looking at their map they can see the features you are discussing in view and find them on the map. They learn what a draw or a steep hill looks like on the ground and on their map and how to read contour lines. Now was the time we'd divide them into teams and assign each a contour line. Their mission was to start at point A and follow the contour line to a designated point B.

We talked about how easy it was to get sloppy and careless, so we kept them on their toes, always reminding them what it took to be a good soldier. Things like cover and concealment, quickness of movement, and the hand signals for forward and back movements were practiced until every soldier had them down pat and was working as a team. When firing and moving, your buddy covered your movement and you covered his. You got the men thinking as they were moving and had to stop: what were you going to do? How long were you going to stay there? What if the movement got stalled? Every situation was different in combat. The thing you didn't know was how long you would be out there, so you secured your flanks and started digging in! You were much better off when those incoming rounds started hitting your position. This was how we indoctrinated the men.

DiCarlo: "Lt. Mehosky's forte in England was training the platoon in small unit actions where his inventive mind found its best form of expression. Correctly foreseeing the kind of combat we were most likely to encounter, he drilled and redrilled us in small unit formations. He stressed rapid deployment techniques and how to use the existing terrain to our advantage. He did his job well; combat did not spring any surprises on us that he had not already anticipated and prepared us for. A rare skill."

Remember the bouillon cubes I told you back at Mackall? Well, even little things like bouillon cubes were all a big part of taking care of my soldiers. When all the other soldiers were waiting for the food trucks to come in after a long day's march, my men were having soup and crackers.

It was cold in England, especially out in the field, and wearing that helmet during night training and foul weather brought chills right through your body. I had seen the British troops wearing the "balaclava," a woolen garment that tucked inside the trousers and pulled over the head, exposing only your face and kept everything else warm. We went down to a merchant and I bought every man in the platoon a balaclava.

Even on the coldest nights in the woods, when that helmet got as cold as ice, we were the warmest platoon out there.

Something new was always coming down to us with which to experiment. It was during this time that the two-wheeled hand-pulled cart, a four-foot by four-foot affair for transporting equipment on the march, was being looked at from the top level. It was a pretty neat little thing. We'd load our gear and rations for three days and move out. Two guys at a time took turns pulling the cart during the march. A day or so out we'd scout a particular village to determine the location of the bakery and butcher shop, then send a party of men to buy breads, meats and other things to supplement our rations. Here the men had to study the map to find the village, note the terrain and prominent features, note how the village was situated, study the roads leading in and out, and determine the best way to get into the village undetected. Then I'd select a squad to go into the village, half to get to the bakery, the other half to the butcher shop. In doing things like this, we were able to combine a lot of different aspects of field training in a realistic setting, and we never, ever went hungry. That was one of my trademarks in taking care of my soldiers, always first making sure my men had what they needed. This decentralized training down to the platoon level really paid off in Normandy when we were so scattered. The men had the confidence in their ability to function on their own and take the necessary steps to survive, which is the name of the game. You do whatever you have to do to survive.

HIT ON THE NOSE

In order to know if you could drop equipment in or near the drop zone, you had to practice, and since we were using the hand-pulled cart, well, they wanted to know how well a piece of equipment would deploy from an aircraft at 1500 feet. On one particular exercise, my job was to check the straps of the parachute fastened to one of these carts and push the damn thing out the door. When we arrived over the drop zone area, the green light came on and I proceeded to push the cart with everything I had. But when that thing hit the turbulence it swung around violently back toward the door, and wham! The handle struck me across the bridge of my nose. The force was like being hit with a hammer. It knocked the heck out of me and I saw some stars. I suffered a deviated septum and black eyes. Not long after that incident they decided it wasn't a good idea to do this. Meanwhile, I had a time breathing through my nose with all that swelling, so I was breathing mostly through my mouth. It wasn't long before I saw the regimental surgeon for the procedure to hopefully give me some relief.

I think it was October when I had the operation. What they did was numb my nose, then started to chip away at the bone tissue in the bridge area where all the damage was. What they used to do this was a mallet and a thin chisel. They just chipped and pounded until they were satisfied they had opened it to where I could breathe. By this time my head was ready to explode! Next they packed what seemed like miles of strips of gauze up my nose to stop the bleeding and promote healing. For the next couple of days I had to endure walking around with a swollen nose twice the normal size of what was already a good size Polish nose, plus two black eyes. The real pain, though, came when the doctor had to take all that gauze out. Now that hurt! But after a few weeks my nose got better, and, more importantly, I could breathe through it again.

There weren't too many jumps I made over my thirty-one-year career that I don't remember, especially when they were followed by something of a profound or significant nature. One that especially stands out, however, occurred in England, in October, in the early morning during a tactical training exercise. I remember it being cold, real cold for that time of the year. Knowing this, the word went out for every man to take extra precautions to keep warm. I'm pretty sure everyone wore two of everything on that jump.

As jumpmaster I was the first one out, and as my chute deployed, I reached up to grab the risers, but my hands were frozen numb. I couldn't feel anything or get proper control to guide myself in. I began to oscillate from side to side while falling at a pretty fast rate (I always dropped faster than the other guys due to my weight, which at that time was about 205 pounds). As the ground came up, I landed hard with my body turned sideways. My right knee was locked on impact and the force bent it unnaturally inward, tearing out a chunk of bone. Within minutes, I could feel the knee swelling and throbbing. I gathered up my chute and walked across the field to the assembly area at the edge of the drop zone. When everyone was accounted for, we moved out across country on a ten-mile march to our objective. It was toward the end of the day when I stopped, having covered the march with my broken knee, which now hurt like heck. My limp was so pronounced that Captain Harwick told me to fall out. In no time the medics had come up. They wrapped a couple of ice bags around my knee and took me over to the hospital. The X-ray revealed a wedge of bone had chipped out from the side of my knee. In time, this piece of bone would work its way around to the back of my leg until it finally dissolved.

Other than that, I was kind of lucky, I guess, considering all that can happen on that kind of a landing! Like the doc said, "No breaks, no separation, but you'll have to go easy for awhile." My knee was wrapped again and I was given a cane for support, and for the next couple of weeks I was placed on light duty. That meant no more football! Colonel Wolverton and I anchored the right side of the line on the regimental football team, he at tackle and I at guard. We played an inter-division schedule against the other regiments of the 101st plus a team from the Troop Carrier Command. I played my first and last game against the 501st. But I believe all things work out for the best, even though you can't always see it at the time.

CHAPTER 19

MISS BEVIS OF ESSEX

An American Red Cross musical and dance show touring group came to Ramsbury during that time to entertain the troops. That evening, we all loaded into the buses and went down to the town hall. That was the first time I saw Miss Bevis out there dancing, doing her high step, acrobatics and everything, and I thought, Boy, oh boy! Look at that! Later, the entire cast was invited to dinner at the battalion headquarters dining hall. As it turned out, I was at the end of the table and Miss Bevis was just two seats away. There I was, sitting across from Miss Bevis and her girlfriends, trying to strike up a conversation. I couldn't get to first base with her. That's the way it was. I was trying to give her the eye, catch her attention, but she wouldn't look my way, and just kept talking with her girlfriends.

They were staying at the Bear Inn in Hungerford, so after dinner, five of us, Colonel Wolverton, Doc Morgan, Bill Reid, Dick Meason, and I, piled into a jeep and followed the bus over to the hotel. We sat in the lounge having drinks and talking. That's when I really first met Yvonne Bevis. I was getting around with a cane, still limping somewhat, and still on light duty. From then on, every morning I would meet the bus and escort them around to the different areas of other units, and Lou, the bus driver, was kind enough to let me on because he knew I liked Miss Bevis. The whole bus knew, too. "I think he fancies you," Lou would shout.

"Oh, don't be so silly," came the reply. We had a big regimental party at Little Cote Castle in the large banquet room that had a huge fireplace and mantel. Around the walls was the coat of arms of English families dating back centuries. It was a very pleasant evening.

By now I was escorting Miss Bevis around. I had a big, black moustache that made me look much older. One of Miss Bevis's girlfriends couldn't understand why she wanted to date that old man, and when I told her I was just twenty-three, she could hardly believe it. Anyway, as the Red Cross bus came around, I'd be right there at the stop. "Here's gimpy, again!" said Lou.

Once I got serious about Miss Bevis, I was making the trip to London, to the suburb of Essex and back, every weekend or whenever I could get away. I always traveled light. I took a little sewing kit and stuffed it with a razor, toothbrush, toothpowder, and a small bar of soap. I wore a short coat with a big collar and I'd just put that sewing kit into my coat pocket and off I'd go. If I stayed overnight I'd wash my shorts at the hotel. But getting back to Ramsbury was the problem. I was way out in West Hamstead and had to get from there to Paddington Station under wartime blackout conditions. It was usually past midnight when I left and there wasn't any transportation to get me to the train station, so I made the five-plus miles from West Hamstead to Paddington Station at a pretty fast clip in order to catch the last train out. Luckily, I always made it in time to catch the milk train in one of the end cars with all the milk kettles and goats. It was a slow moving train that stopped at every village along the way. I usually managed to get a couple hours sleep and woke up when the train stopped at Hungerford. From there, it was about a three-mile sprint to Ramsbury and I was just in time for morning reveille.

Meeting Yvonne was the best thing that ever happened to me. In fact, those were some of the best times of my life, wonderful times I'll never forget. That's why I married Yvonne Bevis on April 4, 1944. You had to have permission to get married, so one day at Battalion, I approached Colonel Wolverton and said, "Sir, what do you think of a guy, a friend I know, who's thinking of marrying an English girl?"

Apparently he had known all along what was going on, because he answered, "Oh, hell, Mehosky, why don't you just marry her?" And that was that.

Yvonne Joy Bevis was born in London on September 19, 1923. She had two sisters, Elaine and June, and a younger brother Derrick; Yvonne was the oldest. She started ballet at seven years of age at Winsor and Langly Hall. By 1936, Yvonne was at the top of her field in ballet and acrobatics. That same year she performed a ballet solo at Alexandra Palace in London. There followed a couple of years working different theaters with her partner doing dance and acrobatic acts before she auditioned and got on with the American Red Cross.

Yvonne was a petite brunette beauty! She was very athletic from her years of dancing and the many miles she walked each day around London to get from home to her job sites and back. I can remember seeing her perform for the first time and wanting to get to meet her. I'd ride the bus to every one of her performances and make every opportunity to talk with her. How overjoyed I was that we eventually began dating. She was a determined and self-assured young lady and somewhat of a perfectionist in her work ethic. Yvonne certainly had a charming way about her, insightful and intelligent, with a love of laughter! She also enjoyed eating hot cross buns and tea with a passion, and because of that I still call her "Buns" to this day.

Being with Yvonne was wonderful and how I enjoyed being with her family and friends and having those great cups of tea. I was almost becoming English. You might say that never before had one drunk so much tea, with so few, so many times, over such a short period of time!

CHAPTER 20

YVONNE'S STORY

When the Americans first arrived we heard that they were rude, crude, rough, not gentlemen at all, and so on. How did I meet Edward? I was with the American Red Cross at the time. I had auditioned for a job as an entertainer for the troops. We were visiting Ramsbury and were invited to the 3rd Battalion mess hall for dinner. The food was very good and plentiful. We were not used to this. I was feeling very miserable, not well at all, and wasn't talking with anyone. Mrs. MacDonald, our Red Cross Director and chaperone, asked if anything was wrong. Lieutenant Mehosky was sitting diagonally across from me, about three people away. He kept trying to get my attention and talk to me, but I was non-committal and didn't want to be bothered. At first I wasn't interested in dating an older man. We left the mess hall and boarded the bus for the Bear Hotel in Hungerford where we were staying. The next morning we went to another camp, then back to the hotel for lunch. As we entered the lobby there was Lieutenant Mehosky, walking with a cane because he had injured his leg during a jump. He was with another officer and they came over to our table to say hello.

For the next two nights there were parties at battalion headquarters. On the third night was the big party at division headquarters at beautiful Little Coate Manor. I remember going through the receiving line and meeting lots of generals and colonels. My girlfriend, Jackie, did not want to be at the party because she was dating a guy in the 82nd, so she was quite annoyed and wanted to leave, but I wanted to stay. I was sitting on a couch near the fireplace in the big room when Lieutenant Mehosky came over, sat down, and started talking to me. The next thing I knew Jackie was fussing with Bill Reid and gave him a good push practically into the fireplace!

I don't know what changed my mind about Lieutenant Mehosky. I found him to be easy to talk to and we seemed to get along rather well.

He was quiet, somewhat shy, and had a low voice. He was a very nice fellow and a gentleman, not anything like I pictured Americans to be. Edward was strong and muscular. I would guess his height at 5' 10", stocky, a ruddy face with black hair, receding somewhat. At first I took him to be in his thirties, as his moustache made him look older. I told him he was sweet and he said he appreciated that very much.

Going through wartime is much different from any other time because you think this might be your last day. You don't know what's in store for you, yet it's a romantic time, a different time with a special feeling. Edward was very protective and jealous, not of his pals like Christianson or Anderson, but those of whom he was unsure.

But back to that party I was talking about. It was a prop blast party as I was to see later. It seemed everyone was pretty much wasted. At some point in the evening everyone lined up on one side of the room or the other. All of a sudden the guys charged each other, a North versus South thing, and a brawl, as it were, ensued. We didn't know what was going on and it was a little bit scary, too. I had never seen anything like it. And then as if nothing had happened, it was all over and the party resumed as before. At one point in the evening I told Edward I had the strangest feeling that I had been here before, and that it seemed like home to me. It's just a feeling I had, that's all. There is one other thing I should mention, perhaps it's a bit silly, I don't know, but it really happened. In 1935, when I was just a teenager, a fortune-teller read my future in my palm. She said that one day I would meet a dark-haired man from across the sea and would take a trip to America!

If someone asked if I believed in fate, I expect my answer would be, "Yes," especially in regard to the story I'm about to tell you.

During the year 1929, my father, Leslie Bevis, left mom and us kids without any money or food. When he did return, there was a big fight between my parents. A separation ensued and that's when Grandfather Petty stepped in. Since neither he nor grandmother, nor my mother could take care of us kids, it was suggested that perhaps the best thing would be to place us in a boarding school. My parents divorced, and Dad moved to Canada.

Reverend Davidson, an Anglican pastor from Norfolk, was contacted by Aunt Rose, Grandfather Petty's sister, to come to London to help resolve the situation. At his suggestion, it was agreed that June, Elaine, Derrick, and I would be sent to the Actor's Orphanage at Langley, in Buckinghamshire, fifty miles west of London. I was six years old at the time. As the oldest, I felt responsible for taking care of my brother and sisters.

The orphanage, which would soon be changed to a boarding school, was well-known throughout England, having been established by such internationally known actors and actresses as Sir Gerald DuMaurier, Douglas Fairbanks, Sr., Douglas Fairbanks, Jr., Evelyn Lang, Noel Coward, Gracie Fields, and Charlton Hobbs of English cricket fame.

Langley Hall, as the school was now known, was very famous for its pantomimes put on every year during the Christmas holidays by the children. The shows were produced and directed by Peter Jackson, a London producer. During early October auditions were held and from that point to our last performance in December we were constantly practicing.

One show in particular that stands out in my mind and ties in with the notion of fate was "Ali Baba and The Forty Thieves". It was one of the songs from the play that was so significant, even a bit weird as it were, for when I met Edward, his platoon had the nickname, "The Forty Thieves." When he mentioned that to me, I was utterly amazed! It was simply uncanny. I used to sing the little ditty from the play to Edward when we went on some of our walks together. I still remember the words: *We are the forty thieves, we loot, and we sack, and slay. We march abroad with fire and sword, and none our hands can stay. Beware of the forty thieves; we scatter death and woe. To those who dare to seek our lair, no mercy shall we show.*

London was an adventure in every sense of the word during the war. From time to time there were the air raid sirens and incoming buzz bombs hitting indiscriminate targets (the supposed German terror weapon, the V-2 rocket) as we walked the city in search of a restaurant. Whenever air raids occurred, especially when we saw or heard an explosion, Edward would protect me by putting his sewing kit over my head, and we always laughed about that. From the afternoon to the evening we managed to visit two or three restaurants, usually ending up at a very fine Chinese restaurant, which became our favorite and probably the best we ever experienced. Once, at a lounge in one of the restaurants we frequented, there were three Jamaican sailors who were being rude and obnoxious, trying to give me the eye while Edward was up at the bar getting our drinks. When Edward got back to our table, words were exchanged and a fight broke out. It was Edward against the three of them! Before long, a Canadian officer came over to help and soon it was over and order was restored.

I saw Edward a lot over the next couple of months. We were married on April 4, 1944, in an Irish Catholic Church in West Hamstead, London. Our priest was a young Irishman. My mother, my sister Elaine and my brother Derrick, Aunt Gladys and Uncle Alex, Grandma and Grandpa Bevis, Grandma and Grandpa Petty were all there along with Captain Harwick and Lieutenant Christianson, the best man. They were in uniform and looked stunning. It was a small but lovely wedding and I was very happy. I married the leader of the "Forty Thieves."

Years later, I composed the following poem to express the love I had for my new country and for my admiration for the men who had given their lives to insure freedom:

<u>Remember, America</u>

To honor God and country was America's freedom born.
For equality and liberty was her justice won.
Let's not forget our heritage. Let's keep those truths in sight.
Stand up America and honor our country's might.
The fathers of our country fought with faith and pride,
To win America's freedom with justice on their side.
Let's not forget our young men who fought for victory,
On foreign shores of battle to stamp out tyranny.
Let's keep our peace America and honor those that died,
And guard America's freedom with justice as our guide.
Stand up America, salute our flag with pride,
To all unite, to keep the peace,
And God with us abide.

Yvonne J. Mehosky
1976

CHAPTER 21

THE AIRBORNE RIFLE COMPANY

We were an airborne rifle company. Our job was designed to strike fast, hit hard, secure the objective, and get out. We were not like regular infantry. A rifle company of parachute infantry had a company head-quarters made up of supply, communications, a company commander with the rank of captain, an executive officer, a first sergeant, and clerks. Runners were used to carry messages from company to platoon. There were three platoons in a company. Each platoon was commanded by a first lieutenant. The assistant platoon leader was a second lieutenant. A platoon had three squads of nine men each. Each rifle squad had a .30 cal-iber, light machine gun manned by a gunner and an assistant gunner-ammo bearer. The rest of the squad were riflemen proficient with the M-1 rifle. Each platoon had a platoon sergeant and a communications man. The weapons squad had a 60mm mortar section composed of a gunner, assis-tant gunner, and an ammo bearer, and a 2.35 rocket launcher or bazooka section made up of a gunner, assistant gunner, and ammo bearer. We moved by foot and carried everything. We were fast going into the attack, knew how to scout and cover the point and rear of the column, and prid-ed ourselves on security. In marching or field training, we were always on the lookout for the enemy, always thinking ahead, and always anticipat-ing. Captain Harwick commanded H Company; Dick Meason was the executive officer, the XO. I had 1st Platoon; Ken Christianson had 2nd Platoon; and James Walker had 3rd Platoon.

The company's top kick was G.G. Bolles, known as "Pop" to the men. His sense of humor was displayed when you least expected it. Bolles stayed with H Company the entire war. Fred Bahlau was the company supply sergeant. J.J. McCollough was my platoon sergeant; a very capa-ble NCO who didn't miss a trick. All in all, when full strength, we num-bered about 120 to 130 men. We were considered light infantry, yet we could unleash devastating fire power upon the enemy. Our strength was in our quickness and maneuverability and this was combined with a hardened toughness, a will to win, and intense competence and teamwork at the lowest level. Our training prepared us for the bloody combat we would soon experience on the European mainland. We were unique. Because of our training, we were quite capable of fighting like a straight infantry unit if the situation called for that. We were trained to kill the enemy and could not wait to get at them. This was not cockiness, just confidence, confidence from the top down. We were Company H of the 3rd Battalion, 506th Parachute Infantry Regiment, 101st Airborne Division, the "Screaming Eagles."

CHAPTER 22

HELEN'S 3ᴿᴰ BATTALION

There is another person I want to tell you about. Her name was Helen Briggs, later known most affectionately as "Briggsey," Miss 506th. She loved the regiment and the regiment loved her. However, it was the 3rd Battalion she fell in love with. When I first met her, she was the American Red Cross (ARC) Director who ran a recreation club for 3rd Battalion called the "Wolverton Donut Dugout." It was a place for the enlisted, but I honestly had trouble resisting those delicious donuts and hot coffee she always had around. She usually chased me out after I brought my soldiers in and got a couple of those donuts. She couldn't do enough for our soldiers. She planned day trips and there was always something going on at her club, like chess or ping pong tournaments.

Helen started a newsletter for the soldiers she called The "Poop Sheet". Here are some excerpts from the second hot "Poop Sheet" dated April 16, 1944:

Sorry this edition is a little late, but it was so darn lonesome with you all away that I couldn't concentrate on anything.

The skating party last Monday was lots of fun. I'd like to learn some of the trick steps the British threw in to the tune of the band.

We will be making final arrangements for the quiz program soon, so sign up your intelligentsia now.

Thursday night seems to fit both Kay Gainey and me for the table tennis playoff between this club and the Aldbourne ARC Club. If Thursday night suits Darby of Headquarters Company, I'll rustle around for some transportation.

Spangler of Headquarters Company and major factotum of the officer's mess, says he's going to reform. He claims he is the checkers champ of the battalion and will accept all challenges to his self-proclaimed title. He'll get it, too, by default in two weeks, if everyone takes his word for it.

Colonel Wolverton says he will play the winner of the chess tournament, if we have a chess tournament. Pick your own first opponents and then let me know whom to pair off. I guess that will be the easiest way to run it.

Next time we have bingo, one of the prizes will be a teeth cleaning job. That used to be my racket before I got on friendlier terms with GI's.

This sounds pretty good to me: "Life can only be understood backwards; but it must be lived forwards."

It looks like the glider boys on the hill are taking a page from the paratrooper's notebook and are using small chutes as brakes.

This paper seems to have become a column by Briggs. How about giving me some material so I don't have to do a monologue?

The people we borrowed the bridge tables from haven't taken them back yet and if there are any bridge players around let me know and I'll rustle up some of my own cards that I've been holding out on you. I'd like a good game sometime, too.

That was some party H Company had the other night. It seems like they wasted a lot of combat energy though.

I can have a load of donuts if you would like to play hosts to the village kids. The donuts have gotten a glamorous appeal and I can't refuse them forever, so how about the proud papas getting together and planning the thing.

His bride (Lieutenant Mehosky and his wife, Yvonne), has joined the chief of Forty Thieves (1st Platoon, H Company). His men are wondering how the British food ration will support his appetite. Sign on newlyweds' car: Results of Careless Talk!

Helen Briggs
Ramsbury ARC Director

Helen continued her narrative fifty years later from a taped interview:

"The men of 1st Platoon adored Lieutenant Mehosky. I was tickled to death to learn that he named his first-born, Ivan, after the same nickname the men had given him. I remember his platoon got the nickname the Forty Thieves at Ramsbury; something to do with an alleged pilfering incident of sterling silverware from a manor house. Colonel Charlie Chase, Colonel Sink's XO, came down to investigate, and I remember hearing how mad Colonel Wolverton was; he called in Harwick and Mehosky to explain. 'OK Ali Baba and the Forty Thieves,' shouted the Colonel, 'what's this about some missing silver?' And I remember hearing how Lieutenant Mehosky stood his ground defending his men and that they, his platoon, could not have done such a thing! But I always was crazy about the guy. He was funny, liked to kid around, and had a sense of humor. He always saw the best in people and was always looking out for his men. One time he brought his platoon in for donuts after a problem and I gave him hell because officers weren't allowed in my club. Did I ever tell you about 'Mehosky Green,' or the airborne cavalry? Or how about 'the invasion money?' He was quite a character and his men really adored him. It was quite an outfit, our 3rd Battalion, Colonel Wolverton and everybody. By the way, 'Mehosky Green' refers to the color he turned and hence proceeded to throw up whenever he flew. He hated flying but loved to jump!

"There was a couple of times when they had two air force nurses per plane go up with them on a jump. And those nurses were all excited and talkative: 'Oh, you're going to jump out? Oh, it's so high. You are so brave and fearless.'

"Lieutenant Mehosky turned to them and said, 'Ladies, you think we're brave? You should see the airborne cavalry! Why, they jump out one side and swing around, and the horse jumps out the other side, and together they swing downward and land galloping!' And I think the nurses believed it for awhile.

"I took a Monopoly game up to the officers' club and left it there for them. And after everybody left for the marshalling for D-Day, I went up to get the Monopoly game to bring it back to my club. All the Monopoly play money was gone! Somebody said Lieutenant Mehosky had taken it to use as 'invasion money.' I never did find out if he got away with it.

H Company I knew better than anyone else. Ken Christianson was badly wounded in Normandy. But it's strange the things you remember, like Ken always gobbling up a #10 can of fruit at the mess hall. I got Jim Morton into trouble once. On one particular skating party, I had worked so hard for a month to get the bus filled. I even refused a dinner invitation from Colonel Sink. We get on the bus to go out to the rink at

Swindon. Lieutenant Morten was on board. 'The boys don't want to go skating,' he said. 'They want to go pub hopping!'

"And I said, 'No, we're going skating.'

"He had let the men vote. They voted to go pub hopping. One guy went skating with me. I was very near crying, as hard as I worked on this, that son-of-a-bitch Morten. So the next day at lunch, Colonel Wolverton asks me, 'Miss Briggs, how did your skating party go?'

"And I said, 'It didn't!'

"'What do you mean,' the colonel asked.

"To which I explained, 'one of the lieutenants got on board my bus and decided the boys would rather go pub hopping, so they put it to a vote and went pub hopping.'

"'What's that lieutenant's name?' inquired the colonel.

"'Oh, I couldn't tell you that, I just...'

"'That's an order!' he shouted.

"'Well. OK,' I replied, 'it was Lieutenant Morton.'

"'Bobuck!' shouted the colonel, 'have Lieutenant Morton report directly to me after lunch!'

"You hear everything. Before the Normandy drop Captain Shettle was commander of I Company. There were grumblings. The men did not like the way he did things, so he said to them that if they didn't like the way he ran things in the company, they could vote him out. So the men took a vote and the result was that they did not want him. This is what the soldiers told me. Anyway, Captain Shettle was moved to battalion headquarters and Captain John McKnight took over I Company. McKnight proved to be much tougher than Shettle was, the way I heard it. I guess I never knew the real reason, but I had my suspicions. Shettle and Anderson didn't get along either. On Christmas Eve, 1944, we were in Paris to meet the hospital train coming in. It was the only one with white sheets, clean linen and pillowcases, and very ill men. And I had a musician come in to play. As I looked down, there was a young Jewish kid. He looked at me and said, 'I hear music.' And I said it was the piano player. 'Oh,' he said, 'that's nice. Where am I?'

"I told him he was in the hospital and he'd be going home soon. 'Home?'

"'Yes.' But the nurse standing behind him was shaking her head that he wouldn't make it. I had to get out of there in a hurry, and I wished him good luck.

"Because of the breakthrough, we had a curfew. The only guys who could get up to the club were the ones who worked at the RTO. I had this huge Christmas tree, didn't have many light bulbs, and I had spent about a hundred bucks on decorations, a little tinsel and some lights. I was up on the ladder, throwing on this tinsel, and I said, 'If you're not going to help me, to hell with it! I'm going to bed.' When I got up in the morning, tinsel was all over the tree and at the end of each branch was a donut. That day the wounded from Bastogne started arriving in Paris by hospital train. Bob Harwick and Knute Raudstein were among those coming in."

In 1994, Helen attended my 70th birthday party at my son's house in North East, Maryland. It was a marvelous time. I will never forget this scene as long as I live: as Yvonne and I entered the house, there was Helen Briggs Ramsey to greet us with a cup of coffee and a donut, and she was wearing her Red Cross uniform. That was the last any of us would see her alive, for a couple of years later, she was brutally beaten in her Washington D.C. apartment when she intercepted a robber. She died shortly thereafter. Rest in peace, Helen. You are dearly loved and missed by us all.

CHAPTER 23

GEARING UP FOR THE INVASION

As we entered 1944, among our usual training duties was a tactical division command post exercise. There was also individual battalion combat firing at Beech's Barn Range several times a month.

In February we had a three-day battalion "isolated platoon problem" plus a Regimental Command Post Exercise (CPX). These exercises were increasing with great frequency.

In March, General Lee developed a heart problem and was replaced by General Maxwell Taylor from the 82nd Airborne. We made two jumps in March; one was a night jump, the other a demonstration jump for Prime Minister Churchill and General Eisenhower.

By April and May things began to intensify. There was a Regimental Combat Team exercise in Torquay, and two night jumps, one of which our battalion suffered 146 hospital causalties. The May jumps were the prelude to the invasion, which would take place in June in the early morning hours, but of course we did not know it at that time. We sure felt we were getting close. Everyone could sense something big was going on, it was in the air, and then we reached a point where we were practicing simulating jumps which emphasized rapid assembly and attack problems. We knew we were getting closer to the big day when everything we had trained for the past twenty-one months would be put into motion. We were ready to go.

Nevertheless, you still managed your platoon without letup, changing things as the situation warranted, and handling problems as they arose. For example, I had to demote one of my platoon sergeants to private and promote Corporal Martin to the vacated spot. On the last night jump before Normandy, Sergeant Martin broke his leg and had to be replaced by Sergeant Estes as squad leader. I made Don Zahn my second scout. Don would receive a battlefield commission to Second

Lieutenant in Holland and be assigned to me in C Company. Then there was the problem with Sergeant Sunquist. He didn't make the Normandy jump because he was under arrest in the guardhouse, which was a pup-tent ringed with barbed wire and a guard posted nearby.

May 22 and 23 became the dress rehearsal for the Normandy drop. The regiment left garrison at 2130 hours for the field where a simulated jump, assembly and attack problem was conducted. After two nights were spent in the field fine-tuning rapid assembly and quick movement to the objective area, we returned to garrison.

On the 27th of May 1944, Third Battalion left Ramsbury at 0800 and arrived at our designated marshalling area camp in Exeter that afternoon. Camp Exeter was a sea of tents, ringed by a high double row barbed wire fence. Military Police were visible all over the place. It was hard for anyone to get in or out because so much was riding on the outcome. Sandtable briefings began on the 29th at 0100 in the morning and continued, with many platoons, right up to our departure to the airfield on June 5th. Sandtable briefings were conducted in large tents, under guard and tightly controlled by the regimental S2 and S3 sections. The sandtables were of various sizes depicting the terrain features of the operational area: those sections of the Cotetin Peninsula in Normandy designated as our drop zone and assembly area, (Drop Zone D, in the Angoville-au-Plain vicinity). Third Battalion's objective was to take the two bridges over the Douve River east of the town of Carentan. Second Battalion was responsible for securing the Utah Beach exits in the Pouppeville area. First Battalion would take and hold the town of St. Marie du Mont. Accomplishing these objectives was designed to support the infantry landings at Utah Beach. We were told by the best intelligence estimates that there were no enemy troops in the area. As we would find out, there were, in fact, several German divisions in the area and had been for awhile, and because their positions were so well dug in and concealed, the Air Force couldn't spot them from the air!

It was imperative to be able to identify each other in the dark so as to facilitate a rapid assembly on the drop zone. To help remedy the problem, each man was issued a "cricket," a small, metal clicker that made a "click-clack" sound when pressed between the thumb and finger; the other feature that would be used to identify units and which proved helpful was painting a white distinctive symbol on the side of each helmet. The 506th was designated by the spade, as in the spade of a deck of cards; the 501st, a club, and the 502nd, a heart.

We were originally scheduled to go in on the 5th of June, but rough weather postponed the operation. Time for one more check. I rehearsed the jump with my platoon in such great detail that nothing was left to chance. Every man knew it by heart. We went over jobs, assignments, and objectives. Equipment loads, weapons, ammunition, clothing, footgear, and food rations were checked. I'd assemble the platoon at all hours of the night to study the sand tables one more time and compare terrain features, coordinates, distances between landmarks and our objectives. Another thing we rehearsed, just in case, was procedures to follow, what to do, where to go, and who could take charge in the event we got separated.

Hank DiCarlo recalled, "During the late afternoon of June 5th, Lt. Mehosky held a final sandtable critique of our primary objectives after the jump. I remember how much he impressed upon us the necessity for a quick capture of the Douve River bridges and his insistance that we keep moving and not get bogged down in any side action that did not immediately impact on the success of our mission. The last words I remember him saying were 'You know what we have to do. Keep moving, don't bunch up and let's meet at the bridge.'"

First Platoon was ready to go. Then a last minute decision was made at the company level to jump holding onto the equipment bag instead of strapping the bag to the body as we had been trained, and as we had done on all of those practice jumps in England. This turned out to be an irritant and a bad idea, especially at this late date when all the men were completely familiar with the equipment and had jumped with it strapped on. Now we had to think about something new and untried, just when we had everything down to a science. I was mad and protested strongly to Captain Harwick about the dumbness of this decision and he agreed, but that's the way battalion wanted it to go, and that was that! As it turned out, most of the men lost their equipment bag as soon as they hit the prop blast on exiting the plane, including myself. We landed in German-held Normandy with little more than our rifles, trench knives, and a few rations.

EVE OF THE INVASION

It was sometime after six in the evening when Lieutenant Colonel Wolverton gathered his battalion around him and spoke from the top of a hedgerow before our departure. He said that after this war was over, he'd like us all to meet him in Kansas City at the Mulebach Hotel for one heck of a reunion. Then he asked us to get down on our knees and look upward to the sky and pray with him. He prayed and after that all was quiet as each of us was silent in our own thoughts. Many, many years later, a copy of the prayer Lieutenant Colonel Wolverton was reported to have said was circulated to veterans around the country. It went like this:

God Almighty! In a few short hours we will be in battle with the enemy. We do not join battle afraid. We do not ask favors or indulgence, but ask that if You will, use us as Your instrument for the right and an aid in returning peace to the world. We do not know or seek what our fate will be. We ask only this: that if die we must, that we die as men would die, without complaining, without pleading and safe in the feeling that we have done our best for what we believed was right. Oh Lord, protect our loved ones and be near us in the fire ahead and with us now as we each pray to You.

With that, he looked around at everyone in the group, smiled and nodded his head, and then with a serious and determined expression said, "I am proud of you. You are a fine group of officers and men. I am proud to be your commander. The battalion is ready and strong. Now let's go do the job we have trained and prepared for. Move out!"

"The thing I remembered most clearly about our walk to the airfield was the utter silence of our passage, marked only by the soft scuffle of our boots on the roadway. The entire route was lined with silent spectators and the very atmosphere was heavy with the weight of what we hoped to accomplish when we reached our cross-channel destination. After all the months of training and preparation, we headed for our destiny like high school seniors approaching their final exams...hopeful, fearful and praying for the best results possible," remembered Hank DiCarlo.

In the early evening of June 5, we boarded trucks for the short ride over to the airfield and from there marched out to the runway. The sight that greeted us was massive-hundreds of C-47s lined up at intervals over the entire airfield. Our parachutes were out there waiting for us, arranged in rows next to our designated aircraft. A couple more hours to go. Now we had everything strapped on and were making final equipment checks, each man checking the other, helping here, adjusting there. They stood facing me in one long row, nineteen men, (about half of my platoon) plus a medic.

I don't recall saying much then, just checking each man and assisting. The hours seemed to pass by quickly. We were waiting for the signal to board. I would board last. Finally, at approximately 2230 hours on the night of June 5, the word was given to board the aircraft. Almost at once the propellers started and kicked out puffs of black smoke as each man mounted through the single door to his assigned position in the bucket seats in the fuselage of the C-47.

"Even the conversations as we fitted our chutes," Hank DiCarlo said, "were few and subdued. The reality of what we were about to attempt was finally penetrating our inner being. The only conversation I remember having was when I asked Don Zahn and Frank Padisak if they were going to use their Dramamine capsules. They both answered in the negative and gave them to me. That's how I got the reputation of being so aloof to the tension building during our flight across the channel. I even appeared to some to have slept most of the way. Just the memory of that night prompts me to recapture the oil and gasoline odor that permeated the aircraft as we taxied into line for the takeoff."

PART VII

AS WE APPROACHED THE DROP ZONE THE SKY WAS FULL OF EXPLOSIONS, SHELLS SCREAMING EVERYWHERE. OUR PILOT TOOK IMMEDIATE EVASIVE ACTION AS WE HURRIEDLY EXITED THE PLANE. THE FLACK AND TRACERS WERE SO HEAVY THAT I CROSSED MY LEGS ON THE WAY DOWN.

Lieutenant Mehosky's Jump into Normandy

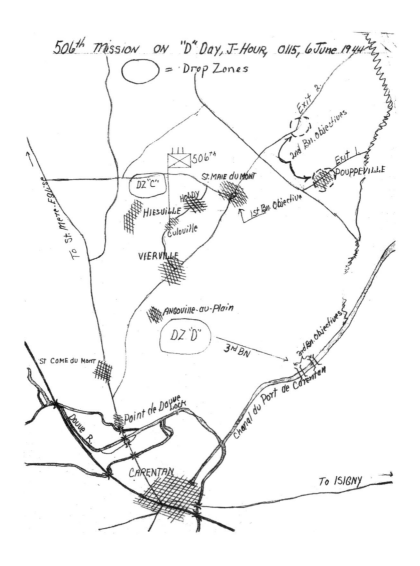

506th Mission on "D" Day, J-Hour, 0115, 6 June 1944

◯ = Drop Zones

To St. Mere-Eglise

506th

DZ "C"

St. Marie du Mont

HOLDY

HIESVILLE

Culouille

VIERVILLE

1st Bn. Objective

Exit 2.

2nd Bn. Objectives

Exit 1.

POUPPEVILLE

Angoville-au-Plain

DZ "D"

3rd BN

3rd Bn. Objectives

St. Come du Mont

Point de Doque Lock

Douve R.

Chenal du Port de Carentan

CARENTAN

To ISIGNY

CHAPTER 24

D-DAY'S FIRST WAVE

Each man was handed a copy of Colonel Sink's thoughts once aboard the aircraft. I read the following to my men:

SOLDIERS OF THE REGIMENT:

TODAY, AS YOU READ THIS, YOU ARE ENROUTE TO THAT GREAT ADVENTURE FOR WHICH YOU HAVE TRAINED FOR OVER TWO YEARS. TONIGHT IS THE NIGHT OF NIGHTS.

TOMORROW THROUGHOUT THE WHOLE OF OUR HOMELAND AND THE ALLIED WORLD, THE BELLS WILL RING OUT OUR TIDINGS THAT YOU HAVE ARRIVED, AND THE INVASION FOR LIBERATION HAS BEGUN.

THE HOPES AND PRAYERS OF YOUR NEAR ONES ACCOMPANY YOU. THE CONFIDENCE OF YOUR HIGH COMMANDERS GOES WITH YOU. THE FEARS OF THE GERMANS ARE ABOUT TO BECOME A REALITY.

LET US STRIKE HARD. WHEN THE GOING IS TOUGH, LET US GO HARDER. IMBUED WITH FAITH IN RIGHTNESS OF OUR CAUSE AND THE POWER OF OUR MIGHT, LET US ANNIHILATE THE ENEMY WHERE FOUND.

MAY GOD BE WITH EACH OF YOU FINE SOLDIERS. BY YOUR ACTIONS LET US JUSTIFY HIS FAITH IN US.

R. F. SINK, COLONEL

We took off at 2330 hours, on June 5, 1944. The battalion's formation consisted of forty-five planes known as Serial 10. At the time of enplaning, the Third Battalion combat group comprised 630 men and fifty officers.

Company H had 132 enlisted men and eight officers. I was the jumpmaster of our plane that carried a stick of nineteen men, which was half of First Platoon. I sat in the first seat across from the door, so I had a good view of the men and the jump door. The only thing I could see outside during the flight over the channel was the blinking wing lights of other C-47's in our formation. The interior of the cabin was fairly dark, yet you could see down the row to the last man. There wasn't much talking; each man was wrapped in his own thoughts. You could sense the mood, a mood of great anticipation and eagerness, a wanting to get at the enemy and get the job done. They shared a quiet confidence you caught glimpses of, reassuring one another with a facial gesture, a handshake, or a simple nod, two rows of paratroopers bundled up in all their jump equipment. Some tried catching a few winks, while others smoked cigarettes. It was more of a somber, serious mood that prevailed. The sound of the engines seemed to help keep the focus of my thoughts as I reviewed procedures again. In my mind's eye I could see us exiting the plane, chutes deploying, hitting the ground. We would have to assemble fast, move out and link up with the rest of the company. We had to be ready to encounter the enemy just in case. After all, we'd be roaming around in their backyard. One of my men was humming the popular hit tune of the day "One O'clock Jump." I didn't pay too much attention until the irony of it hit home: the first phase of D-Day, the airborne landing in Normandy which we were now approaching would take place somewhere around one o'clock in the morning on June 6, 1944. We were the first wave of the allied invasion.

THE GERMAN HELD COTETIN PENINSULA, NORMANDY, FRANCE

We passed over the channel islands of Guernsey and Jersey, and entered the continent from the southwest. As we approached the Beaumont-Angoville-au-Plain-Vierville area, our designated drop zone area, Drop Zone D, the red light by the exit door started flashing, signaling that we were just minutes from the drop zone. That's when all hell broke loose! In no time the men were on their feet, hooked up, checked, and ready to go, eagerly waiting to exit the plane! Explosions of anti-aircraft fire filled the sky with red, yellow, and white tracers flying up at the aircraft in all directions, flack pinging off the aircraft. During this time, when seconds and minutes seemed like an eternity, the pilot of our aircraft took evasive action, dramatically increasing airspeed instead of slowing down to required jump speed. He banked the plane in a southward direction away from the drop zone. Now the green light flashed and it was time to go. Our tightly-packed line flew to the door and out into the pitch black night with a furry. I was the first one out, and what hit me was the prop blast, a violent force that ripped my equipment bag out of my hand! A second or two later came the opening shock of my parachute deploying, savagely jerking my body as I struggled to grab hold of the risers. I did not see any other parachutes around me and yet my men came out fast, right behind me (jumping at airspeeds of 120 mph will cause between each jumper a wide gap of great distances, even miles). Most of my candy bars and most of my equipment were gone. As I floated downward, I could see a barn that had been set on fire; small arms fire criss-crossed the horizon. It was cold, bitter cold, and black, except for the tracers from enemy fire zipping all around me. There was so much stuff coming up that I feared I'd get hit, so I crossed my legs and held on tight to those risers during my decent. I wanted to get below this as fast as I could.

I don't remember much about that landing, but I landed in one piece in a field bound by hedgerows. As I was getting out of my chute, I heard a paratrooper clunk down near me to my right, and at the same time another dropped down to my left. They were from the 501st. Then we heard machine gun fire. We hit the ground and crawled to a cluster of tree saplings in the middle of the field. As we prepared to fire on the enemy position in a corner of the field now to our front, I had pulled the pin on a hand grenade and was ready to throw when I heard what reminded me of the clicking sound my platoon's machine gun made when they were getting ready to fire. I hesitated and listened again. No, that was clearly not ours! Now I heard German voices. "Here, you hold this and throw it after I fire a couple of rounds in there," I said as I handed the grenade to the soldier on my right. (I had always carried a folding stock carbine, but

I had lost confidence in the weapon because it had the tendency to malfunction, so I took a reliable M-1 with me into Normandy. My thoughts in preparing for the jump were that I would use tracer rounds since we would land in the darkness). Damn! I hadn't remembered those trcer rounds I loaded until after I squeezed off three rounds. That immediately drew fire on our position. The guy who was on that machine gun had to be an experienced gunner because we received a traversing fire that raked our position! We practically had no cover, save the tiny saplings which still exposed our legs. One of the rounds hit me in the left thigh, going completely through, and another burst hit me in the right foot with enough force to numb the whole leg. The guy on my left was dead. I pumped in another couple of rounds and then the next thing I knew there was an explosion and all was quiet. The fellow on my right had thrown the grenade.

We waited there for a moment, then the two of us crawled off in the opposite direction to a hedgerow to our rear when we heard the "click-clack" sound of a cricket. We returned the identification sound. As we inched closer we came upon a dozen paratroopers of the 501st waiting there in the hedgerow. Greetings were brief, and being the only officer there, I took charge. Two of the soldiers volunteered to scout. One told me there was a dirt road on the other side of a gate at the end of the hedgerow. A plan was formulated that we would cross that road and see what was to our front, the direction of the sound of small arms fire we kept hearing. We moved out in three groups, single file. It was just starting to get light. From the gate we could see a farmhouse on the other side of the road. We got across the road fast, by two's, and held up on the other side. Here was the situation that confronted me: I knew there were enemy troops to my rear; I did not know what was down this dirt road we had crossed, a road which was higher than the surrounding terrain; and now facing us to my front, right, and left, were hundreds of yards of swamp! Far off to my extreme right, I could make out the shape of what appeared to be a lone sentry pacing back and forth, as if guarding something on the high ground. That was odd and didn't look too inviting. To my immediate front, to the left, was a tree line that stair-stepped down into the water until they disappeared, a hundred yards distance or so. Beyond that, say two to three hundred yards, was a vast expanse of water (the German's had flooded the fields as a deterrent against airborne troops), and about a couple of hundred yards beyond that was an embankment and a road. I could see what seemed to be activity with soldiers holding that area, and I knew they had to be our troops. Yes, I thought, that's where the 501st was supposed to be. So I figured that's the direction we would head (in fact, we would come in through the left flank of the 501st, just below Addeville). I informed the men.

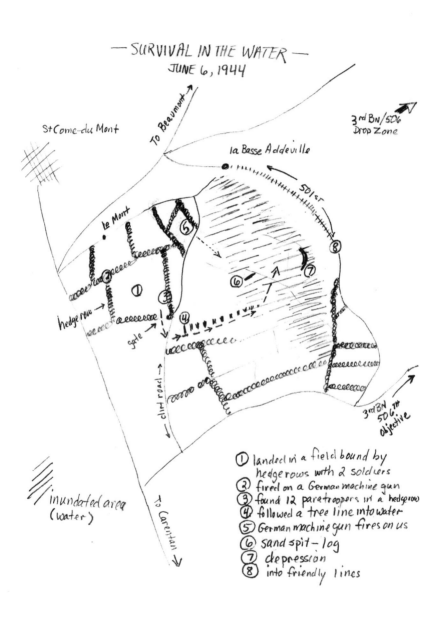

— SURVIVAL IN THE WATER —
JUNE 6, 1944

St Come-du Mont

TO Beaumont

3rd BN/506 Drop Zone

la Basse Addeville

le Mont

501st

⑤

⑧

②

①

⑥

⑦

hedgerow

③

④

gate

dirt road

inundated area (water)

To Carentan

3rd BN 506 7th objective

① landed in a field bound by hedgerows with 2 soldiers
② fired on a German machine gun
③ found 12 paratroopers in a hedgerow
④ followed a tree line into water
⑤ German machine gun fires on us
⑥ sand spit — log
⑦ depression
⑧ into friendly lines

CHAPTER 25

SURVIVAL IN THE WATER

The plan now was to follow this tree line down into the water to its end. That would give us cover before entering the water. At that point, when the tree line gave out, we would then veer off to the left in a diagonal direction toward the embankment in the distance, where our troops were holding along the road. We would have to negotiate hundreds of yards, in knee-deep water, and then further on to the road to friendly lines. I put the scouts out in front of our line and took up a position about mid-way. We followed the tree line into the water. When we reached the last tree, approximately waist high, we moved off to the left and headed straight for what looked like a dirt bank, a small depression less than a hundred yards off near a cluster of trees. Then, as we were about fifty yards out in the water, we got hit! Our column was raked with automatic fire coming from the left from up on the road we had crossed earlier! We were caught in the open, in knee-deep water, and in a hell of a fix! It was every man for himself as we instinctively dove to the water.

As I dropped to the water, I caught a glimpse of some of the men trying to run through the water, and in the next instance, they were cut down. I took a deep breath and scrambled with all my strength and energy, zig-zagging under the water like a madman. I remember bullets ripping through the water in every direction I moved, like a nest of angry hornets! Finally, gasping for air, I came up behind a small sand spit and log that provided cover from the enemy fire still peppering our position. One of the soldiers was already there when I reached it. That tiny piece of earth in the middle of this expanse of water was a Godsend. It was just enough protection to shelter us as we lay there pinned down, half in the water, half out, facing the direction of fire. There were bodies all around us of those soldiers who had tried to run for it. Three or four of them had made it to the depression. It looked like the machine gun fire coming from the high ground, about 300 hundred yards off to my left front.

The Germans zeroed in on my position and raked us again and again with fierce machine gun fire that chewed away a chunk of our protection on each pass. We could scarcely move a limb without receiving withering fire. The one time I returned fire, they poured it on heavier! They had us pinned down. "Son-of-a-bitch!" I shouted, "those bastards won't even let me fire at them!" The soldier with me was very restless. He said that he wanted to join his buddies who were safe in that depression out there. He said he thought he could make it, but I told him to stay put, to stay with me for the time being because there was no chance of doing anything. I told him he'd get killed if he tried to move out. We could now see that the two scouts had made it along with two other guys. The next thing I knew this guy got up and started running like crazy, screaming at the Germans, and moving as fast as his legs would go in that water. He had gone fifteen or twenty yards when he was cut down! All through the day I could hear moaning out there in the water. Then it was quiet. There was nothing I could do, so I just stayed there all day long in that damn, cold water.

Unknown to me as I lay there pinned down in the water, the 501st in the vicinity of Addeville le Basse was up against heavy enemy pressure in the St. Come du Mont area and had called in gunfire from a ship offshore to neutralize the enemy to their front. I guess the forward observer had seen the Germans' fire on my column. I was in a greater world of hurt, because what sounded like a freight train express was those big 16" shells that were landing in the water all around me! "Just don't use me," I cursed in my mind. The earth shook as each shell exploded with a terrible force raining down great columns of water and mud. It was an experience I'll never forget. I mean, the sound of those incoming shells and the concussion from the explosion was deafening and earth shaking, something you don't want to be near if you can help it! My entire head was ringing and my body shaking as if I were holding a jack-hammer! I guessed they were adjusting their fire on each salvo, trying to get the range of the coordinates right on the road from where we had received that devastating fire. But those rounds still came in, tearing the swamp to pieces! Those things were so close that I thought one was going to drop right on me at any time. When I lifted my head, I saw they had found the range and blasted everything on that road to hell! I was not going to take any chances at that point. No, I decided to wait until dark and make my way across to the depression and hook up with the soldiers waiting there. I was down to my last piece of chocolate I had hidden in my jacket in case of emergency.

At the break of daylight, our little group, the five of us, moved out toward the 501st lines. We approached cautiously and signaled by waving our arms. Someone on the line signaled and passed us through their lines. We were now with the 501st and mighty happy to be with them after that ordeal in the water! Thirty hours had passed since I landed.

Elements of the 501st, under Colonel Johnson and Major Allen, had set up a defensive perimeter along the road between le Basse Addeville and la Barquette near the river. We came through on their left flank. They had been holding against heavy enemy pressure for two days. Meanwhile, like the small group I had collected, groups of varying numbers were coming in throughout the day from different directions. One of the sergeants took care of the men I brought in with me, while I was escorted to the command post. At the command post, a lieutenant informed me that elements of 3rd Battalion, 506th, were up on the Douve River, holding two bridges at le Port. Later that day I was released from the 501st and, with a group of other 506th men, led them to our lines. It was late afternoon when we checked into the lines. There wasn't much of the battalion there. I reported to the aid station to have my legs examined and the wounds dressed. I got hold of some rations and took care of my hunger.

We didn't have much equipment to speak of at that time. We were holding our objective area and waiting for more of the battalion to come. A group had gone out earlier to make contact with the regiment. Since night was coming on, the temperature dropped quickly. I was still wet, and getting colder as I looked for a good place to get some sleep. I had to try to keep warm. There were no blankets, no extra coats or anything like that. You had to fend for yourself as best you could. My uniform had not completely dried, but sleep was over taking everything. So I pulled out my gas cape and put it over me, but I still couldn't get warm. I was shivering when a little stray dog happened by. He was a friendly little thing and I gave him a morsel of my ration which seemed to make him happy.

Then I grabbed him and put him under the cape with me, and I stayed pretty warm the whole night. The little dog was gone when I woke up in the morning.

SOME OF THE REST OF THE STORY

While there on line, we were just a collection of elements of the battalion. I wondered what had happened to my men and if their experiences were similar to mine. I was never able to catch up with them all. DiCarlo's letter to me, years later, filled in some of the pieces:

Dear Lieutenant Mehosky,

We were all scattered during the Normandy drop. Couldn't find anybody. Like all the other guys, we were trying to survive and find our way back.

I was in the other stick with Lt. Bolte. I remember nothing of what happened during the flight until I was awakened when the red light came on. When we counted off for equipment check at the red light, I discovered I was number thirteen, with Frank Padisak in front of me and Don Zahn behind me. Talk about a sudden sense of doom. The plane was being fired on and we could see tracers rising to meet the incoming aircraft. We were flying pretty close to the ground at this point and I could see a burning barn below us. Within a minute the green light came on and we tumbled out of that C-47, having no idea where we were or what was next, but with the knowledge that the army waiting for our descent was going to be as hostile as hell. As soon as my chute opened I became aware of anti-aircraft tracers lighting up the night sky. I landed in an open field between a stream and a paved road. Once I struggled out of my harness, I assembled and loaded my M-1, donned my homemade bandoleers and started in search of some friendly company. Making my way to the road I had observed on the way down, I crossed it and crouched in the ditch that was on the other side. Nothing around me seemed in the least bit familiar. It appeared that the air force had dropped us in the wrong place!

Just as I was rising to follow the roadway, I heard someone running toward me. I prayed they would be paratroopers. They were Germans! And here, Lieutenant, is where all those tedious training problems and solutions we had undergone in England paid off. While the mental side of me dealt with the shock of suddenly seeing real enemy soldiers, the physical side of me lifted my rifle and fired a full clip of eight rounds into the bunched target of three men running toward me. As they hit the ground, I sought cover, reloaded and approached them from behind. When I finally worked up enough courage to check the bodies, I discovered all three of them were dead. I could almost hear your words, Lieutenant, "Don't bunch up! Don't ever bunch up!"

Fearing additional enemy company, I worked up a concave slope. I still had not seen one American trooper. Then I heard a "click-clack" sound coming from a bush to my left front. Heart in mouth, I clicked on my cricket the counter signal and was soon united with Otto Dworsky from my company. As we made our way westward in search for more troopers, we could hear sporadic small arms fire all around us. Here and there we ran into more of our men, although some of them were not only from different regiments, but from the 82nd Airborne. Wow, we wondered, were we in their assigned drop zone or were they in ours? The Germans didn't have this identification problem, because they just fired at everybody. The rest of the night and next day was just one more deadly game of hide-and-seek.

Well, that's about it, Lieutenant. Over the years the guys and I always thought that had we landed in our drop zone and assembled as a unit, what a load of damage we would have given the Germans! But I guess it wasn't meant to be. Anyway, we survived and went on to fight another day, thanks to your leadership and training.

My best wishes,
Mario 'Hank' DiCarlo
1st Platoon, H Company

Chapter 26

A MAN WITHOUT A PLATOON

Most of my platoon was still missing. Some had found their way to the battalion's current position, not many though and certainly not enough men to reconstitute my platoon as a tactical unit. Those who did make it in were integrated into a group to resemble a company. At this point our battalion consisted of only nineteen officers and 117 enlisted men. Since I no longer had a platoon, I was designated to assist the acting H Company commander, Lieutenant Dick Meason, since Captain Harwick's whereabouts were still unknown. Captain Shettle was in command of the battalion. During this time we continued to hold the two bridges on the river and improved our defensive position. Patrols were sent out to make contact with the other battalions of the 506th.

Around June 8, D-Day plus two, the battalion was relieved by the 327th Glider Infantry at 2000 hours and moved to a bivouac area near the village of Hiesville. We moved out in the dark along a sunken dirt road. Then something caught my eye—the glint of a shiny object off to the side of the road. "What's that?" I said. It was just lying there, not buried or attached to anything. I picked it up, and to my surprise it was a medallion! On one side was a picture of Napoleon; on the other was King Neptune sitting on his throne holding a trident in his right hand. I was stunned. Can you imagine the significance of it all? Shivers ran up and down my back. Why was I the only one to see this? What did it all mean? The invasion of France, D-Day, was code named "Operation Neptune," and the country we were invading was once Napoleon's kingdom! Convinced this was my good luck charm, I kept the thing in my pocket.

During this time we were continually joined by officers and enlisted men who had been widely scattered during the jump and had fought with other units during the first couple days of operations before being released to us. By June 9, the battalion's strength reached twenty-four officers and

278 men, still below half-strength. That afternoon, Captain Harwick rejoined the battalion and took command. He had been captured, but managed to escape. We were now in regimental reserve. Then the saddest news to filter down to us hit like a ton of bricks: Colonel Wolverton, our battalion commander, Major Grant, Battalion Executive Officer, and most of the command staff were killed in their chutes when they landed in trees miles away from the intended drop zone! They never had a chance. Damn those Germans! Orders were received on June 10 to relieve 3rd Battalion, 501st in out-posting the inundated area from the Carentan-Valognes Road to Liesville-sur-Douve. The battalion command post was set up in the village of Houesville.

TWO WOUNDED SOLDIERS

On June 11, the battalion was ordered to relieve 1st Battalion, 506th, who were in contact with the enemy on the Carentan-Baupte Road west of Carentan. We were relieved at 2300 hours by the 2nd Battalion, 502nd, and marched to St. Come du Mont, where we were taken by truck to Carentan. Then we got the word that we'd be attacking to the west on the Carentan-Baupte Road, echeloned with G Company in the lead. The 2nd Battalion, 506th, would be on our right flank and elements of the 501st on the left. I was serving as an assistant executive officer for H Company. My role during the attack was to follow one of the platoons and provide assistance where needed.

The attack got underway at 0500 hours following an artillery barrage to soften enemy resistance. We would be crossing open fields and attacking one hedgerow at a time where the Germans had taken their positions. While moving forward with the command element, I came upon Lieutenant Ken Christianson sitting against a hedgerow, dazed and in shock. He had been wounded in the shoulder and a medic had just administered morphine and was dressing his wound. "Ken, are you all right? Ken, can you hear me?" He didn't say anything or recognize me.

I left him and continued moving forward. The column was making progress through the thick underbrush when the lead elements of the company came under heavy fire in a field in front of a hedgerow. Enemy machine gun fire stopped all forward progress. Heavy mortar fire exploded all over the field as men lay out there dead or wounded. I was in the corner of this field and I could see two wounded men waving their arms about twenty-five or thirty yards from me. The enemy fire did not slacken. The next thing I knew, I was crawling to the soldier nearest me. He was caked with blood and couldn't speak. The mortar fire now seemed to be pin-pointed right on me as explosion after explosion hit all around me, shell fragments sailing over my head. Somehow I managed to flip the soldier on my back and began inching my way to safety as fast as I could. The fire followed us. "Hold on tight, buddy," I said, "I'm going to get you and me out of here!" There was a medic near the command post to my left at the base of a hedgerow, and that's where I dropped the soldier.

The other wounded soldier was lying more toward the middle of the field and was still alive. Out I crawled on the double, machine gun fire altering my route, yet I was able to get to him. I could see he'd been hit in the arm and both legs and couldn't move. "This kind of stuff can be damaging to our careers," I said when I got him. That brought a clenched teeth smile on the soldier. "Now, when I flip you over on my back, I want you to hold on for dear life! Don't think about anything! Just hold on!" I made my way back on the crawl zig-zagging away from the fire and at one point, he fell off my back. I managed to get him on once more and resumed crawling toward the hedgerow where the command group was located, with machine gun fire tearing up the ground along my path. "Do you think someone's pissed-off at us?" Once more I had crawled out of that field of hell and blood with a soldier who never once made a sound. That was my part in the battle for Carentan. I never knew the names of those two wounded soldiers and I can't remember what they looked like. I have always wondered what became of them. Anyway, our attack came to a halt and we withdrew to the original line of departure at the village of Douville. There we set up a defensive perimeter and dug in for the night. We were relieved by the 401st Glider Battalion and moved to a bivouac area along the canal at Basin a Flot.

On June 13, our battalion was attached to the 501st holding a defensive position astride the Carentan-Periers Road in the vicinity of

Auverville. There we held for four days, then shifted over to the area at St. Quentin until we were relieved by the 501st. It was during this time that Major Horton took command of Third Battalion.

Edward Stanley Mehosky, age 9, received his first Holy Communion, June 14, 1931, Reading, PA.

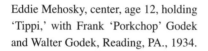

Eddie Mehosky, center, age 12, holding 'Tippi,' with Frank 'Porkchop' Godek and Walter Godek, Reading, PA., 1934.

Home visit, 1941, Mehosky's Cafe and bar, 11th and Muhlenberg, Reading, PA. From left to right (rear): Wellington Manning, Edward Mehosky, Edward's father, Stanley. Front: Augusta Manning and her daughter, Sundra.

Corporal Mehosky, Arlington Cantonement, 1941.

Lt. Mehosky, 1st Platoon, Company H, 506th PIR, Combat gear, Camp Mackall, N.C., 1943.

2nd Lieutenant Mehosky after Officer's Candidate School, Fort Benning, GA, 1943.

Camp Shelby, Mississippi. 85th Infantry Division, August 17, 1942. Left to right: 2nd Lt. Hebert, Cpt. Mudget, 2nd Lt. Griffith, and 2nd Lt. Mehosky.

Lt. Mehosky, 506th PIR, Toccoa, Georgia, 1943.

Yvonne and Edward, the happy wedding couple, West Hampstead, London, April 4, 1944.

Kathleen, friend of Yvonne, and Ken Christianson, best man, with Yvonne and Ed, London, 1944.

Edward, also known as
"Ivan," and his bride,
Yvonne, April, 1944.
London, England

Left to right: Lt. Mehosky,
1st Platoon, Cpt. Harwick,
commander, H Company;
Lt. Christianson, 2nd Platoon,
and Yvonne's sister, Elaine,
London, England, 1944.

Members of 1st Platoon, H Company,
506th at Mourmalon La Grande, France,
November, 1944. **Left to right**: Vecchi,
Martin, Zahn, Padisak, and DiCarlo.

Louis Vecchi, 1st Platoon,
H Company, 506th, just
before the Normandy jump,
May, 1944.

Lt. Bobek, 3rd Batallion, 506th PIR, checking his men
on the eve of the Normandy drop, June 5, 1944, Exeter, England.

Pvt. Keener, 3rd Batallion, 506th, at his anti-tank position near Bastogne,
December, 1944.

Major Mehosky, Korea,
1953.

Paratroopers of the 101st AD moving to positions at Bastogne, Belgium, December, 1944.

Newly promoted Major Mehosky near Regimental Hqs. 160th Reg., Korea, 1953. (40th Inf Div.)

Cpt. Mehosky and Cpt. Mike Chester on the ridge of Hill 851 near Mundung-ni, Korea, 1952. (40th Inf Div.)

511th PIR, 11th Airborne Div on review at Ft. Campbell, Ky, 1955.
Col. Cassidy front, Major Mehosky center.

Discussing communications during Exercise "Follow Me."
Left to right: Col. Norman Carnes, Col Cassidy, 1/Lt. Zamparelli, Major Lee
Southerland, Brigadier General Derrill Daniel (now Commanding General, 11th
Abn. Div.), and Major Edward Mehosky, 1954

Major Mehosky
502nd Airborne Battlegroup,
during an exercise in Germany,
1956.

LTC Mehosky
at the Pentagon, 1963.

US Advisory Group, 21st Infantry
Division (AGVN) at Bac Lieu, Vietnam,
1963. Lt. Col. Mehosky, front left, and
General Cushman, center.

The 4th Brigade, 16th Battalion say 'good-bye' to
Lieutenant Colonel Mehosky at Fort Knox, Ky, April, 1966.

Colonel Edward S. Mehosky
at Fort Ritchie, MD proir to promotion
to full Colonel, 1967.

PART VIII

WHEN I GOT BACK TO CAMP, THE WHOLE PLACE WAS
PRACTICALLY DESERTED...THEY HAD ALL LEFT FOR HOLLAND

Lieutenant Mehosky, H Company

CHAPTER 27

HOMECOMING

We moved north up the peninsula to an area south of Cherbourg. It was in this area that a French farmer invited me and another officer to have dinner with him and his family. That evening we walked over to his farm. We were greeted at the entrance of a stone farmhouse by Monsieur Lavasiour, who led us down to the cellar, which doubled as a bomb shelter, and where they mostly spent their time. It was pretty dark down there; the only light was provided by a couple of candles on a long, wooden table. There we met his wife, two children, and grandmom, whom the children called, "Nana." We brought along some gifts for everyone that were very much appreciated, things like C-rations, socks, candies and chocolates. We spoke practically no French, they no English, with the exception of a couple of words, yet we got along just great. On the table were individual piles of salt in which to dip your potato. The meal consisted of a bottle of red wine, hard bread, and a small bucket of boiled potatoes. It was a wonderful, wonderful meal, and they were warm and gracious hosts. They didn't have much, but wanted to let us know how thankful they were for what we were doing in saving the country from the hated Germans. They were very poor, but very proud people. It didn't take much for anyone to see the cruelty and suffering this war had brought on the civilian population.

From Tollavast, we boarded trucks on the morning of July 13 and headed south for Utah Beach, where, after thirty-seven days in combat, we returned to England. Third Battalion jumped into Normandy with thirty-nine officers and 562 enlisted men. Our losses resulted in twenty-two officers and 262 men killed, wounded or missing in action.

By late afternoon we were aboard landing craft that carried us to Southampton, England. On hand to greet us was the 101st Division band, playing the "Beer Barrel Polka." Waving excitedly from the docks were

Helen Briggs and her American Red Cross staff who had come down from Ramsbury to welcome us home. They served hot coffee and those famous donuts. Helen's beloved 3rd Battalion was back home.

It was early evening when we left Southampton by bus for our camp at Ramsbury after nearly six weeks of combat. But the first order of business was a much needed rest, to get away from it all for awhile, and so we were granted a seven day furlough. I telephoned my wife, who was living in the London suburb of West Hamstead at the time, that I would be up on the first train out of Hungerford.

Normandy had been our baptism by fire. We had accomplished our objectives despite the horribly scattered landings and key command and staff losses; we were now seasoned, veteran troops. The 101st went into Normandy with 14,000 troops: 6,600 by parachute drop, 7,400 by glider. Of the 3,836 casualties suffered during the campaign, 868 were killed—roughly 28%. Consider this: due to the severe scattering of the division during the drop, only 38% (or 5,320 men) assembled with their units at the close of the first day on June 6. That meant that there were about 8,600 troops out there, on their own, struggling to survive! But we were extremely objective oriented. That was always one of the huge, overriding factors in the make-up of the airborne soldier. Why, paratroopers who were dropped as far north as Cherbourg made it back to their unit within days, and in some cases, weeks, but they made it back. Later, we even heard of paratroopers who were dropped in the channel and came ashore on Omaha Beach hours before the invasion troops, and came through the German lines there.

By August we were back to our old, quick pace. It was a time of regrouping, of honoring those who died, of receiving replacements for our losses, and a time of getting back to being a company again. The men were drawn closer to each. There was lots of talk among the officers and men about the Normandy Campaign, especially things that went right and things that went wrong. Of course, there were many, many stories of heroism, courage, and determination that never made the history books and probably never will. Invariably one's thoughts turned to the men who had been lost; men you knew so well; men you would miss. But you never dwelled on it, and certainly did not let it dominate your thoughts.

My job, like everyone else's, was continuous, repairing from the last mission and getting ready for the next one. I was back in charge of 1st Platoon again, and Bolte, who had fared well and had done a good job in Normandy, was still my assistant. Captain Harwick was back in command of H Company. Major Oliver Horton was the new battalion commander. However, part of us had died when Colonel Wolverton was killed. One could sense how deeply he was loved and missed by everyone.

Platoon training once again intensified as we began to integrate our new equipment and fill our thinned ranks with new replacements. By August 14, our parachutes arrived, and then we received our first briefing on the next combat operation, code-named "Transfigure." Plans called for a daytime drop by the 101st, near a French village, south of Paris. The British 1st Airborne Division and a Polish parachute brigade were to land near Rambouillet. Our goal was to help destroy the German 7th Army. The "go" date was to be August 17. Then word came down that, due to General Patton's swift movement on Rambouillet, Operation Transfigure was canceled.

SILVER STAR TURNED DOWN

The action around Carentan had probably been the most severe of the entire Normandy Campaign. I had been told by my superiors that because of what I did in rescuing those wounded soldiers pinned down in that field by machine gun and mortar fire, I was being put in for the Silver Star. Someone even furnished a bootleg copy of the narrative for me. I remembered the incident again and couldn't help thinking that all the German guns were trained on me at that time and place.

I saw huge chunks of earth flying in the air from exploding shells, the ground chewed and raked by machine gun fire, soldiers out there lying face down or on their backs in blood and dust. I heard the distinct roar of battle on all sides, and men yelling, screaming and moaning. I don't remember in great detail about bringing in those two soldiers, but I can still picture that first soldier out there, moving his arm back and forth, not saying a word, his shirt saturated with blood, and that look in his eyes when I got to him. We ran into a meat grinder out there, a wall of lead that stopped us cold. Later, I was informed that instead of a Silver Star, I would receive the Bronze Star. That's the way the ball bounces in the army as in all sectors of life. You've just got to be able to field what's thrown your way, let it go, and land on your feet. I let it go.

I suffered in Normandy with a raw, inflamed cyst that had grown the size of a half-dollar at the base of my spine. Since our new mission had been aborted and it was uncertain as to when something else might develop, I decided to have this thing looked at properly. Captain Harwick knew I was having a lot of discomfort and sent me over to regiment. There, the regimental surgeon sent me off to Army Hospital Headquarters, near York, where they would operate. It had reached the stage where I was barely able to walk.

About three weeks later, in September, I was released from the hospital and, upon checking in at division headquarters, was told the 101st had left for the jump on Holland. Arriving back at Ramsbury was like being in a ghost town. There remained just rear echelon personnel, the handful of soldiers and officers needed to take care of business. I was brought up to date on events. The jump took place so fast that no one had a forewarning of what was to happen. The 506th landed in the vicinity of Son and St. Oedenrode and had fought their way north to the Neider Rijn River and the town of Opheusden. The overall plan was called "Operation Market Garden," and along with the 82nd, they were to provide airborne support to the British forces trying to outflank German forces supposedly in retreat. The Germans, in fact, were fiercely counter-attacking everywhere in that sector.

BALANCING FEAR

You hear the men talking about fear. Fear is a constant in war. It's something that is always present, everywhere, from the foot soldier to the commanding officer. It's a delicate balance between doing your job or caving in under its weight. In view of this the troops are always looking at you. This factor is heightened when individual soldier's visibility is reduced due to darkness, clouds, or fog. You must know where you are, what's around you, and what's in your front. It is in circumstances like this that many a good man will break from the weight of fear. Robert E. Lee and Thomas J. Jackson had an unmatched faith in God, perhaps unparalleled in recent history from a military standpoint. Lee said that "courage is doing your job in the face of fear." And who can ever forget Stonewall Jackson's famous admonition to his subordinates to "never take counsel of your fears?" If there is one constant in war, besides that men will be killed, it's that amid danger, fear is ever present. Our job is to manage it rather than let it consume us. Don't dwell on it, but keep busy, keep your mind occupied on the job you were sent to do and all will be well.

CHAPTER 28

JOINING THE REGIMENT IN HOLLAND

Having missed the Holland jump, I was eager to get over there with my unit. By the time I got orders to proceed to the forward area it was October 22. Lieutenant Croon and I caught a hop on one of the C-47s heading for France and landed at an airfield somewhere near Paris. There we were able to get a jeep and driver to get us to Holland to the present location of the 101st. We drove all that night and all morning. I had never seen such total, absolute darkness before; the landscape was black. We went up through Belgium, crossed two rivers in Holland, and finally located military police who directed us to division headquarters located in the narrow stretch of land between the Neider Rijn River and the Waal River, called the "island." Further to the west, at a town called Opheusden, at the narrowest point of the "island," the 506th and the 327th Glider Infantry Regiment bore some of the heaviest of the division's fighting, where, on their left flank, they met head on and repelled heavy attacks by the German 363rd Volksgrenadier Division.

On October 23, at one o'clock in the afternoon, I reported in to division headquarters. A warrant officer checked me in, then the G-1 contacted the S-1 at Regiment. "Oh yeah, send him down." I saw Lieutenant Leach, the S-2, and we talked for a minute. Leach quickly brought me up to date on what had transpired since September and that the 1st Battalion had a new commander who just arrived from England, Lieutenant Colonel James LaPrade. I had met Colonel LaPrade in Ramsbury after returning from the hospital. I didn't know it, but in less than a week I'd be working for him. After clearing regimental headquarters that was located in the town of Zetten, and stopping in to pay my respects to Colonel Sink and the staff, I went over to Third Battalion.

Third Battalion at this time was in regimental reserve with their headquarters on the other side of the town of Zetten. Captain Harwick, now in command of the battalion, was happy to see me and greeted me with a big smile, "Good to see you, Ed. You've been sorely missed!" By this time Fred Anderson, Dick Meason, Bill Reid, Joe Doughty and other officers stopped in.

I learned that Major Oliver Horton had been killed at Opheusden. And Bolte, my assistant, had been killed at Einhoven in a house to house clearing operation. I seem to recall meeting Lieutenant Andros, now in charge of H Company, and Lieutenant Stroud, who had my old 1st Platoon. At that time, there was no job for me in the 3rd Battalion. I was excess.

NIGHT PATROL

The next day I was informed that I would lead a nine-man reconnaissance patrol from I Company. I joined the men that evening at battalion headquarters where we were briefed by the intelligence officer. Our mission was to cross the river and reconnoiter the enemy-held town of Wageningen. At that time I met a man from the Dutch underground who would lead us through German positions on the other side of the river. We moved out at 2030 hours through 1st Battalion's sector along the dike and down to our designated departure point at a boathouse at the water's edge.

This boathouse was a long, wooden building, open at both ends. In the middle of the building was a boat of sufficient size to transport the patrol. As we prepared to lift the boat, an oar dropped and we hit the dirt! No sooner had the sound died than we saw this blazing, red hot ball of fire coming right at us! It had to be a round from a German 88. That round passed only a few feet above us, went the length of the boathouse and exploded on the dike. The quick response of the Germans' fire indicated they had the boathouse zeroed in as a primary target. This was not a good start. We continued to lay still, barely breathing, anticipating a second round. That second round never came, but just in case, we waited awhile longer. Then we moved out and proceeded across the river. From that poin to the other side I doubt there was ever a patrol as quiet as that one.

Someone messed up selecting such a prominent feature as a boathouse as the starting point for a patrol. The crossing, however, was uneventful. We exited the boat and crossed flat, open land. The Dutch guide took us through German positions and up an escarpment. A path was soon joined that led to the edge of town. We left the guide and started down a wide street with houses and trees on both sides. On the street and sidewalk were millions of acorns! Even as quiet as we tried to be, there was no getting by those stinking acorns! Every step produced a loud crunching sound. It was starting to get pretty tense, because if we could hear the sound, someone else could, too, and this was an enemy-held town. It was then that I said something like, "Those god damn peanuts!" This seemed to break the tension among the men.

At an intersection we heard piano playing and voices singing. I decided we should investigate the source of the raucous noise. My scouts came back and identified the building from whence the sound originated and the voices as German. I briefed the men and placed them in position. A reconnaissance by fire was the only way to develop the situation and acquire much needed information about the enemy. On my signal, we opened fire. We killed the sentry and about four or five others who came running out, firing their weapons blindly. There were still enough of them in the house to continue firing on us. Not wanting to stay around too long least reinforcements come in, we disengaged, regrouped, and retraced our steps back to the edge of town. The guide was waiting. His face displayed a broad smile. We crossed back over the river, moved up in the dike, then passed through 1st Battalion lines and reported to the Regimental Command Post. It was now 0330 in the morning. After debriefing and providing the S-2 with information, the patrol was dismissed. They liked the idea of what I said to my patrol, the peanut comment, as being the right thing at the right time. They liked the damage we inflicted even more. The men of my patrol conducted themselves admirably. I was very proud of these fine men from I Company. I hit the bunk at 0600.

The next day a group of officers got together at battalion headquarters over some hot coffee. Fred Anderson and Joe Doughty had just come in and wanted to hear all about it, especially the details, "the fun parts" as they liked to say. By then the word of our little encounter had circulated all over the battalion. I guess my actions generated a lot of excitement. I think what we shot up was either a German officer's club or NCO's club. In the final count we probably killed eight or ten of them.

506th S-2 Journal...D-Day plus 37...24 October 1944

Unit dispositions unchanged. Two, officer-led, nine-man patrols crossed the Neider Rijn during darkness. One patrol reports having located and shot up some sort of soldier's club. The other patrol reports no contact. One casualty suffered.

Extract of Unit Journal

22 October 1944.....0700......Lt. Mehosky and Lt. Croon leave base camp for forward area.

23 October 1944......1530......Lt. Mehosky arrived at the Regimental C.P.; 3rd Battalion in Reserve at Zetten.

24 October 1944......2030.......Two patrols went out at night led by Lt. Andros of H Company and the other led by Lt. Mehosky of I Company.

25 October 1944......0100.......The patrols that had left on the night of 24 October located at Wageningen what they thought was an enemy N.C.O. club. They shot the sentry and about four or more of the enemy at the club.

25 October 1944.....0500.......The two patrol leaders reported at the Regimental C.P. giving above information.

The Germans retaliated on October 25 and 26 with an intense shelling of our lines. An enemy force of about forty men hit B Company on line.

CHAPTER 29

TAKING COMMAND

Captain Fred Anderson, who commanded I Company and was one of my closest friends, awakened me. He had a hot cup of coffee for me. He told me what his men had said about the patrol. "I like the acorn story, Ivan, and you referring to them as 'god damn peanuts' because of the loud crunching sound they made. That was pretty good. It was not only humorous, but well timed, exactly the right thing at exactly the right time to settle them. Then shooting the hell out of that German club, why, I have never seen my men so fired up in a long time. They told me they'd go out on another patrol with you anytime, anywhere. I want to thank you for taking care of my boys." Nothing got by Fred. If anyone knew what was going on, it was Fred Anderson. Then in the next moment he asked, "How'd you like to command a company?"

"Sure," I said, "but nothing's open in the battalion for me."

"Not 3rd," Fred said, "I'm talking about 1st Battalion. I hear they need a good company commander down there real bad at C Company."

On October 30th Captain Harwick called me to his office and told me to report to Colonel Sink at regimental headquarters. "Ed, it looks like they have a job for you!"

A regimental commander knows the situation in his battalions at all times. Colonel Sink was acutely aware of casualties suffered in each company, in losses of officers and men up to that point of the campaign. He knew some of the companies, like C Company, for example, were at half-strength, and he knew there were some problems. He came right to the point. "I need a company commander over at 1st Battalion, Lieutenant. How'd you like to take command of C Company, starting today? Good! That company is down to half-strength and morale is pretty low. They've got some problems I want straightened out. I want you to get them in shape and up to standard. The battalion is now in reserve. Colonel LaPrade will be expecting you. Any questions? Well, good to see you again, Lieutenant."

"Thank you, sir," I replied, saluted, and left.

'C' COMPANY

C Company was located on the outskirts of Valburg in a house and barn in an orchard. I was met and escorted inside the barn where the men were assembled, about 65 of them. Morale was low. Discipline was lacking and some of the men became vocal. It was not a favorable first meeting. This brought on a strong response from me in soldiers' language that they clearly could not mistake. They knew now who was in charge and what was expected. After the men were dismissed, I met with my officers and NCO's at my jeep and formed my command group. The afternoon of October 30, 1944 was coming to a close and we had a lot of work to do.

I observed improvement on a daily basis although there was still some resistance. During this time we had periodic meetings and assemblies in the barn where, later in the evenings, we were entertained by local talent from the company, a Lieutenant Coker and his magic show. It was good to see the men laugh.

On November 9, 1st Battalion relieved the 3rd Battalion in the 506th defensive sector along the Neider-Rijn River and the Arnhem-Elst Railroad. My orders were to cover a 1,500 yard sector along the dike between Driel and a railroad bridge, and tie in with the company on my left and the one on my right. I met with the company commander I was to relieve, shown the extent of his flanks, and brought up to date on the situation. Relief was completed at 2330 hours without incident. Platoons were put in position along the dike facing the river. The area we covered on line boiled down to roughly thirty yards a man. My command post was located in the basement of a farmhouse in an orchard next to a jam factory. From my location I could see the railroad bridge at Arnhem was still in enemy hands.

A slit-trench had been dug in the farmyard whereby the men relieved themselves. As previously mentioned, everything was under observation by the enemy across the river. On occasion, someone out there doing their business could receive fire from those German 88's. On at least one instance of which I was aware, one of my men had to take evasive action because of incoming fire and dove in head first. His quick thinking saved his life.

Vigorous night patrolling by both sides marked this period of activity. There was occasional artillery fire on our positions by the "hostiles," as Colonel Sink always referred to the enemy. The Germans still had command of the high ground across the river. One of the reasons my command post was in the basement of a farmhouse was because German gunners could easily knock out any structure above ground. I was always aware of that and tried to instill this attitude in my men. After all, why make it easy for the enemy? But we had a problem with our communication lines getting blown out all the time. I had the greatest respect for those communication guys, out there in all sorts of weather, splicing wires day and night, stringing up telephone wire so the company commander could have communications with his platoons and battalion.

On one night in particular, I remember being with my command group in my command post, when suddenly the main lines were yanked off the table! We knew the Germans had been patrolling on this side of the river. The lights were quickly doused as we dove to the floor, expecting a hand grenade to come tumbling down the steps. It was pretty tense there for awhile. Finally, after nothing happened, we went up to look around and someone burst out laughing. What had happened was a pig had gotten tangled up in the telephone lines and was making quite a fuss! "Incoming bacon, Sir," one of my men said.

"Well, let's get that thing fixed," I replied, "and radio the platoons that I'll be coming down tonight."

We were relieved on November 15 and went into reserve at Lienden. Over the next six days we received heavy shelling. On November 23, my command post took a direct hit, wounding three soldiers. I had been visiting one of my platoons when I heard of the incident and rushed back. At 0600 hours, November 25, we were alerted for the move by truck to Mourmalon la Grande, France for reorganization and preparation for future deployment.

The 506th, along with the rest of the division, had been in Holland for seventy days. Casualties amounted to 3107 men killed, wounded, or missing in action during this time. As we entered France, this chapter was concluded. Unknown to us at the time, our biggest test, and probably the best piece of soldiering we did the whole war, was right around the corner. The crack 101st Airborne Division would be called north again, but this time to a place called Bastogne, in the Belgium Ardennes, where a date with destiny awaited. We were to become the hole in the donut in the epic defense of Bastogne, a feat which would come to symbolize American resistance not only in World War II, but for all time. There, as in Normandy and Holland, we would write our history.

CHAPTER 30

MOURMALON LA GRANDE

On the afternoon of the second day of our long truck ride, we arrived at our new base camp at a place called Mourmalon la Grande, a small town some twenty miles east of Rheims, France. The town of Mourmalon grew up around the old French army garrison there. The Germans had used the garrison as a tank depot when they occupied France, but now it was being used by the U.S. Army as a troop replacement center and supply depot. It was our new home for the time being, and we were here for a well-deserved rest, to refit, and otherwise upgrade our current situation. Once the men got situated and cleaned up, finished the hooting and howling about the French latrines (instead of a toilet seat there were two footprints in the cement and a drainage hole in the middle, no toilet paper, just a water faucet on the wall), it was off to the mess hall. I never saw men eat such enormous quantities of steak, potatoes, green beans, milk, bread, and ice cream. Of course, the coffee consumed that first evening reminded me of 3rd Battalion's arrival at Ft. Benning after that long, blistering march.

Early the next morning we were off to the training area to resume morning activities, which included PT, where the five-mile unit run took priority. Often we would see Colonel LaPrade running through the training area. He was a distance runner of reputation. The only time I got a chance to talk with him one on one was the time he came over to where we were training and we talked while observing the men.

I usually had breakfast with Dick Meason, who now commanded Company A, and Herbert Minton, Commander of B Company. Minton and I were the same age. I got to know Minton pretty well through our mess hall chats. He was a great guy and a fine soldier. It was during this time that Lieutenant Albert Hazenthal, who commanded C Company prior to getting wounded in Holland, returned as my executive officer.

Hazenthal was a good officer and we got along well.

We had a party for Don Zahn, now a new lieutenant in the company, who had received a battlefield commission. We had an opening and I had asked for him.

There was a lot of work to do at Mourmalon. Replacements were coming in every day. One morning during company formation, the men assembled for roll call were a total mess, disheveled, looking more like a bunch of bums than soldiers. It just so happened that Colonel Sink had come down unannounced to check the morning formation and was lurking about in the shadows. Luckily, I spotted him. I immediately wheeled about, saluted, and said, "Sir, this company is not ready for inspection!"

"Carry on, Lieutenant," the colonel said, "I can see you have work to do," and left the area. Facing my men, I told them in no uncertain terms that that was the last time I ever wanted to see them in formation not properly dressed!

There is a story among many stories I heard about Colonel Sink I'd like to relate. It seems one day he came across a soldier who didn't salute, had no military bearing, and was woefully sloppy. The colonel dressed that soldier up one side and down the other, leaving that poor soldier quaking in his boots. "Now private," the colonel said, "when you see this insignia again," pointing to his eagles, "you had better know what to do!" There was a momentary pause, then the colonel said to the soldier, "And if you think I'm mean and tough, well, you ain't seen nothing yet! Just wait 'till one of those officers gets hold of you who wears those single gold bars on the shoulder, because son, those guys are the meanest, nastiest men in this whole damn army! And they are always looking for soldiers like you!"

In early December, the 101st was reorganizing under a new table of organization patterned after straight infantry divisions. It was in this environment, as we were receiving new weapons and replacement troops, that all hell broke lose north of us in the Belgium Ardennes. We would soon be called up to help stop the last great German counteroffensive of the war.

PART IX

HITLER HAD DECREED THAT ENCIRCLED BASTOGNE BE TAKEN AT ANY COST. HE REFUSED TO UNDERSTAND, SEPP DIETRICH GRUMBLED, THAT EVEN THE ELITE DIVISIONS OF THE SS COULD NOT EFFORTLESSLY OVERRUN THE AMERICANS. IT WAS IMPOSSIBLE TO CONVINCE HITLER THAT THESE WERE TOUGH OPPONENTS, SOLDIERS AS GOOD AS OUR OWN MEN.

Albert Speer, *"Inside The Third Reich."*

101ST AIRBORNE DIVISION
DEFENSE OF BASTOGNE, BELGIUM
DECEMBER, 1944

NOUILLE

BOURCY

LONGCHAMPS

FOY

502

506

CHAMPS

502

506

BIZIRY

BASTOGNE
327

501

101

10

NEFFE

MANDE
ST. ETIENNE

SENONCHAMPS

327

327

327

501

MARVIE

REMOIFOSSE

xx xx xxxx 101ST Defensive
Perimeter

CHAPTER 31

BASTOGNE

Camp Mourmalon, France, December 18, 1944

The priority was training and reorganization. New weapons had been arriving in the company area in large, wooden crates. A big part of the day involved uncrating weapons and cleaning off the thick grease called cosmolene. No ammunition had been received yet. The men were in various phases of receiving and cleaning their weapons when the jolt came that morning. We got word that something big was happening north of us, something about a breakthrough! We were alerted for imminent deployment. Rumors became the main topic of discussion. Then the first trucks began arriving.

We'd be going north in open cattle trailers. The men collected their clothing and gear, assembled, and began loading by squads. They were arrayed in various combinations of winter combat uniforms. As for foot gear, we still wore the brown, leather combat boot. As it would turn out, this singular item, more than any other, was the second enemy we would face where we were going. It would cause us problems so severe as to tax our resourcefulness in the days and weeks to come. Other items like cigarettes, candy bars, crackers, and bouillon cubes were crammed into whatever pocket was not filled with extra socks.

There had not been much time to prepare, and most of my men were still cleaning their weapons when we pulled out.

We were part of a vast ten-mile long convoy of the 101st, some 12,000 strong. It was dark and snow began to fall as we headed in a northeasterly direction toward Belgium. As the temperature fell, the men huddled on the floor of the trailers to keep as warm as possible. The only stops made were relief stops or for trucks that had slipped off the road. On December 19, between 0200-0300 in the morning, we arrived at the designated assembly area in a large, snow-covered field west of the town of Bastogne. By 0500 hours the entire 101st Airborne Division had assembled.

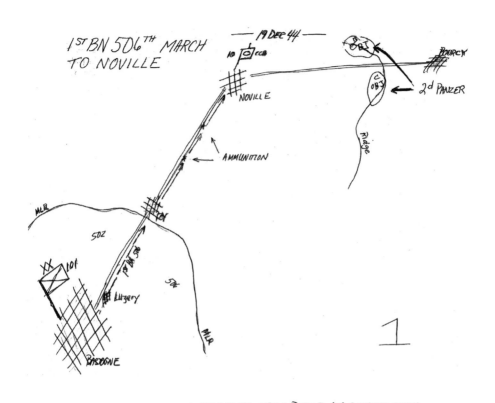

1ST BN 506TH MARCH TO NOVILLE

— 19 DEC 44 —

10 ☐ CCB

BOURCY

B OBJ

C OBJ ← 2d PANZER

NOVILLE

Ridge

AMMUNITION

MLR

SDZ

101

1st BN 506

506

FOY

Luzery

MLR

BASTOGNE

1

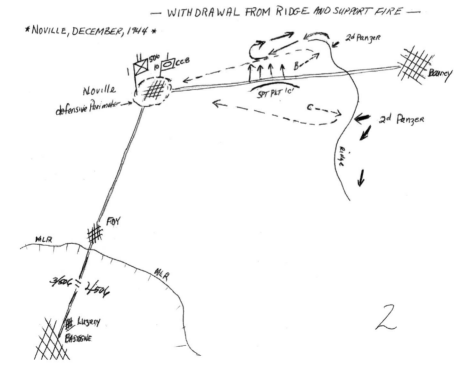

— WITHDRAWAL FROM RIDGE AND SUPPORT FIRE —

* NOVILLE, DECEMBER, 1944 *

1 ☒ 506 10 ☐ CCB

Bourcy

Noville
defensive perimeter →

2d Panzer

B

SPT PLT 'C'

C

2d Panzer

Ridge

FOY

MLR

3/506 ⤴ 2/506

MLR

Luzery
BASTOGNE

2

CHAPTER 32

FIRST BATTALION AT NOVILLE

Lieutenant Colonel LaPrade assembled his company commanders and told us that German armor and infantry were northeast of us and that they would probably move to capture the town of Bastogne and its vital road net. Our orders were to defend and hold Bastogne and the surrounding area. First Battalion would be in division reserve, while 2nd and 3rd Battalions would set up a defensive position to the northeast, tying in with the 501st on their right and the 502nd on their left. At 0700 hours, we marched out of the assembly area toward Bastogne.

As 1st Battalion marched through Bastogne to a reserve position in the village of Luzery, we received a change in orders: we were to get up to Noville, a village five miles north of us, to reinforce a combat armor team heavily engaged, and to secure and hold Noville.

BACKGROUND: TEAM DESOBRY

On the 18th of December, three German divisions, the 2nd Panzer, the Panzer Lehr, and the 26th Volksgrenadier were moving on Bastogne from the east. Noville, a village about five miles northeast of Bastogne, was the focal point of the 2nd Panzer Division. The only American force in Bastogne at this time was a combat command battalion from the 10th Armored Division, commanded by Colonel William L. Roberts.

By the morning of the 19th, Colonel Roberts sent Major William Desobry up to Noville with fifteen medium tanks and a platoon of tank destroyers (609th Tank Destroyer Battalion) as a blocking force. This force was known as "Team Desobry." His orders were to hold at all costs. After several fierce fire-fights with elements of the 2nd Panzer Division, Major Desobry requested permission to withdraw, but he was told by his commander that Noville had to be held. In the meantime, Colonel Roberts told Desobry a rifle battalion of paratroopers and a platoon of tank destroyers (705th Tank Destroyer Battalion) were on their way to Noville. When Major Desobry learned that the 1st Battalion, 506th was coming but sorely in need of ammunition, he sent some of his service company speeding off to the VIII Corps ammunition depot located west of Bastogne. By late morning, Desobrey's supply people had placed piles of ammunition crates in the middle of the road at two places between Foy and Noville.

The battalion marched through the village of Foy that cold, gray morning through a light snow that covered the ground. C Company was at the point. The men were eager to get there and we still did not have ammunition. The word was we'd get ammo before we reached the town, so nobody worried about it. Ahead on the other side of Foy, in the middle of the road, was one of the best sights the men and I had ever seen— opened crates of every kind of ammunition we would need. It didn't take long for each man to stock up as the column continued forward. There was another pile ahead in case you didn't get what you needed at the first pile. We could hear tank fire from Noville as we approached.

THE HIGH GROUND

Noville was a small farming village north of Foy that had grown around a major road juncture. Two commanding ridges dominated the village, one running from north to northeast, the other to the southeast which rose gradually to a height of 500 meters at the crest, and was approximately 800 yards distance from Noville.

Major Desobrey had his tanks and tank destroyers positioned on the outskirts of the village facing north and northeast, and they were engaged when we got there somewhere around one in the afternoon. The company momentarily assembled on the south side of the village. By the looks of things, Noville had taken a pounding. Lieutenant Colonel LaPrade issued orders to his company commanders: "To defend Noville, we're going to have to take those ridges—the high ground there to the east," he said, pointing in that direction. "About 800 yards out there's a gradual sloping to the top, so you'll be going uphill most of the way. We'll guide on the Noville-Bourcy Road. Company C, you'll attack on the right flank of that road, and Company B on the left flank. You've got embankments along that road. No signs of any activity up there. Get your men ready. We'll move out at 1400 hours sharp."

We moved out of the assembly area on the edge of town to the line of departure. Based on the commander's plan, my implementing plan was to have two platoons attacking abreast with the left platoon guiding on the Noville-Bourcy Road. Platoon leaders were given their instructions. At the designated hour, the company initiated the attack to secure the high ground. I took my position between the lead platoons and my support platoon.

We moved out quickly and my platoons were half way up the ridge when the enemy suddenly opened fire. My men continued upward in the face of this fire, covering each other and nearly reaching the crest. By now the fire had intensified; mortar, artillery, and machine gun blasts blunted their steady forward movement. Casualties were mounting. I ordered them to withdraw from the ridge and take up defensive positions around Noville. They withdrew in good order and the enemy did not pursue. During the withdrawal of my lead platoons, I observed B Company in the distance off to my left withdrawing from the high ground on the other side of the Noville-Bourcy Road, being closely pursued by German armor and troops. I swung my support platoon into action and directed them to take firing positions along the road embankment. I tell you, we opened up on those German forces with a fury, hitting them with a severe and punishing fire on their flank (enfilade fire) that stopped them cold and sent them reeling with what looked like pretty heavy losses. They withdrew to Bourcy. Company B was able to continue its withdrawal to Noville. There was only sporadic fire now from the enemy on the high ground, and it was late in the afternoon when we joined the rest of the company on the southeast side of Noville.

I firmly believe our aggressive action caught the Germans off-guard and that they reacted with everything they had to prevent us from taking that hill. It was later learned that we had run head on into a German counter-attack intent on taking Noville, one that had kicked-off at the same time as ours! The end result of that fierce encounter was that they held the ridge and we held the town, and most importantly, we had delayed their attack plans, forcing them to regroup. We gave them a good punch in the nose that let them know they would not just walk into the area we held, as they were accustomed.

I would be remiss not to mention those I call the stalwarts of Noville-the tank destroyers and the medium tanks, the Shermans. Those things, especially the tank destroyers, were quick and could turn on a dime. They gave the Germans fits, inflicted punishing blows, and kept them at bay, preventing their tanks from getting into Noville. It was really something to see those tankers work, but their numbers were dwindling.

The road to Bastogne was still open. Wounded and killed were taken by jeep and truck to Bastogne. To get around during the artillery rounds, you had to zig-zag from building to building. My runner was hit in the leg during this time and evacuated.

I put my company in a defensive position in the Noville perimeter where we faced to the southeast. Mines were placed at intervals in front of our position. We had mortars and bazookas in each weapon's platoon to nicely augment the fire we'd bring on the enemy coming this way. The men dug foxholes as best they could in the hard earth. I located my command post in the basement of one of the bombed-out houses nearby. Upon returning from a meeting with the other company commanders, I noticed a number of abandoned vehicles, tanks, half-tracks, trucks and jeeps about the village that looked in good operating order, so I put the word out to have platoon leaders get the names of soldiers who could drive those things. When the time was right, I'd see what we could do.

At 1600 hours, December 19, Lieutenant Colonel LaPrade called us to a meeting at his command post located at the center of the village in a building on the second floor. The room where we met was dark. There was a table in the center of the room with a map sprawled across it. I noticed the windows had been boarded and a large center window had a tall, wooden chest pushed in front of it to protect the occupants from shrapnel. To my surprise, I was greeted by Major Harwick, executive officer of the battalion, who had just arrived in Noville only a couple of hours ago. He had been in Paris on leave when we left for Bastogne and made his way to us on his own. Once he got to Noville, he said he had to dodge and sprint from building to building because of the mortar fire coming in.

All commanders were present. The meeting was brief. LTC LaPrade got the casualty report, then the ammunition status. Company positions and armor were marked and adjusted as necessary. "We are to hold Noville indefinitely," said the Colonel. "The enemy is going to keep shelling us and probing—looking for a weak point to attack. Then they'll move around us and try to cut us off from Bastogne." That's the last time any of us would see Colonel LaPrade alive.

We resumed our duties on the perimeter. It could not have been more than fifteen or twenty minutes later when I got the call from Major Harwick to come right away to the command post! We assembled in the basement this time. Major Harwick was shaken and his voice grave. "Men," he said, "Lieutenant Colonel LaPrade is dead! Most of the men who were in that room were killed. After you left, we received a direct hit. It came right through that damn window that had the chest in front of it! The whole damn room exploded. Major Desobry was critically wounded. We've evacuated them to Bastogne. I was in the next room and luckily escaped! So command of the Noville force has now fallen on me. Regiment was informed of the situation, doesn't like it, but said we'd have to hold here for at least one more day." As night came, we could hear enemy vehicles on the move.

HARWICK RECALLS NOVILLE

Dear Ed,

I am sending you a copy of an article I wrote for a magazine some years ago to better let you know my recollections about Noville. In our last meeting at your house in Reading, we talked about that part of the war that got me to thinking and searching my memory of events as I remember them from my point of view. Let me know what you think.

Best regards,
Bob Harwick

I reported and started to set up a message center in an adjoining room and in general set up for operations. As I did this, a shell came through the window of the command post and I found myself in command of the forces in the town.

There was a quick consultation with the new armor commander. We set up a defense around the town, spotted our tanks and tank destroyers, and sent a report to regimental headquarters explaining the situation and asking for a doctor to replace the one who had been wounded.

As night came on, the intensity of the fire decreased. We set up mines and flares and waited for the attack we knew was coming. We sent our wounded back with the dead.

We could tell what the Germans were doing. We could see gun flashes as they moved around out there, probing. They kept up their fire all through the night. The road to Bastogne was still open, but by daylight, we felt sure they'd have us surrounded! The battalion was alerted. We could not reach Bastogne by radio. We braced for those tanks that would come down from the hill.

In those private minutes, the thought of death goes with a shrug. The fear is not of the enemy, but of yourself. What will the fellows think when all this is over? Will I be the one to give? By God! Not me! And that passes. How is it at home? I'm glad they don't know the spot I'm in. Glad I wrote that letter last night. I wish I had some coffee, now. Hope those tanks are set. Wish we had more than six. At least there are nine tank destroyers, but those Krauts sure have a pot full. Tanks are all over the place!

So it went, with thoughts tumbling but always returning to the attack we knew was coming. The men were tense and staring out into the darkness. They could see nothing, but it was too quiet. The time rolled past the daylight hour and still it was dark. It was unreal. At least you could count on nature being the same. Then as the black slowly melted into a clinging gray, we saw the reason: fog!

With this first visibility came the warning shriek of approaching shells. As the men ran for cover, the barrage was upon us. Smoke and dust added to the fog. To see beyond twenty yards was impossible. A warning call came from the outposts. They could hear German tanks moving.

The battle took on a weird aspect. The country became a confusion of clanking treads, fleeting glimpses of dark hulls, and dirty yellow flashes as the tanks fired into the town. Formation disappeared and each engagement was a tank and a few men probing here, trying there. Our tank destroyers held position and at the range of those few yards, the effect of their fire was murderous. Yet the fog was a mixed blessing. German units slipped past and through our defenses, but were knocked out. One was knocked out just fifty feet from the command post by one of our partially disabled tanks which had been placed in front of the building for protection. Part of the church steeple came down with a crash of dust and large stones bounded down the street.

Our aid station was full and we opened another cellar. It was obvious our losses were making gaps in our line which could not be plugged. The command post personnel, switchboard operators, clerks, and slightly wounded men were sent to the companies.

There was a lull, but we could see the tanks reforming. We had no communication with Bastogne. A half-track, which contained radio equipment that wouldn't work, was loaded with several badly wounded men who obviously were going to die without attention and was ordered to force its way back to Bastogne. The message I sent was: "Casualties heavy. No more armor-piercing ammunition. Request reinforcements, ammunition, and medic supplies." The vehicle left but did not return, although I found out later that it forced the roadblock and had gotten through.

About ten o'clock we briefly contacted the regiment by radio. I was afraid to tell our true situation over the air, and the message we received was to hold at all costs. That cost began to mount with a tank attack right down the road. Part of our infantry positions were lost, but the tank destroyers got their 20th tank, which burned at the edge of town.

The situation was so acute that I called in the company and tank commanders. Another attack or two would end the affair for us. We drew up plans to fight a withdrawal. A jeep with two wounded men and a messenger who volunteered was sent down the road. The message was to General McAuliffe. It just said, "We can hold out, but not indefinitely." There was no answer.

About 1230 a radio operator in a tank picked up a message telling the armored units to assist the infantry in fighting out. I took this as a legal means to do what I knew had to be done in this situation. I ordered a withdrawal at 1330 hours, keeping the message as evidence. I still have it.

Four tanks and Mehosky's C Company left first with orders to push and engage any enemy without further orders. The tank destroyers with A Company formed the rear guard to prevent the Germans from following. All of the wounded were placed on vehicles. Disabled vehicles were set afire and a five-minute fuse put on what ammunition was left.

WITHDRAWAL FROM NOVILLE
— 20 DEC '44 —

2d Panzer

NOVILLE

BOURCY

Ridge

2d Panzer

German Tank

C, 1ST BN

FOY

3/506

2/506

MLR

MLR

Luzery

XX 101

BASTOGNE

3

CHAPTER 33

WITHDRAWAL UNDER FIRE

Enemy armor was observed moving on the high ground in a south-easterly direction on the morning of December 20. From my post, it looked like they were trying to move around us by moving toward Foy. If successful, their forces could encircle Noville and cut us off from the rest of the division at Bastogne! At 1330 hours Harwick ordered the withdrawal from Noville.

When I received the order that we would withdraw, I immediately informed the platoon leaders to have the designated drivers move out and secure the vehicles they were going to drive. This was accomplished by groups of two or three. Those soldiers made it happen, for in no time they brought to the company area a tank, a half-track, a truck, and a couple of jeeps!

CORPORAL JIM CADDEN'S STORY

During the fierce Noville encounter, I was summoned by Captain Mehosky, through a courier, to the company command post which was located in the basement of a partially destroyed house. He asked me if I had ever served in the armored forces. When I replied in the negative, he asked me if I would go with a tank operator and retrieve an abandoned Sherman tank located in front of the company's 3rd Platoon sector. I naturally agreed and he had the courier take me to the guy who was going to drive the tank. The guy was a trooper from the 2nd Squad of my platoon, 1st Platoon, named Fred Zavasky. Well, Zavasky and I and Sergeant Ted Hentz of the 2nd Platoon, who saw us crawling out to the abandoned tank, followed and the three of us entered the tank. Now we're inside and come to find out Zavasky knew very little about driving a tank. He drove a farm plow in Illinois. After about five minutes of fooling with switches, he finally found the starter and started the tank. When he put it into gear, it started to move with jerks and stops. We were moving in the direction of German tanks who fired at us! So then Zavasky abruptly turned to the left and headed back toward the 3rd Squad foxholes that sent the guys running and dodging for cover. Zavasky lost control of the vehicle and we were roaring over pig pens, chicken coups and fences like the Keystone Cops! We finally stopped when we smashed into a storehouse in the middle of town. If our escapade could have been filmed it would surpass a Laurel and Hardy comedy venture. It presented hilarity during a tense situation.

ENEMY ROAD BLOCK

The withdrawal began in the afternoon. C Company was designated the lead echelon, and would be accompanied by four Sherman tanks. The abandoned vehicles I had commandeered were placed in the rear of my company and used to transport casualties.

The Noville-Bastogne Road is a straight shot to Bastogne, about five miles south. It was a banked road wide enough to support our column of vehicles. The road had a shallow ditch on the left side, and in places, high embankments on the right side. First Platoon took the point. I took my position near the front of the column on the left side of the road in a shallow ditch. The lead tank was next to me on the road. That way, I had good communication with battalion.

As we approached the village of Foy, the lead tank received direct fire from our left front, and the column stopped. I deployed two platoons abreast to the left side of the road to engage the enemy roadblock—a tank, machine gun squad, and panzerfaust (rocket launcher). My support platoon took up firing positions on the right side of the road behind an embankment. The tanks in the front of the column were returning fire and at the same time moving forward and back so as not to be an easy target. Knowing the lead tank was the primary target, I tried to distance myself by crawling back, but the tanker had the same idea as he rammed his vehicle in reverse right beside me! I quickly crawled forward and he did the same. Once more I crawled back away from the tank. There was no other place to go because of the heavy fire focused on that tank. Then the tank exploded in flames from a direct hit! I crossed the road and joined my platoon. A couple of my men lay motionless on the road, including 1st Platoon Sergeant Mike Paros. From this observation point I could see the combined fire of my attacking platoons and fire from the other two tanks was taking its toll on the enemy roadblock, and soon the threat was eliminated.

I was only aware of what was happening to my company at the front of the column. I did not know what the rest of the column was doing, but I assumed they had engaged the enemy.

Having taken care of one threat from the left, a new one was developing on our right flank. I could see enemy units advancing towards us from the west, from the woods adjacent to Noville, approximately 700 to 800 yards from my position. At the same time, elements of 3rd Battalion, 506th began counter-attacking from their positions below Foy. There was a medic nearby attending to one of my men who had been shot in the head. I was in a prone position along the road embankment, watching the attack, when I saw something small and black that reminded me of a bee heading straight for me! As I tried to roll out of the way, I felt a sharp pain and a numbness in my left hip, and at the same time a burning sensation on my left thigh. I knew I was hit! Fearing the worst, I called to the medic to check me. He did, and not finding any blood, said I was fine, yet I could still feel something burning my leg. I quickly felt around and discovered something had entered my left trouser pocket. What I pulled out of my pocket was a hot chunk of lead, a spent bullet that had probably ricocheted. The tip of the bullet was painted black, which meant it was an M-1 armor-piercing round. Whew! That was close! It could have killed me, but the amazing thing is that I could see it at all!

Meanwhile, the German attack on the right flank was stopped by the energetic attack of 3rd Battalion as well as the flank fire from the column. The enemy withdrew toward Noville. Now that the threat had been neutralized, the column continued its withdrawal and entered the division perimeter and went into reserve in the village of Luzery. Most of our vehicles had gotten through. It was now 1700 hours and dark as a weary battalion regrouped. I was proud of the men of C Company. Colonel Sink was one happy man that day when he saw his 1st Battalion coming through the lines.

HARWICK'S VIEW OF THE WITHDRAWAL

Ed, In case you did not receive the information I promised to send along regarding my views of the withdrawal from Noville, here it is. I am looking forward to seeing you and your family soon.

Regards,

Bob Harwick

The column got off in time under the cover of wonderful fog, and how the men did a brilliant job of changing position, loading wounded, and gathering or destroying ammunition and equipment. The last of the wounded had just been put on a vehicle when sounds of fire told of trouble at the front of the column. As I hurried forward, the first tank was on fire and C Company hotly engaged, but we had to push on.

Part of the column now moved across fields and into the village of Foy. There we encountered a force of Germans and after a sharp engagement without the loss of one soldier of our group, took thirty-five prisoners and a major. I did not count their dead. All of the wounded came in safely. We had just broken our way through the German ring and the battalion was moving down the road through the six buildings that made Foy. It was no column. The fighting had scattered the groups, and they now reformed and filed past me and on into the barns at Luzery. They were dirty as only fighting men can get—clothing torn and mud-caked. Two days' beard had just made them appear dirtier. A few of the men were bloody. Most of them had a shovel, or pick or axe, mostly German or taken from the farms. If you don't dig, you die. But they were happy. They had been in a tough spot. Through their own strength they had gotten out. They had done a good job and they knew it. The spring in the step of the tired, dirty bodies, and the look in the eyes told that. Almost 600 had gone in. There were less than 400 who came out.

After we got the men settled, we had a hot meal. The officers met that night around nine o'clock at Major Harwick's command post. There we had hot coffee and donuts and talked. Colonel Sink stopped by. Then it was back to the company area for a couple hours of sound sleep. Where they got those donuts no one ever knew.

Thus ended the first major encounter with the enemy in the Bastogne epic. In summarizing the results of the Noville action, 1st Battalion and Team Desobry, as a unit, lost thirteen officers and 199 enlisted men were killed, wounded or missing. But the Germans paid an even greater price: they lost thirty-one armor vehicles and a full battalion from the 3rd Panzer Regiment was badly crippled.

The men and officers of the 1st Battalion, 506th and units of Team Desobry had performed admirably and could take pride in knowing that they took part in the defense of Noville that helped stall the attack of the 2nd Panzer Division. We had held for two days against numerically superior forces, slowed the enemy advance, and bought time for the regiments to set up a defensive perimeter. Then we conducted a successful withdrawal in the face of enemy fire. Colonel Sink's 1st Battalion returned intact. We were never defeated.

On the 20th of December, word was passed to all units that the Germans had cut all roads leading to Bastogne. We were surrounded! In the days to come there would be fierce battles in various sectors of the perimeter as the enemy probed and attacked, trying to exploit a weakness. Each time they attacked, they were counter-attacked and the perimeter held. First Battalion was in division reserve at this time.

CHAPTER 34

ENEMY PENETRATION

Extract from the Diary of Lieutenant E.S. Mehosky, C Company/1st BN/506TH PIR

* *0200 hours 21 Dec'44—1st Battalion is in division reserve at Luzery.*

* *0600 hours—1st Bn called up to eliminate enemy threat, a penetration between 2nd Bn, 506th sector and 501st sector, below a railroad station.*

* *0900 hours—Bn leaves reserve area, line of departure for attack: Bastogne-Foy Road.*

* *1100 hours—counter-attack initiated in an evergreen wooded area; "A" attacks on the left, "C" on the right; "B" in reserve.*

* *1600 hours—counter-attack successful; line restored; sixty-five enemy KIA and eighty prisoners taken; eighty-five more driven into 501st sector, killed or captured.*

* *1800 hours—Bn arrives back at Luzery.*

It was after six in the evening when C Company got situated in the barns at Luzery. Along with my command group, there was an artillery officer staying with us. In the midst of all that was going on, he livened up the place with his fondness for mint juleps. How he missed his drink! He was an industrious fellow too, for before I knew it, he had gone out and scraped some snow in some cups, shaved slivers of chocolate on it and presented us with nice chocolate snow cones. Not a mint julep, but pretty darn good for considering where we were.

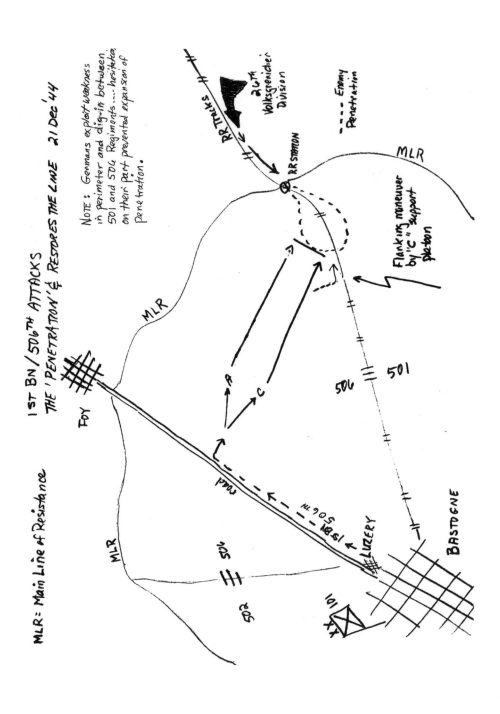

MLR = Main Line of Resistance

1ST BN / 506TH ATTACKS
THE "PENETRATION" & RESTORES THE LINE 21 DEC '44

NOTE : Germans exploit weakness
in perimeter and dig-in between
501 and 506 Regiments ... hesitation
on their part prevented expansion of
penetration.

RR Tracks

26th
Volksgrenadier
Division

- - - - Enemy
Penetration

RR STATION

MLR

MLR

FOY

A

C

Flanking maneuver
by "C" support
platoon

506   501

1st BN 506 TH

LUZERY

502

501

503

101

BASTOGNE

The morning of December 21 was cold. It had snowed. Intelligence reported that the area near division headquarters in Bastogne had been shelled at 0100 that morning by a railroad gun somewhere to the east of town.

We had been there in reserve some thirteen hours when we got word that there had been a penetration by German forces down the Bourcy-Bastogne Railroad tracks, and that they were dug in between the 506th and 501st sector in a wooded area southeast of Foy. Information received at division estimated nearly a battalion of infantry in position near the railroad tracks in the rear of 2nd Battalion, 506th. This was a very serious threat to us because if left unchecked, the enemy could bring armor right through Bastogne and cut the 101st in half! The situation was critical.

At 0700 hours Major Harwick received an order to eliminate an enemy penetration. Harwick assembled his company commanders. I had left word with my platoon leaders to get the men ready and where to meet me. Major Harwick greeted each of us as we arrived. His voice was quiet and serious. He looked at each of us, nodding his head as if he were talking personally to each one of us, not as a group. His demeanor was informal. "Regiment has informed me that the enemy has penetrated our lines between the 506th and the 501st sector," he said. "They're in a wooded area southeast of Foy along a railroad track below the Halt Station, here," he said pointing to the area on his map. "Division estimates possible battalion strength in there. I mark their position right about there at the cluster of woods on this side of those railroad tracks. And it looks like they're only a mile or so from headquarters! Well, we're going to root them out! I plan to attack with two companies. Meason, your Company A will be on the left, and Mehosky, your Company C will be on the right. I want to hit them at the weakest point, on the shoulder of the penetration, about here. Probe until you make contact, then knock the hell out of them! We move at 0900 hours sharp."

First Battalion departed the assembly area outside the village of Luzery at 0900 hours. Our designated order of march facilitated deployment of the attacking companies. We marched a distance of about

1500 yards northeast on the Bastogne-Foy Road, then left the road and deployed. We were now facing southeast in the direction of the railroad tracks where the Germans were dug in, about 800 to a 1000 yards from our present position, between Bizory and Foy. As we began moving through the woods, we experienced incoming artillery which exploded above our heads in the tree tops. Tree bursts, as they were called, made a loud cracking sound. We were moving through what appeared to be a Christmas tree farm. There were lots of evergreen trees with thick boughs. The deeper we advanced, the thicker were the tree boughs, heavily laden with snow, their lower branches touching the ground. Even the slightest movement knocked snow to the ground, revealing our position to any observer. Snow was above ankle deep. About 300 yards from the railroad tracks where we believed the enemy to be, A Company veered off to the left, C Company to the right. Machine gun fire and rifle shots rang out as A made first contact. My forward platoons closed to within 200 yards of the tracks and drew fire. Movement became difficult. Our forward progress momentarily stalled. The enemy had the advantage of well-concealed positions for the time being. They had cleared fire lanes underneath the tree boughs at ground level and sighted in weapons. It looked like their fire was coming straight out of the trees and snow. We couldn't see them, but now we knew where they were. My two forward platoons movements were stopped by heavy fire and pinned down.

It was that moment I committed my support platoon! With sprints and dashes, we moved around the right to flank the enemy. I felt this maneuver would be decisive, and it was. I closely followed my flanking platoon on the run. It was tough running through the snow, even infuriating, trying to move with those heavy wrappings around our rotting boots! Heavy automatic fire was being received along with sustained rifle shots as my platoon continued the flanking attack. As soon as the enemy detected our flanking movement, they started bolting from their positions and the pocket began to disintegrate. The coordinated movement between my two lead platoons and the maneuvering platoon enabled the attack to continue with sufficient firepower to cause the enemy heavy casualties. It was here that the enemy was either killed or captured. Those who escaped the killing zones of fire from our two companies were chased across the railroad tracks into the 501st area by elements of 2nd Battalion, 506th. The enemy was written off by late afternoon, 1600 hours, the line was restored and the perimeter remained intact.

First Battalion's attack against the German penetration resulted in sixty-five of the enemy dead and eighty taken prisoner. The 501st killed a score more and took about eighty-five prisoners. We learned later that it was the 1st Battalion, 77th Regiment of the 26th Volksgrenadier Division that had penetrated our lines, and were in the process of calling their armor forward when we struck!

As we marched back and came within sight of Luzery, on hand to greet us were the division commander, General McAuliffe, Colonel Sink, and their staffs. They heartily congratulated us on a job well done. As division intelligence was so apt to say, "the penetration was quarterized and sealed by our 1st Battalion, 506th. This was not an infiltration. The situation was critical and we committed our division reserve."

After we got the men settled, I went to the mess area for coffee and a sandwich when the Battalion S-2 came over and began telling me the event he had witnessed. By now a couple of other officers came over, too. He had observed the attack and said the Germans had me zeroed in as I followed my flanking platoon. "Unbelievable," he said. "Those tracers were coming right between your legs on each stride you took that whole twenty-yard sprint. I don't see why you weren't hit! By the way, Ed, I didn't know you were that fast." Looking back, I was never aware of it during the entire action. I was aware that we were being fired on, but that's about it. I suppose with every soldier who has been in combat, there are close calls with death of which they are never aware.

CHAPTER 35

DIVISION RESERVE

We were back in division reserve in the barns of Luzery after that sharp engagement the previous day when, on December 22, we got the word about the German ultimatum to surrender Bastogne or else, and General McAuliffe's famous reply: "Nuts!"

When a soldier asked his platoon sergeant what the general meant by that answer, the sergeant replied, "He told the Germans to go to hell!" To the division as a whole, it was a huge morale boost, a shot in the arm just when we needed it.

I went over to the aid station in Bastogne to check on my men. While there I looked in on Dick Meason who had been shot in the stomach during the attack yesterday. He was heavily sedated and awaiting evacuation. The place was full of wounded soldiers.

The defense of Bastogne had reached a critical stage at this point. All supplies had run dangerously low. Bad weather prevented supplies from being dropped in by parachute. Then, on December 23, a cold, clear day, the first air drops came floating to earth inside the Bastogne ring, in fields located between Senonchamps and Bastogne. Ammunition had at time reached rationing levels, especially for the artillery. I still had with me those vehicles we brought out of Noville, so naturally I was determined to put them to good use. I sent my supply people out to the drop zone to see if they might lend assistance bringing in the supplies dropped on the 23rd, 24th, and 26th of December. I made sure we never missed an opportunity to help out. You always look out for your men first, in any and every way you can. I had pretty much impressed on my men that nothing was to be wasted. In that cold, wet environment, you use everything you can get your hands on. We used every part of those parachutes, cut up canvas bags, and took the felt that lined the wood crates, things no one else was going after, and put all those discarded items to good use. When we were on the move, for example, bedding down in the woods for the night, we'd cover a part of the ground with evergreen boughs upon which canvas was placed. On top of the canvas went strips of felt, and the parachute panels became a blanket. What you had then was a nice, warm sleeping area that could sleep six soldiers warm as toast.

Our feet were always wet because our boots were always wet! Our boots were literally rotting off our feet. That was one of the big problems. We were inadequately supplied at Bastogne for the winter weather. It made us angry that the army hadn't supplied us with winter gear as they should have when we were at Mourmalon. I don't think the American public was aware of the deplorable conditions we endured for want of proper equipment. Our boots were deteriorating so fast that the soles began separating from the boot. Men's feet were always wet, so protection for the feet was a prime consideration against frostbite. Keeping your socks dry was a constant challenge. It paid to be doubly sure to keep an extra pair dry all times, usually by keeping them under your arms under your uniform. The constant drying out of the wet boots hastened their rotting. What you had were men who kept their boots together by wrapping them with strips of blanket, bed sheets, felt, canvas, and whatever materials were on hand to keep the feet dry. It was during the first air drop that we received a small number of rubber overshoes. Since there were not enough to issue to each man, they had to be rationed according to the most severe cases. My supply sergeant thought I was one of those severe cases. The sole of my boots had separated from the rest of the boot and were beyond repair. To prevent them from flapping when I moved and keep my feet somewhat dry, I'd tie strips of cloth around the boots, then wrap canvas around them and tightly bind them with cloth strips. I wore booties on my feet which one of the women in Luzery made for me from felt from wooden boxes we got in the parachute drop. Once the platoons reported, the most severe cases received rubber overshoes. I then accepted a pair from the supply sergeant.

I was ordered to turn over my vehicles at this time. I knew I was not authorized to keep those vehicles, but what the heck, I'd make good use of them until the time came to turn everything in. "You've got to get rid of those things," Harwick said. "You have more vehicles than regiment!" Nevertheless, I was able to retain a couple of jeeps.

The enemy kept probing and attacking, and they kept getting repulsed. We kept on our toes, anticipating the next emergency that could come at any time.

A HORRIBLE SHELLING

On December 26, 1944, elements of the 4th Armored Division reached the Bastogne perimeter in the 327th Glider Regiment's sector to the south and the siege was broken. The 101st transitioned from defense to offense as the Germans were retreating. Even though they were on the run, they struck back savagely time and again.

We were now on the offense following 4th Armor attacking out of Bastogne. It was now January, 1945. Considerable enemy forces were still in the area and putting up a stubborn resistance.

As 1st Battalion moved to regimental reserve at Savy, we got strafed by enemy aircraft that wasn't supposed to be anywhere around. We relieved 3rd Battalion, 502nd and defended the Recogne-Monaville area for the next couple of days.

Two dates in January, 1945 stand out in my mind. The first is January 9, the day we received one of the heaviest poundings from German artillery and tank fire I ever experienced. Someone forgot to tell the enemy that they were supposed to be on the run. It happened in the Recogne-Noville sector. The 506th was on the left flank of the 101st setting up in a triangular defense in the Bois-Fazone Woods west of Noville. We were in the process of digging in for the night. I had just finished checking my platoons and was returning to my command post, located by a tree, to dig a foxhole and get some coffee. Lieutenant Hazenthal, my executive officer, had just arrived from making the rounds. We were talking and preparing to dig when all of a sudden a flare lit the sky right over us. That meant trouble and we dove for the ground! As soon as we hit the ground, an artillery barrage of severe intensity began exploding. Shell after shell after shell exploded with ferocity in our area, with no let-up. The noise and concussion were terrific and unforgettable.

Feverishly clawing at the hard, frozen ground with our canteen cups and making no depression, we began scratching sideways like madmen,

trying to make even a little depression in which to lie. The intensity of the
barrage increased. Seconds seemed like days as chunks of earth and metal
flew skyward and rained down on us like hail. During all this, Hazenthal
hurt his back and went to the aid station. That's the last I ever saw of him.
I was alone. By that time, I managed to scrape a small depression in the
ground and pressed myself in there as close to the earth as I could. Then
it was over. Smoke filled the air and trees were still smoldering. One of my
platoon leaders came running toward me as I got up. "Lieutenant," he
shouted, "Where the hell did that come from? That was the nastiest
shelling I've ever seen! We took some hits. You all right?" The company
had come through in not too bad a shape, but there were casualties. Then
I found out the battalion command post had been hit. Major Harwick and
his executive officer, Captain Raudstein, were badly wounded and evacuated. Captain Shettle took over command of the battalion, but he was
wounded the next day as the Germans continued hammering our position. Captain Kessler from regimental was now in command of 1st
Battalion. Over in the 3rd Battalion area my good friend Jim Morton had
been wounded in the same barrage and was evacuated.

In light of the constant shelling of our positions duringthattime, command had the engineers bring in truckloads of logs three to five inches in
diameter to be used as coverings for our foxholes, especially for protection
against the shrapnel from tree burst explosions. Overall, it was a good idea
that saved lives. Yet in one of those freak happenings in war, I came across
one of our officers dead in his foxhole, the logs covering the opening tightly together and still intact. What had happened was a tiny, thin sliver of
shrapnel had found its way through some small opening between the logs,
pierced his helmet and entered his brain, killing him instantly.

No one ever found out how that flare was set off so close to our area,
but during all the commotion I lost my two good luck charms: the
medallion I found in Normandy, and the black-tipped M-1 bullet that
landed in my pocket at Foy. I lost them somewhere in the Bois-Fazone
woods in Belgium.

The other January date that stands out in my mind forever, an event I
was told when we arrived at our new assignment in February, was the birth
of my first son, Ivan Paul, on January 7, 1945!

MY GUARDIAN ANGEL

We moved forward in the direction of Houffalize in pursuit of the Germans. The column had stopped after marching eight miles. The battalion commander was at his jeep looking at his map. The men were sitting on either side of the road awaiting orders to resume the march. I sat down with my command group in a snow bank along the side of the road. I was pointing out terrain features of the Houffalize area when a soldier whom I did not know, nor had ever seen before, came over to me, saluted, and said the battalion commander wanted to see me right away. As I got up, I couldn't help chuckle, for my weight had made a deep impression in the snow and it sort of reminded me of a snow angel I made in the snow when I was a little kid. When I got over to the captain, he looked surprised. I saluted. "You sent for me, sir?"

"No, Lieutenant, I did not," he replied. "But look here," he said, his finger on the map. "We'll be veering off in this direction away from the high ground, on the flank of Third Battalion. Pass the word; we resume the march in ten minutes. Good to see you, Lieutenant."

When I returned to the spot where I had been sitting in that snow bank only moments before, there were a couple of my platoon leaders and sergeants gathered around. "It's a good thing you left when you did, sir," one said, pointing to the impression my body had made in the snow. "That thing would have killed you!"

I was jolted! There, right in the middle of the imprint, was a jagged chunk of hot metal five to six inches wide. There had been no explosion on impact, just a quiet "thud" someone close by had heard. It must have been a piece of shrapnel from an artillery round that exploded somewhere and sent bits and pieces of metal in all directions. Whew! I always wondered if someone else, someone in another unit nearby, someone I didn't know, was injured or even killed by a piece of metal from the same round? I think my guardian angel was working overtime.

A couple of days later, while observing my company moving forward, one of my platoon leaders, Lieutenant Reed, I believe, joined me. The company was doing a hell of a good job, he thought. "We had it all wrong," he said. "Had you all wrong! Just wanted to let you know how me and the men felt for the rough treatment you received by some in the company." He said he and the men were proud to serve with me. I told him I appreciated that and that I was just trying to do my job. After all we had been through together, Company C had performed admirably and they could be proud, as I was, for a job well done.

At one point during our chasing the Germans out of Belgium, I saw some of the men of my old 1st Platoon when H Company was on our flank. Hank DiCarlo remembered this as the last time he and the men would ever see me.

"It was like meeting an old friend," DiCarlo recalled. "We were under some heavy mortar fire at the time, but he still retained that sense of humor and that aura of command that had first impresssed us many months before at Camp Toccoa."

On 16 January, 0825 hours, C Company led off 1st Battalion's attack against German positions in the vicinity of the village of Vaux, northwest of Noville. We flanked their positions and by 1030 that morning, we were in possession of Vaux. That evening we dug in on a line east and north-west of Rachamps, tying in with the 17th Airborne Division.

On January 17, at 2110 hours, 1st Battalion closed in on the assembly area in a wooded area south of Sonne Fontaine. There, we were joined the following day by the other battalions of the 506th. We had been in Bastogne and the surrounding area for a month and were now on our way south once again. On the 20th, we encountered heavy snow and slick roads. The weather was bad, and the roads went from bad to worse as ice covered them. Movement was slow and dangerous at times. At one point, the convoy was badly broken up. But we got through, and by January 21, we were in the German town of Weisslingen. From Weisslingen we moved to Printzheim, then on to Bossendorf as January closed out.

Intelligence reported that battle casualties suffered by the 101st Airborne Division and attached units during the Bastogne Campaign resulted in the loss of 130 officers and 2014 men. The enemy paid an even higher price trying to take some prime real estate held by as fine a group of men as ever there was: tough, determined men who fought and died there for a way of life, for freedom, for their country and loved ones, and for each other. That was the 101st Airborne Division.

Extract From Diary of Lieutenant E.S. Mehosky, C/1BN/506th PIR

19 Dec '44, 0400 hours—unit arrives at assembly area near Champs, west of Bastogne-1st Bn receives initial briefing to secure Noville and hold. Make contact with Desobry Task Force (CCB, 10th Armor).

March distances...Bastogne...5000 yards; Foy...5000 yards; Noville...2500 yards.

1050 hours—Bn starts march to Noville via Bastogne...necessary ammo for op plans placed in center of road—Foy to Noville.

1300 hours—1st Bn reaches Noville.

1430 hours—Attack begins—1st Bn attacks east and north of town to secure high ground—ridge line 800 yards distance—sloping to 500 meters elevation. Intense small arms and artillery fire from the ridge stop our attack—objective never reached. Attack stalled and superior fire influence order to withdraw and establish defense around Noville.

1445 hours—Enemy counter attacks with sixteen tanks and a battalion of infantry from left side of ridge...pursuing B Company withdrawal.

1500 hours—C Company support platoon assists in stopping enemy counter attack.
We hit them with heavy flank fire!

1530 hours—C Company sets up defensive line of the perimeter on the southeast edge of the village.
1600 hours—meeting at battalion CP of all company commanders.

1630 hours—LTC LaPrade killed, Major Desobry wounded as shell rips through Bn command post. Major Harwick, XO, in command.

1800 hours—company commanders assembled and told of the situation—hold for one more day. Wounded and dead evacuated to Bastogne. Main road still open.

1900 hours—artillery fire heavy—casualties mounting.

20 Dec '44, *0100—1300 hours—shelling continues. My runner hit by shrapnel in the leg and evacuated with other wounded. Enemy maneuvering on flanks. Looks like intention is to encircle Noville.*

1300 hours—Maj. Harwick orders the battalion and combat team to withdraw from Noville.

1405 hours—Withdrawal from Noville begins. Order of march: C Co.—tanks at point, half-tracks—B Co.: Headquarters Co., tank destroyers and Co. A form rear guard.

1500 hours—C Co. lead platoon receives small arms and tank fire from direction east of Foy. Two platoons deployed and attacks road block; enemy attacking in force on our right. Third Bn on line south of Foy attacks to relieve 1st Bn. Part of column broken up.

1645 hours—Noville forces reenter division perimeter through 3rd Bn/ 506th lines on main road south of Foy.

1700 hours—1st Bn at Luzery in reserve.

1900 hours—All roads leading to Bastogne are cut by enemy armor; they have encircled the town. They think we're surrounded and have us at their mercy…think again!
2300+ hours—Enemy force reported penetrated our lines down the Bourcy-Bastogne Railroad between 2nd Battalion, 506th sector and 501st sector southeast of Foy in a wooded area.
Get ready! This looks serious! Better inform the men.

PART X

A QUIET SECTOR OF THE WAR

CHAPTER 36

ALSACE-LORRAINE, FRANCE

It was stop and go most of the way as we encountered lousy weather on the snow and ice-covered roads. After forty-two hours, we arrived at night near the German border in eastern France, the region known as Alsace, on February 1, 1945.

First Battalion set up camp in the village of Pfaffennhoffen, a deserted place save a few stray dogs and cats. We were in what was considered a quiet sector of the war, holding the line. But it was almost too quiet, the type of situation that could lull you into a false sense of security. I set up my command post at the railroad station in the station master's house in the basement. Our observation points were from the windows at street level. My orders were to defend a position along a canal that paralleled the Moder River. You could see Germany on the other side of that river. When you take up positions on an inactive front, you do a heck of a lot of patrolling, extensive and frequent, so as to continue to get information as to what's in front. This primarily occupied the short time we were there.

As the weather transitioned into early spring, the ground began to thaw, and this development brought new problems. We were dug in on the slope of a hill, but because of the high water table and melting snow, all the foxholes filled with water. We had to move to still higher ground and establish our defensive position. Some men thought it was all right if their heads protruded above ground in their foxhole, but that was unacceptable. When we checked, if their heads stuck out, they knew they'd have to dig it deeper on the spot until they got it right. This was standard procedure in all companies.

We began to receive truckloads of supplies. There we were in Alsace, France, a quiet sector at this time, and wouldn't you know it, just as soon as the temperatures began to warm, our winter boots arrived! Those sorely needed rubber overshoes that we so desperately needed up at Bastogne finally caught up with us. Well, needless to say, that got a lot of hoots and cat calls from the men! And my supply sergeant was as mad as hell!

COMPASSIONATE LEAVE

A cablegram from the American Red Cross found its way through channels. Battalion called me to report in and at the same time informed me of the birth of my son. I was surprised when compassionate leave was granted, something the commander and the chaplain worked out. I was given a jeep, a driver, extra cans of gas, identification papers, and authorization for ten days of leave to England and back. The next morning, we took off. It took us almost two days to get to an airfield outside of Paris. My driver's orders were to wait for me until I returned. I hopped a flight over to England, arriving at Northholt Airport, northwest of London. Yvonne and the baby were staying with friends in West London. She was surprised when I showed up. Two weeks earlier I never imagined I'd be back in England so soon. Words just cannot express my thoughts of that occasion. Within seconds, as I hugged and kissed my wife, it was as if all the training and war I had been through flashed before my eyes and I realized the Lord's guiding hand. I was safe and sound and back home with my family. The war seemed far away then.

As in any war, you never know when your number is up. It can happen suddenly at the most seemingly innocent time. I was one of the fortunate ones, saved for things I could not imagine then. I came through the hell of combat, first as a platoon leader, then as a commander leading a top rifle company against a tough, disciplined, well-trained and well-equipped foe. I was one of the youngest to hold such a position at twenty-four years of age. But this had hardened and matured me beyond my years. I was an officer and a seasoned veteran with four campaigns to my credit. I don't know if ever there was a more dramatic period in human history or a time where so many titanic events that reshaped the world were crammed into a space of ten short months. Even the years of preparation seemed like only yesterday. We were all deeply affected in one way or the other. It changed us. I still hold dearly to those memories of events, and most of all, to those wonderful characters I shall never forget. It was a time that has passed, yet lives on, but never to be repeated the same way again. The blessings that God saw fit to bestow on that mighty cause, one that enveloped the entire world, a cause that extracted its cost in sweat and blood and lives, forged the strongest bonds between people. I can still see those moments framed as pictures in my memory as from a thousand cameras. They have always been there; they have never left. It was much later in life, when I had grown old, that I had the opportunity to verbalize some of these thoughts into narrative.

But I'm getting ahead of myself.

CHAPTER 37

JEEP ACCIDENT

Five days later I was back at the airfield in Paris and my driver was there waiting for me. Retracing our steps, and driving at night so as to make good time, I relieved my driver so he could get some sleep. I guess I was in a hurry to get back, because I was driving pretty fast. There were still blackout conditions. Suddenly there was a sharp turn in the road! I mashed down on the brakes, but went into a slide and hit an embankment. All I remember was the jeep flipping over and being airborne for a second. When I regained consciousness, I realized I was pinned under the steering wheel of the jeep! Then I remembered my driver and wondered what had happened to him? "Lieutenant, are you OK?" came a voice out of the dark.

"Yeah, I'm OK, but I can't move." The next thing I knew my driver was tugging at me and pulling me out from under the jeep by my feet.

"Lieutenant," he said, "I was having a good sleep when all of a sudden I had this sensation as if I was flying through space! When I opened my eyes, I was face down on the side of the road, and then I realized I had been thrown out." Once we collected ourselves and got situated, we flipped the jeep over, got her started and continued on. We both felt damn lucky and thankful to have come out of the crash with only a few cuts and bruises. Not much else was said other than our praise for the tough, sturdy jeep. It was one of the best things our country ever produced during the whole war. A little farther down the road we saw signs to an army field hospital. We reported in and were treated for abrasions. The doctor also determined I had suffered a concussion, and just to be safe, decided to keep me overnight for observation. I slept one of the deepest, soundest sleeps of my life. I was released in the morning and after breakfast we got under way. We arrived in the early evening of the tenth day at regimental headquarters in the town of Hagenau, in Alsace, France. Things were still pretty quiet.

CHAPTER 38

MEDICAL EVACUATION

On February 25, First Battalion, along with the rest of the regiment moved by truck convoy to Saverne in preparation to entrain for the move to our base camp at Mourmalon. First Battalion boarded the train and departed at 1100 hours. I think all would agree that this was by far the most comfortable mode of transportation for soldiers yet encountered, and the straw-covered floors in each boxcar added to the warmth and good spirits of the men. We arrived in Rheims at first light and boarded trucks for the last leg of our journey to Camp Mourmalon.

First Battalion was billeted in hundreds of four-man tents, each tent equipped with a pot belly stove, lighting fixtures, four beds, and a wooden floor. In no time we got the men situated, oriented, and immediately began a rigorous schedule of training two days after our arrival. Replacements began arriving and so a large portion of our time was allocated to getting each company up to standard and in shape. It was during this time that I was promoted to captain.

PRESIDENTAL UNIT CITATION

In March, on the vast parade field at Camp Mourmalon, we all turned out looking our best, the entire 101st Airborne Division. On this breezy but sunny day, we were to be awarded the Presidential Unit Citation by General Dwight D. Eisenhower, Supreme Allied Commander. Lieutenant General Matthew Ridgeway was also present. General Eisenhower and Major General Taylor, 101st Commander, reviewed the division. The citation read:

These units distinguished themselves in combat against powerful and aggressive enemy forces composed of elements of eight German divisions during the period from 18 December to 27 December 1944, by extraordinary heroism and gallantry in defense of the key communications center of Bastogne, Belgium. Essential to a large scale exploitation of his break through into Belgium and northern Luxumberg, the enemy attempted to seize Bastogne by attacking constantly and savagely with the best of his armor and infantry. Without benefit of prepared defenses, facing almost overwhelming odds and with very limited and fast dwindling supplies, these units maintained a high combat morale and an impenetrable defense, despite extremely heavy bombing, intense artillery fire, and constant attacks from infantry and armor on all sides of their completely cut-off and encircled position. This masterful and grimly determined defense denied the enemy even momentary success in an operation for which he paid dearly in men, material, and eventually morale. The outstanding courage and resourcefulness and undaunted determination of this gallant force is in keeping with the highest traditions of the service.

THE EAGLES SCREAM 'HOORAY!'

BASTOGNE'S BASTARDS BATTER WAY INTO HALL OF FAME

(by Jules Grad, *Stars and Stripes* staff writer)

101st Airborne Div., Mar 16—there's a hallowed place in the United Nations' Hall of Fame today for the Battered Bastards of Bastogne. They received their life-membership awards in the sacred shrine yesterday from the President of the United States.

The Presidential citation, first in U.S. military history ever awarded to a division, was presented by Gen. Eisenhower to the 101st Airborne for "extraordinary heroism and gallantry in defense of the key communications center of Bastogne."

On a sun-drenched field, which once rocked with the noise of battle from World War I artillery and mortar blasts, the heroes of the Belgium Bulge stood at stiff attention while reconnaissance planes droned lazily overhead.

"It is a great personal honor for me to be here today to take part in a ceremony that is unique in American history," Gen. Eisenhower began. "Never before has a full division been cited by the War Department, in the name of the President, for gallantry in action. This day marks the beginning of a new tradition in the American Army."

NAME ALWAYS ASSOCIATED

"With this tradition, therefore," Gen. Eisenhower said, "will always be associated the name of the 101st Airborne Division and of Bastogne.

"Yet, you men, because you are soldiers of proved valor and of experience, would be the last to claim that you are the bravest and the best.

"The proved valor and experience came on the starry night of June 6, 1944—D-Day, when the 101st's parachutists dropped out of the skies onto Normandy and became the first Allied soldiers to descend on Hitler's Festung Europa. And then a battalion of the 502nd Parachute Inf. Reg. carried out the first large-scale bayonet attack against the German troops defending the approaches of Carentan. Out of this action came the division's first Congressional Medal of Honor.

"So far as I know, there may be many among you that would not rate Bastogne as your bitterest battle. Yet it is entirely fitting and appropriate that you should be cited for that particular battle," Gen. Eisenhower said.

These heroes of Belgium, perspiring by now from their long-fixed position at attention, needed no reminding that Bastogne may not have been their bitterest battle. Recalling their valiant stand at Bastogne, Gen. Eisenhower pointed out that their position in the Belgium bastion was of the "utmost importance to the Allied forces."

"You in reserve were hurried forward and told to hold that position. You were cut off, surrounded. Only valor, complete self-confidence in yourselves and in your leaders, a knowledge that you were well-trained and only the determination to win, could sustain soldiers under those conditions. You were given a marvelous opportunity, and you met every test."

And then Gen. Eisenhower opened wide the gates of the sacred Hall of Fame for his Battered Bastards: "You have become a fighting symbol on which the United Nations, all the citizens of the United Nations, can say today: 'We are proud of you.'"

"AWFULLY PROUD OF YOU"

"It is my great privilege to say to you here today, to the 101st Division, and all attached units, that I am awfully proud of you."
Absent from the review was Maj. Gen. Anthony C. McAuliffe, who com-

manded the Division during the Bastogne epic and who had gone to a higher command. It was he who fashioned a typically terse American answer to German demands for surrender on the forth day of the siege when he replied "Nuts" to the enemy commander's ultimatum.

But the 101st's men, who answered in their own way to von Rundstedt's order, were there on that field of honor at the end of the parade and their sentiments were perhaps best expressed by Wilburn Moore, a gangling Fayetteville, Tennessee private.

"Sure I'm proud," he said. "We did what we were supposed to do, but there's more to be done. So let's get goin'."

I can vividly recall that morning in March, when a stiff wind was blowing across the plain, and the men were assembled and standing at attention in company formation on that great parade field at Mourmalon La Grande. When General Eisenhower had finished his remarks, we proudly passed by the reviewing stand, our flags and banners fluttering in the wind, looking sharp and polished, all of us, proud to be members of the mighty Screaming Eagles of the 101st Airborne Division.

A BULLY

One evening at the officer's club, I noticed this big hulk of a lieutenant bothering to no end a smaller fellow officer at the bar, butting heads with this guy who was trying to mind his own business. This poor guy just couldn't get away no matter what he did. Every time the big lieutenant took a few gulps of beer, he'd obnoxiously yell out, "Come on, let's butt heads!"

Watching this, I was getting angrier by the minute, and damn it all, I couldn't stand a bully picking on someone smaller. I'd had enough! I went over and stepped between them. "He's had enough, Lieutenant. Why don't you leave him alone?" The bully turned on me and an altercation ensued. Words were exchanged and before anything could happen, a group of officers got between us and escorted him to another part of the club while he was making threats and acting like a jerk.

Disgusted, I left the club to return to my quarters. As I reached the tent area someone jumped me from behind and hit me a good one, square on the bridge of my nose! That got me as mad as hell and I tore into my attacker. It was that obnoxious bully from the club. I knocked him to the ground, daring him to get up, then walked away. But he jumped me again, and again I knocked the heck out of him. "Now, tough guy," I said, "if you know what's good for you, you'll get the hell out of here!" He was still on the ground when I reached my tent. A couple of hours later, I heard a commotion outside. This same dumb lieutenant was now out there with his brother, calling me out. "Go home! You're drunk," I shouted, having thought it better to let it go rather than having to explain this incident to the commander. Then it got quiet. I drifted off to sleep. In the morning, at the mess hall, someone told me that the trouble-maker from the club had been medically evacuated by ambulance—something about getting beat up pretty bad last night. That was the last thing I ever heard about it.

Resuming a vigorous training schedule (early morning runs and long marches) caused the cyst at the base of my spine to become inflamed again to the point where I was having trouble even walking slowly. It wasn't long before I checked in to the aid station to have them take a look and hopefully get some relief. They told me they would have to send me on to the field hospital in our sector. The doctor at the field hospital said I would have to be evacuated back to England to get proper treatment. I was in the medical system where they tagged me and evacuated me without my being able to let my commander know what was going on. They informed him later that day. My wife visited me in the hospital in England during my short stay; however, the doctors there determined they did not have the proper facilities to do the job right, so they sent me back to the States. I wound up at Fletcher General Hospital in Cambridge, Ohio, on May 18, 1945.

At Fletcher, during the rest of May, I was under the care of the chief surgeon, Colonel O.E. Nadeau, who examined me and diagnosed the problem as a scarococygeal-congenital, recurrent cyst. In June, I was granted thirty days leave to Reading to visit my parents. Upon release from Fletcher in July, I spent the next two months in Ashville, North Carolina at a redistribution center for more rest and recuperation. In September, I reported to the separation center at Indiantown Gap

Military Reservation, Pennsylvania for processing out of the army.

On December 30, 1945, I was a civilian again. I was a different man from the one who enlisted in the army in 1940. I was older, more mature, more serious, and experienced beyond my years. I felt much older than twenty-four. I had seen and experienced the hell of war, had seen men die, and seen men horribly wounded. I had escaped serious injury in the face of many close calls. The war had changed me in ways hard to explain. I had a family now and the most important thing on my mind was getting Yvonne and the children over here.

PART XI

THERE WAS AN OVERFLOW OF CAPTAINS, SO I GOT BACK
INTO THE ARMY AS A SERGEANT.

Edward Mehosky, 1947

CHAPTER 39

BACK INTO THE ARMY

The year 1946 came in quietly. At my home I did a lot of bartending for my dad and saw a lot of the old timers, the regulars, and my old buddies from school once word got around I was back from the war. You would have thought I was some kind of a celebrity or something. Everyone was coming around with greetings and expressing their thanks that I was back home safe and sound. "We were praying for you, Eddie. Your pop kept us informed of your whereabouts and what was going on. Thank God you're home safe and in one piece. What was it like? Did you kill any Germans? Any close calls? How about a couple of beers on me, Eddie?" I appreciated them and got a kick out of their genuine interest and sincerity. It was a nice feeling, but I was still pretty quiet about it all.

I was never one to be a loud sort of person; rather, in my own way, I tended to be more reserved. I was serious, perhaps, but not standoffish or anything like that. I wasn't funny, but I had a sense of humor and always enjoyed a good laugh. That was me.

Being back from the war, I could catch up on events. Some of my friends I met at Toccoa, like Frank Reis, came around to take me golfing, and from time to time Bob Harwick, my old company commander and battalion commander, and Bill Reid, 3rd Battalion, would drop into town whenever their jobs brought them to Reading.

MY FAMILY ARRIVES

It had been almost a year since I last saw Yvonne and the kids. How I missed them! Finally the day arrived. Dad and I drove to New York to meet Yvonne and the kids at the disembarkation port, but failed to find them. We were informed that they had taken a train out, so we raced back to Reading and made it just in the nick of time as the train was pulling in.

Dad and I waited anxiously. I had gained some weight. I guess my face was fuller and my frame larger. We were standing on the platform directly in front of the train door when suddenly there was Yvonne and the kids. She looked great and my heart was racing! The kids had grown. Upon exiting the train with the kids, Yvonne first looked our way, then in different directions trying to spot me, not realizing that it was me and Dad right in front of her. My word, had I changed that much? Finally, she looked my way again and this time she recognized me and ran toward us, pointing and telling the kids, "That's your father and grandfather!" Dad took the kids as we embraced and kissed and laughed and hugged. Oh, what a wonderful day! A couple of *Reading Times* reporters were on hand to record my family's arrival and reunion on that day of February 11, 1946. I didn't know it would make the front page. The city of Reading went out of their way to make British war brides welcome and to feel right at home. It was a nice touch. I have kept that newspaper article all these years.

JOINING THE RESERVES

In the spring of 1946, I joined the reserves with the rank of captain in the 339th Replacement Battalion, Eastern Pennsylvania Military District. Lieutenant Colonel Raymond E. Kunkleman commanded the unit. I also enrolled at Kutztown College and took a couple of courses. But Yvonne was not happy with my tending bar or living with my parents at the café in Reading. She didn't like the environment or what it was doing to me, and she and Mom were not getting along that great either. I quickly grasped the situation and started making plans to get back into the army. I left the army as a temporary grade captain, Army United States (AUS). What I wanted to do was obtain a permanent grade in the regular army. Frank Reis and I went to sign up, but they told us "no way," there were too many captains still in the army. The only option left was to re-enlist in the enlisted ranks. At one of our monthly meetings we received a memorandum from 2nd Army Headquarters, Fort Meade, Maryland on the subject of competitive tour of active duty for reserve officers. I wasted no time in acting. Yvonne was thrilled!

FORT DIX

On March 31, 1948, I received notification of authority to enlist in the army as a tech sergeant and was assigned to the leader's course, Company C, 47th Infantry Training Regiment, 9th Infantry Division at Fort Dix, New Jersey. Up to this point my military career consisted of five years, seven months of active duty, and two years, two months of inactive duty. I was further assigned to the leader's course, commonly referred to as the "La De Da." My job was as an instructor and supervisor of various phases of military science and tactics, in addition to running the physical training program. My health was good. I was 5' 10" and 220 pounds, a little heavier than at previous times. Within a month I dropped ten pounds. During PT, I used to race the younger guys in the fifty-yard dash and often beat them. They couldn't understand how a fellow my size could do that. They loved trying to beat me in push-ups and pull-ups every morning. I used to kid with them and tell them what Grandmother Babush said: "If you eat your cabbage and pierogies (dumplings), you will get big legs." I always said this to them in Polish and they loved it.

COMPETITIVE TOUR

I worked under the adjutant, Captain Joseph Michaelski, who took a personal interest in me, and who I give all the credit with helping me get into the competitive tour program.

On July 25, 1948, my competitive tour commenced. That morning I was honorably discharged from the army, T/Sgt. Mehosky, Edward S., serial number RA 13005159, and was put on duty as a captain, serial number 01284551, Infantry, for the purpose of pursuing a regular army commission.

Having been initially assigned to Battery C, 42nd AAA Battalion, 9th Infantry Division at Ft. Dix, I was now assigned as commanding officer of Company A, 39th Infantry Regiment, also at Ft. Dix. This was the start of my required three separate ratings at three different posts within a one year period.

Following a satisfactory rating from the battalion commander, and endorsed by the regimental commander, I received orders for Camp Pickett, Virginia.

Camp Pickett had been inactive. When they activated the 17th Airborne Training Division to meet the need of an influx of draftees at that time, they selected Camp Pickett. The problem was that the camp had been left in poor shape and was now overrun with weeds. It was located in a remote part of Virginia.

On September 1, 1948, I received orders to report to the 513th Airborne Infantry Regiment, 17th Airborne Division at Camp Pickett, Virginia, as company commander of Replacement Company. Only cadre was there when I reported. I was surprised to find my company personnel having to make up the bunks for the incoming draftees due to arrive, as ordered by the regimental commander. This was a little known fact of how the army had changed in a short time since I left. I was assigned to Headquarters and Headquarters Battery, Division Artillery. It was at this time we got word that Camp Pickett would be closing, so a lot of the work focused on cleaning up in preparation for closure. After I received my second satisfactory rating, I received orders in March assigning me to the 5th Infantry Division at Fort Jackson, South Carolina. My reporting date was April 17.

At Pickett, we lived in a farmhouse, Yvonne and I and the kids, Diane, Ivan and Stanley. Stanley was just a baby. It was twenty-five miles from camp, since there were no quarters on base. Then, after a couple of months, they opened the old barracks for family housing. The second floor was given to us along with its twelve toilets and a few pieces of furniture. Our beds were army cots. There were no carpets so we used cut-up cardboard boxes. As it was still cold, the only thing available for heat was a coal stove in the middle of the room. Yvonne got the stove going every morning and maintained it throughout the day. The floors were rough, unfinished wood that caused a lot of splinters in the kids' feet. When it was time to move on to Fort Jackson, those quarters had to be cleaned, including those twelve toilets!

We arrived at Fort Jackson, South Carolina, home of the 5th Infantry Division on April 18, 1949. I was assigned commander of I Company, 2nd Infantry Regiment. As this was a training center, my primary job was to train recruits and turn them into soldiers. In June, I was assigned to take over Headquarters and Headquarters Company. It seemed they wanted me there to straighten out a company that was operating under different standards, a company, I had heard, which was being protected by the adjutant and executive officer. Word had it that whenever someone came down hard on them, they'd go running to these officers. That was the situation when I took over, and the first thing I did was put them back in the army! The second thing I did was to leave them with no doubt whatsoever as to who was in charge and who was now running the company!

Well, when the new commander, Colonel Shanze, arrived, neither the adjutant nor the XO put in a good word for me. In fact, they kind of stirred the pot, and the very first day the new commander came to see me, he was loaded for bear! Can you imagine a commander coming to inspect my company with a mirror and white gloves? Oh, shit! I thought, What's going on?

He marched right to the latrines, lifted the toilet seat and stuck that mirror under the rim of the inside of the bowl where all that green stuff lingers since the day the toilet was made. Well, that's what he checked! What did I do? Back off? No way! I did my job and that was it. After a while, the colonel saw what I was doing, saw the place gleaming according to his white glove standard, and could see steady improvement in the men. From then on, he left me alone. That lasted four months. On November 2, I was assigned command of C Company.

Pit bull dogs were the rage at Jackson. One day I bought a pit bull terrier from one of the officers and brought it home to Yvonne and the kids. About a week or two later, the dog started snarling and foaming and running in circles, showing symptoms of an animal gone mad with rabies. I contained him with chairs in a corner of the house until our next door neighbor, a military policeman, arrived and shot the dog! It was years before we got another dog, but when we did, he was part wolf.

My third and final rating was contingent on a fitness report from the medical officer. No sweat, I thought, until he said, "You're overweight, Captain. You are going to have to lose twenty pounds in one week or else I won't endorse your report!" There was no "or else" about it. I had come too far and worked too hard for my captaincy to blow it now. There was only one thing to do. I went on a high protein diet, ate mostly hard-boiled eggs, drank strong laxatives, exercised and ran my butt off. The regular doses of laxatives weren't working, so after a couple more days I switched first to another stronger laxative, and finally Epsom salts. I was taking so much I probably ruined my insides dropping those seventeen to twenty extra pounds. When I went back to see the doc, he was more than satisfied and signed my medical report. By mid-November I received my third and final successful rating. I was now regular army. My date of rank for captain was January 25, 1950.

Diary note: Received today, November 16, 1949, a letter from Lieutenant General Gillem, Jr., Commander, Third Army.

Dear Captain Mehosky:

I have noted with a great deal of pleasure your appointment to the regular army and wish to take this opportunity to express my personal congratulations.

You are to be especially commended for your fine record during the course of your competitive tour. I feel sure that your services as a member of the regular army will be equally outstanding.

Please accept my best wishes for a most successful military career.

Sincerely,

Alvan C. Gillem, Jr.

From December 1 to the end of March, I held the job at 3rd Battalion as assistant executive officer, and then from April to July, I was assigned to the post transportation section under Major Rex Bayless. Here we met and became good friends with Harry and Edie Borgia from New York. At every post the Borgias were assigned, they had insisted in living in a trailer so they wouldn't have to entertain their relatives. The Borgias were wonderful friends and a fine couple. Harry was in the Quartermaster Branch when I knew him, and after that, went on to become a pilot. Later, when I was at Ft. Benning with the 508th, Harry was sent to Korea. It was during this time that I got word his plane had been shot down and all aboard killed. We were grief stricken and felt Edie's loss deeply. Harry was a fine officer.

CHAPTER 40

THE 508TH REGIMENTAL COMBAT TEAM

My next assignment was the Infantry School at Fort Benning, Georgia. I was one of 177 officers of the student detachment assigned to the nine month Infantry Advanced Course #2 that September. There were sixty course problems covered during this time. My class standing was 136. Those few courses I didn't excel in were subjects in administrative categories which I naturally associated with sedentary desk-type assignments. I always wanted to be with the soldiers, commanding, training out in the field, and not confined to a desk job in some office. I guess that's why I never showed a great enthusiasm for the administrative aspects of the army and maybe had a mental block. Toward the end of school, word began circulating about assignments and who would go where. There were about twenty of us who were pretty sure of airborne assignments. Anticipating this, we started a voluntary PT program. We'd meet at a designated hour after class, assembling in shorts, T-shirts, and jump boots and run out to the Sand Hill area of the post and back. Within two weeks I was pretty much back in shape. The army assigned me to the 508th Regimental Combat Team, 82nd Airborne Division at Fort Bragg, North Carolina.

I reported to Fort Bragg on March 31, 1951. Upon checking in, it struck me that the only personnel on duty were an officer and a few NCOs and clerks. They informed me that everyone else was down at the airfield making their qualification jumps. I drove to the airfield, reported in, and was introduced to the senior officer there, a Major Flowers. "Glad to have you here, Captain Mehosky. Hey, there's an extra chute right over there. Why don't you put it on and join us?" As I put on my chute I thought maybe they were going to give me some quick training on that new T-10 parachute they had been using, or perhaps a word or two about the new parachute landing fall.

The Story of a Soldier • 219

These guyswere on jump status, and it had been seven years since my last jump. Well, next thing I know I'm in the middle of the stick in a plane a thousand feet up! The red light came on. At that point, we immediately stood up, hooked up, checked equipment, and shuffled forward on the command, "Stand in the door!" Each man was pressed in tight to the man in front of him. When the green light came on, we were quickly pushed out the door as the fellows in the rear gave a tremendous, continuous shove until they too had exited. There was no hesitation and no time to think. My chute deployed in an easy jolt, nothing as violent as the old T-7. As I descended, I thought about the landing, feet together or apart? What was it they said about the new parachute landing fall? Then I landed. It was the best jump and softest landing I ever made.

Colonel Joseph Cleland commanded the 508th Regimental Combat Team. My immediate boss was Lt. Colonel Ralph Burns, who commanded 1st Battalion. I had A Company. Lieutenant Angel Torres was my executive officer, and Hardy Batchelor was my first sergeant. Captain Kutchinski, who commanded C Company, and I, were always competing as to who had the best company, best mess hall, most range qualifications and things like that. One thing I was noted for throughout my career was my mess halls. Nobody beat my mess halls. I mean they were spotless, efficient and had the best prepared food around. You could get a sandwich anytime, and it was usually where my bosses frequented from time to time.

Reactivation Day for the 508th was held on May 5th, beginning in the morning with a review and presentation of colors. Major General Thomas F. Hickey, Commanding General, 82nd Airborne Division spoke the greeting:

Troopers of the 508th. We welcome your regiment back into the ranks of the airborne units. As before in WWII, we of the 82nd Airborne Division are proud to have you with us, even though it be for a short time.

The troopers of the 508th, living and dead, who fought with valor on the battlefields of Normandy, Nijmegen, and Germany, have passed to you a proud heritage and a fighting tradition. Let those gallant men be your example in moving the 508th Airborne Infantry forward to further achievement and distinction, a regiment which our army, our armed forces and our nation shall hold in esteem.

We were just getting settled at Ft. Bragg when the regiment was ordered to report to Ft. Benning.

At Benning, the 508th was billeted in the Sand Hill area. Our mission to become the honor guard for SHAPE Headquarters in Paris, France remained unchanged. We had been designated by the army, and activated by the army with high hopes and expectations. To meet these expectations, the regimental commander implemented a highly organized, rigorous training schedule that reflected his commitment to the highest standards expected of an elite airborne unit. Physical training was comparable to what I experienced in the 506th. But unlike the 506th training, everything here was centralized.

The commander made it clear to officers and NCOs how he visualized the elements of tactical training, and this was accomplished through the use of lecture and demonstrations, with keynote talks by the commander emphasizing his main points and how he expected his commanders to perform. "Now this is the way I expect you to conduct yourself on a patrol," he would say, and went on in depth and clarity, not leaving anything to guesswork. "You've got to be smart, go by the book, rehearse, know what you're trying to accomplish, and above all, blend in with the scenery. You work together as a team!" Colonel Cleland went by the book and expected the same standards from everyone. He was one for follow-up, of that you could be certain. If you weren't doing it right, you heard about it real quick. He and his staff were always checking, always critiquing and making corrections on the spot. That year was some of the best training I ever experienced, different from the 506th, but just as good. We soon jelled into one solid, tough and ready unit—a unit that could be deployed anywhere. That was the kind of combat team Colonel Cleland molded.

A NASTY LANDING

First Battalion was making a demonstration jump before civilian and military dignitaries. As I was descending and preparing to land, suddenly my chute collapsed and the next thing I knew I was on the ground on one knee. I was dazed and a swarm of people were around me. Then the ambulance and medics arrived. As they were checking me over, I became aware that whatever just happened put everybody in the stands in an uproar. They saw the whole thing and it upset them. As I was placed in the ambulance my executive officer and first sergeant were nearby and were telling me what had happened. "One of the troopers near you had been oscillating like crazy and crashed into your chute, causing it to collapse. You dropped like a rock and hit the ground head first," they said, "and we thought you were dead!"

Even the medics were astounded. Said one, "Dropping from that height, at that speed, is like jumping off the roof of a three-story house, Captain."

Even their talking hurt my head as a wave of sickness came over me, but I managed to reply that I felt like a cracked, hard-boiled egg, now trying to fight this sick feeling that had set hold of me on the way to the hospital. I was confused, dizzy, and everything above my shoulders, including my brain, hurt intensely. It was a weird feeling.

After a thorough examination by the attending emergency room doctor, followed by a battery of x-rays, they determined I had suffered a severe concussion to my head and extreme trauma to my neck and shoulders. They kept me overnight and the next day for observation just to be safe. Yvonne and the kids came to see me, as did a lot of other people. I was released and sent home the following morning and placed on light duty.

A day later I decided to go in to work. My head was still so sore that it even hurt to wear my fatigue cap. The battalion was starting the beginning phase of an army training test (ATT) when I reported. Lieutenant Colonel Dillinder, who had replaced Colonel Burns as battalion commander, was surprised, but glad to see me and asked if I was able to participate. I told him I thought so, but I couldn't wear a helmet. He immediately got the OK from the regimental commander and informed the Infantry School umpires, those conducting the exercise, that I would be wearing a fatigue cap.

The field problem assigned to the regiment, "The Company in Defense," involved a tactical situation consisting of how to deploy your troops and how to best defend the terrain selected by the umpires. My mission was to establish a defensive position for my company. What I did was put my company in a reverse slope defense. Under the close observation of the umpires, I conducted my reconnaissance of the assigned terrain and gave the necessary instructions to my platoon leaders for deployment. They hit it on the run and quickly took position. When it was over and the umpires were huddling, Colonel Dillinder came over to me, beaming. "Ed," he said, "that was great work! Your company looked good. We got it! We sure got it! You hit it right on the head!" Out of the entire regiment only my company, A Company, got the school solution to the problem, and I was starting to feel pretty damn good.

In this exercise, like any other training or combat, I pretty much followed the book, but did some things in a more unorthodox manner. I probably knew the terrain better than most, and here was one of my basic and strongest fundamentals: able to place your men and weapons to attain maximum effectiveness in the area of operation. I think this and the ability to infuse the men with a sense of realism in their training, the idea that you perform as you practice, was one of the hallmarks of my career. People began to take notice of our prowess, for example, during raids and ambushes on other companies in the swamps. Our quick night marches, and intelligence gathering by patrols, our concealment techniques and keeping them off balance by doing the unexpected, were my trademarks. Soldiers spoke of these kinds of things to other soldiers as the word got around. I suppose you might say our reputation was based on action and results.

In any rifle company, platoon or squad, you try to utilize each man's skill so as to take advantage of it for the good of the whole. That's one of the essentials in building a good company. We had in A Company a fellow named Boggs, a second lieutenant who hailed from Tennessee. Boggs had the reputation as a good raccoon hunter, one who knew the land like the back of his hand. Well, that's what he did in the swamps around Ft. Benning on weekends. Pretty soon Boggs and his number one dog, Trump, were conducting regimental coon hunts. Now that guy had perception. He didn't need a compass. He was a natural and could find his way anywhere. When you consider that these activities were usually conducted at night, and the fact that old Boggs never once got lost, it was an amazing thing to witness. One can quickly grasp the advantage of having a fellow like that in your company. You've got to take advantage of each man's strength. If someone at regiment wanted to go hunting, they would call me to ask if Boggs was available for a night of racoon hunting in the swamps. Boggs never paid much attention to his popularity. He was always happy and at home in the wilds. That was Boggs.

One of the things I employed in my company was the use of luminous paint to mark our equipment so as to be easily identified and easily retrieved during an exercise, especially any tactical jump or night drop. We got orders to move from Fort Benning to San Angelo, Texas to perform for dignitaries and reporters. We would do a regimental jump to demonstrate the capability of an airborne regimental combat team in action. San Angelo was selected because of its wide open spaces. The weather was clear but windy, and so the jump had to be postponed for two days. On the third day the decision was made to go ahead, regardless, even though the winds never got below twenty-five miles per hour. When we hit the ground, equipment was flying everywhere, and men were being dragged for yards before they could recover. The wonder of it all was that no serious injuries were sustained. By the time the jump was completed, Regimental Supply Section, the S-4, had accumulated a mountain of equipment there in one giant pile. Everything was thrown in there together so no one knew where their stuff was. Every company supply sergeant was being turned away, except mine. He told the S-4 that because of the identification system that had been employed in A Company by Captain Mehosky, he could retrieve every backpack, canteen and whatnot in no time at all. He proceeded to the amazement of all. It was days before the other companies got their equipment back.

One of the things that made my company such a solid unit was First Sergeant Hardy Batchelor. Hardy was one of the finest NCOs I had the pleasure to serve with during my military career. He was highly respected, competent, tough, no nonsense type of soldier, and all business. He kept a baseball bat near his desk as a conversation piece. Whenever a soldier who thought he was tough conveyed this attitude to the first sergeant, Hardy simply closed his office door and corrected the problem. He was my eyes and ears in the enlisted ranks.

When Colonel Cleland left for Korea to become Assistant Division Commander of the 40th Infantry Division, Colonel Joe Lawrie took over the regiment and intensified the program Cleland started. But when France backed out of NATO in 1952 and, consequently, the 508th's mission got canceled, it was like letting the air out of a balloon. Everything we had trained so hard for and the level of readiness we had achieved to that point went out the window. The 508th was scheduled to be disbanded and people began leaving in all directions for new assignments. Things were pretty dead, so it was at this juncture I volunteered for duty in Korea.

Postscript: No question, the 508th RCT was one of the elite regiments of the day and one of the finest I had the honor to serve in. Had our mission not been canceled, or had the regiment been sent into combat, anywhere, there is no doubt in my mind whatsoever that it would have performed to expectations and probably even exceeded them. You fight like you train.

PART XII

BUG OUT TRENCHES? THERE WILL BE NO BUG OUT TRENCHES UNDER MY COMMAND! BLOW THE DAMN THINGS UP!

Captain Edward Mehosky

CHAPTER 41

JOINING THE 40ᵀᴴ INFANTRY IN KOREA

July 31, 1952. To Major General Cleland, Commanding General, 40th
Infantry Division, APO #6, San Francisco, California:

Dear Sir:

*It is with great pleasure that I extend my heartiest congratulations on your
assumption of command and recent promotion. Also, I can say with a great feeling of pride that I had been a member of your command.*

*The 508th is quite dormant at present, fulfilling ROTC commitments and
an interim training schedule. Many of the old faces are gone bringing a nostal-
gia for the early days of the regiment. However, the training will start humming
again, very soon, when we begin our field training, but by that time I will be on
my way to FECOM. While in that theatre I can't think of a better unit to serve
with than the one the general commands. After discussing this matter with Col.
Dillinder I am taking his advice and submitting an extract copy of my orders and
hope that I may be of service to your command.*

Trusting that you are in good health, I wish you luck and success.

Sincerely yours,

Edward S. Mehosky, Captain, Infantry.

On August 14, I received a reply from General Cleland.

To Captain Edward S. Mehosky, 508th Airborne Regimental Combat
Team, Fort Benning, Georgia:

Dear Mehosky:

*I certainly appreciate you taking the time to write to me. Please know I will
do everything I possibly can to get you, particularly, and any other member of the
508th into the 40th. I know what you people can do and it would be a particular*

The Story of a Soldier • 229

benefit to this division to have as many of you fine officers along here with me that I can possibly have.

We already have Hyman, Armstrong, McDonough, Dubsky 82nd, Tuttle 82nd, Tolar 82nd, Captain Parks 508th, Durand 82nd and any number of others from the 11th and Fort Benning.

If you know me, I am for building a second 508th in this division. We have a lot of fine officers and men whether or not they are from the airborne, but we are doing everything to bring the standard up to the top.

I am sure you will like this division. I hope this finds you and Mrs. Mehosky well. Please accept my kindest personal regards. Thank you again for your letter.

OVERSEAS AGAIN

I received orders to report to the Fort Lawton Personnel Center, Seattle, Washington, for overseas movement to the Far Eastern Command, Yokohama, Japan, on October 15, 1952, but since my wife and kids would be residing in Reading, Pennsylvania and school was to start in September, I requested and was granted an additional fifteen days, making my reporting date October 31. It was in St. Louis where I met Captain James McKee, who was also slated for the 40th and wound up as the regimental adjutant. We rode the train to Seattle and from there flew to Japan. We became good friends.

General Cleland had his men flagging orders of all incoming airborne officers assigned to him. Upon arriving at the replacement depot in Japan, we were intercepted by personnel people from the 40th, walked through the paperwork, and flown to Korea. From Seoul it was a seventy-five mile jeep ride to the front by way of Chunchon and up to X Corps. The land was devastated; villages everywhere were knocked down and people were trying to rebuild.

This phase of the Korean War had settled into fighting along the Demilitarized Zone (DMZ) on the 38th Parallel, on the ridges and in the valleys. The line of defense held by 8th Army spanned the width of the Korean Peninsula, snaking north and south of the 38th Parallel. It started on the western side at Munsan-ni, continued in a great arc to Ch'orwon and Kumhwa, then dipped slightly to Mundung-ni, and completed the line north to Oemyon-Ni on the eastern coast. X Corps, comprised of the 45th Infantry Division, the 40th Infantry Division, and the Republic of Korea's (ROK) 7th Division, manned the center portion of the eastern sector line in the Mundung-ni area, with the 40th in the middle, the 45th on the right flank, and the 7th Division on the left.

After reporting to division headquarters, I ran into General Cleland as he was on his way to a meeting. He talked with me for a few minutes, expressing how glad he was to see me and have me in the outfit. I can tell you the feeling was mutual. From there I went to regiment and reported to Colonel Monk Meyers. I ran into my old boss from the 508th, Colonel Dillinder, who was now the executive officer (XO). I was assigned command of a rifle company, Company L of the 3rd Battalion, 160th Regiment, currently holding a key ridge in the 40th Division's sector on the 8th Army's line of defense. At battalion I was given a more detailed briefing of the situation, problems I could expect to encounter, the disposition of our troops, enemy positions, the climate, and terrain. I was told that decent roads were nonexistent and that the ridges in our sector were some of the steepest and nastiest around. The ridge where my company was dug in was roughly a thousand meters high, situated between Heartbreak Ridge on the right, and on the left the village of Mundung-ni and the Mundung-ni Valley.

CHAPTER 42

COMPANY 'L' AT MUNDUNG-NI

I assumed command on November 14, 1952. From battalion I was taken by jeep over what could be called roads in name only, to a valley at the base of the ridge I would come to call home for the next three to four months. There were two Quonset huts there that served as the company's administration, communication and supply section. The first sergeant gave me a briefing of his operations as well as introduced me to the rest of the soldiers. He then called to the command post (CP) to tell the outgoing commander I had arrived. After a cup of coffee, the first sergeant and I began the hike, arriving about an hour later at the CP on the forward slope after a strenuous, wringing wet climb. I was then taken on a tour. My impression of the situation was not very good. For example, the CP was located directly under enemy observation, sticking out there and looking like old Abe Lincoln's hat. You couldn't miss it, nor could the enemy. I don't think battalion would ever have tolerated that had they seen it, but after climbing up there, perhaps nobody from battalion ever got that far. It got progressively worse. Upon meeting my platoons, I observed poorly constructed, unsafe bunker after bunker; filthy, below-standard conditions characterized each stop. That would change fast. The connecting trench between bunkers was in bad shape, too.

Then I noticed another perpendicular trench heading back toward the ridge line. "What is the purpose of this trench?" I inquired.

"Well, that's our 'bug out' trench, sir," came the reply, "in case we have to 'bug out' of here in the event it gets too hot!"

"Bug out? There will be no bug out trenches in my command! Is that clear?" I retorted, coldly. "First Sergeant, take a note. Get hold of the engineers first thing and have those damn things blown up. And another thing. I don't ever want to hear that defeatist word ever again. We are here to fight!"

By the end of my first week there, I had the engineers construct a new CP over the hill on the reverse slope, out of the way of the damn enemy's direct observation and fire. The former CP was destroyed.

From my CP to the forward bunkers on line I had to traverse a lot of open ground where there was not a stitch of cover, so anytime there was movement in this area, even at night, we usually got shelled by the Chinese. I'd check my platoons at night. I never set a pattern, but varied the days and times in which to conduct my rounds, and I never moved without my radioman, either. The Chinese never fired on me going down to the bunkers; I was usually fired on when returning to the CP, uphill. I had the engineers and the Korean Service Corps come and build some zig-zag trenches up the slope from the bunkers. They had a hell of a time working in that frozen ground and eventually wound up dynamiting the whole area, but those guys got it done.

When a company commander's meeting was called at battalion down the ridge, I'd go to a waiting jeep at my administration hut on the valley floor, then to battalion headquarters approximately five miles away. I sweated like all get out coming down that ridge and was ringing wet by the time I reached the bottom. If that waiting jeep wasn't warm, it would be a chilly ride to battalion.

We all faced the same ordeal of going up and coming down that ridge, yet the Korean Service Corps made that climb three times a day, every day, supplying us with hot food carried on their backs in insulated containers. There had to be a better way. That's when I came up with the idea of having a staircase cut into the side of that mountain, one that would traverse or zig-zag its way up to the top, ending in the area near my CP. Once approval was obtained, I again called on the engineers and the Korean labor force to blast a staircase out of that rock and frozen ground. It took them about two months. Rope handrails were added and the result was a staircase up that ridge that was so magnificent I named it the "Golden Staircase." Right away it proved its worth. Now it was much safer and faster to get up and down that ridge, not to mention fewer injuries. The biggest thing, though, was that it enabled those supplies, especially the hot food, to get up to us faster.

Our bunkers, or "hootchies" as they came to be called, including my

CP, were made of sandbags and timber, and covered with branches and camouflage netting and whatever else you could come up with. It kind of reminded me of the trenches I had seen from pictures from World War I. My CP was of adequate size with enough space for two rooms with flooring. I had a small table and a lamp next to my cot in the smaller area off to the right from the entrance; the left and larger part of the command post was occupied by the rest of my staff: a lieutenant who served as my executive officer, a communications sergeant, an enlisted radioman, and a Korean houseboy. We had a nice cozy stove in the middle of the bunker that kept the place warm. We mostly slept in long underwear, and sometimes in our field gear, but always in individual sleeping bags augmented by layers of blankets. I had an outhouse built adjacent to my CP. It was a two seat job complete with fur-lined seats so your butt would not stick to the frozen toilet seat.

There was a saying, "There is no cold like Korea; nothing compares." That's why the tents and bunkers had pot belly stoves. But this caused big problems with fires, even to the point where some of the bunkers in other companies had caught on fire. This got the division commander so upset that he threatened swift disciplinary action to any commander who allowed that to happen.

The men began anticipating my platoon visits at night. During the day I'd go to front line bunkers and observation areas to see what improvements could be made. My idea of defense was an active, aggressive defense, making things happen, constantly harassing the enemy, and playing with his mind. We would take the initiative, not sit back. That wasn't my style. Nothing was overlooked, everything was checked, and everything was rehearsed. The men not only began to look sharp, they acted sharp, with confidence. They were doing things the smart way, the right way. Morale was up. We became a well-knit fighting team.

The Korean cold is the most severe one can ever experience, and being up on those mountains at night during the winter months is a different thing altogether. Regardless of how good our equipment was, it was only effective when each soldier practiced good winterization techniques. For example, the "Mickey Mouse" boots were perfect for this kind of weather and terrain, but because they were so well-insulated, your feet would sweat to the point that they'd be sloshing around in there and cause foot problems. It was imperative soldiers changed their socks on a regular basis. One of the things I instilled was each soldier would carry an extra pair of dry, clean socks underneath his coat at all times.

To make sure we kept the rat population at bay, we did not store food on line as there had been breakouts of hemoragic fever caused by rodents. I had a large tent erected on the reverse slope that served as a mess hall for the men. Hot food was brought up twice a day and the company ate in shifts by platoon. The other meal consisted of C rations. There was always hot coffee.

There wasn't much patrolling before I took over, but that changed. A commander must always know what is in his front and on his flanks. I probably sent out more patrols than anyone, and that's the way I always operated at night. My patrols were my eyes and ears, my listening posts gathering useful intelligence. Every piece of equipment was checked and rechecked; every detail rehearsed and every man's role discussed. Nothing was left to chance. Every one of my patrols knew what they were going to do and how they were going to do it, expecting the unexpected, reacting to any situation that may have arisen.

One of the most competent and energetic platoon leaders in my company was Lieutenant Robert Leyh from New Jersey. He was solid. I liked him and could count on him. His platoon was squared away and could always be counted on. One night, I had Lieutenant Leyh lead a patrol to scout out the area in the valley between me and Heartbreak Ridge to see what was on my right flank. They were about a mile out when I got this hushed call on the radio from Lt. Leyh that they had entered a mine field! Talking in whispers, I began to extricate them by having them carefully retrace their exact steps with no deviation, slowly, carefully, step-by-step, maintaining the utmost calm throughout, until every man had cleared the point from which they crossed into the mine field without alerting the Chinese. It was tense, touch and go, but finally they arrived intact. I was never so glad to see a patrol in my life. The word was passed to all companies that that area was "no man's land." Another patrol was sent out to see what was on my left and ran head on into an advancing Chinese patrol, resulting in a firefight. They handled themselves well, but I had to get them out of there fast. One soldier suffered a slight wound, otherwise they were all OK. That incident proved to be a big lift for the men and something to talk about.

I was always working to improve our position on that ridge. What could the enemy see on my position, I wondered? What did my lines look like to those Chinese watching us everyday? I sent out a patrol to observe our position. That night, I assembled a seven-man patrol to be led by Lieutenant Leyh. "I want you to move out tonight at 0215 sharp, cross the valley, and set up a concealed position at the base of the enemy's ridge, directly under their noses. Your objective starting first light until dark is to make a panoramic sketch of our position, as if you were the enemy scouting our position. What would he see? I want as much detail as possible. Look for weak points, obvious tell-tale signs of living quarters, poor concealment, things like that. Everything you notice, sketch it. Whatever looks like a good target to you is exactly what the Chinese see. I'll see you back here at 2215 hours tomorrow night. Any questions? All right, move 'em out. Good luck, men."

They returned without incident. What they brought was very revealing and confirmed my suspicions. In front of every bunker the ground was littered with C rations tins as if drawing an arrow for the enemy directly to where our key positions were. We were easy targets. In short order the tell-tale evidence was removed and strict adherence to camouflage discipline was enforced. My report to headquarters highlighted the manner in which I obtained the information and what the information revealed. Furthermore, I believe that report was forwarded through channels all the way up to 8th Army Headquarters. I mention this because of a memorandum that was handed to front line commanders from the new commander, Lieutenant General Taylor, who, upon taking command, cited the need for "better concealment efforts of skyline positions of front line troops."

Toilet facilities in the front lines consisted of holes dug into the trenches. After one completed his business, it was that soldier's responsibility to cover it over with lime. Lime kept the trenches sanitary and disease free. We weren't going to let sloppiness or forgetfulness claim casualties in this company.

Telephone wires had been laid, so I had good communication with battalion by telephone. Should the lines be cut for any reason, or by the enemy, my emergency backup was the reliable PRC-10. I usually had the communication sergeant follow a patrol at night, laying wire behind them as they advanced toward their objective.

The 40th had a pretty neat program started by General Cleland called "King For a Day," whereby they would bring back to division headquarters a front line company commander who was picked as "company commander of the week." The commander selected would be brought off line and picked up in the general's jeep and taken to the general's mess. I was treated to this honor twice during my tour up on that ridge.

I was on good terms with the assistant division commander, Brigadier General Rogers, and Colonel Hennessey, the division's artillery commander. Colonel Hennessey liked to call me to go shoot our 45s at targets and talk about various situations. General Rogers visited my command post once or twice a month and also liked to do a little target practice, except with artillery instead of side arms. We went to the forward observer's bunker, and General Rogers asked, "Well, Captain Mehosky, what should we fire at tonight?"

"We just might catch them asleep today, sir," I replied. I ordered a fire mission, gave them the coordinates, and within no time a couple of salvos streaked through the night air and impacted on the enemy's position on the ridge across the way. There followed a series of huge explosions and fireworks that could only mean we hit one of their ammo dumps. The general was gleeful and slapping his side with his hand, yelling, "Hot damn, did you see that?" From that time on, every time we met in the presence of other officers and VIPs, the general would bring up that topic with as much enthusiasm as the day he visited me on that ridge.

It was too quiet on both sides. We needed more activity. It was during this time I devised my "Mad Minute," an idea headquarters loved and for which they quickly gave me the go ahead. I had the men do a panorama of the enemy's entire position across the valley. Each man studied those positions so they knew those targets cold! Then, once a week at the prearranged time, we'd open up with everything we had:

mortars, machine guns, .75mm recoilless rifle, rocket launchers, and small arms! For one full minute we gave them hell! We plastered them good. It was one awesome display of a rifle company's firepower. That became the highlight of the week, something the soldiers looked forward to with much enthusiasm and anticipation. Once word got around, visits from senior officers increased in our sector.

Personal hygiene was preached so much it became second nature with the men. To help enhance this, I had the engineers build hot water showers in the valley next to our administration and supply hut area. We had more success with our front line showers than the units in the rear were having. This proved to be a tremendous morale boost to the men.

There were times we got shelled by the enemy and times we got shelled by our own people, but the most severe bombing of my position was done by the navy! Word came down to me that navy aircraft from one of the aircraft carriers would be making sorties against enemy positions in our area. To ensure these aircraft would not bomb and strafe friendly positions, we were instructed to mark our positions with serese panels that would be visible to pilots. What we did was stake out a large rectangular area in an open field near my CP. This area was then covered with chicken wire affixed to wooden stakes in each corner. On top of the chicken wire was placed the serese panels in the design of a cross, and covering these was another layer of chicken wire. It was intact and could not be blown away. On a particular day when I had been called to battalion, the navy planes bombed and strafed my CP! Part of the blast had penetrated the entrance and damaged the area where I slept. Fragments from that blast tore into the arm of my houseboy, causing him to be evacuated. When the report went through channels citing that the navy pilots had screwed up, they denied any mistake and claimed there were no panels on that ridge, and that it was the army that didn't follow orders. However, my commander and others had seen the whole thing from the next ridge back at their observation post, and they clearly saw the panels. A second message from 8th Army Headquarters went back to the navy exonerating me and putting the ball in their court.

As much as a company commander drills things into his company about exposing oneself to the enemy, there is always going to be one guy who just never paid attention or didn't care about himself or anyone else for that matter. The men were repeatedly told not to expose themselves to the enemy in sunlight and warm weather. One man acted contrary to the standing instruction and decided to sunbathe on the roof of his bunker. It wasn't long before some observant Chinese soldier across the valley directed fire on that bunker! The second round was a direct hit! The only things found were part of his boots and a severed dog tag.

DOING MY JOB THE ONLY WAY I KNEW

THROUGH: Commanding Office   1 September 1953
          160th Infantry Regiment
          APO 6

TO: Commanding General
    40th Infantry Division
    APO 6

SUBJECT: Recommendation For Award (Bronze Star-Meritorious Service)

Sir:

Major Edward S. Mehosky, 060688, former Rifle Company Commander, Company 'L,' 160th Infantry Regiment is cited for meritorious service during the period 14 November 1952 to 30 January 1953, and superior performance.

Major Mehosky, then captain, distinguished himself by his selfless devotion to duty, working tirelessly to strengthen his company's defensive position, and, through an extraordinary display of leadership and sound knowledge of tactics, the creation of a highly efficient combat team.

Major Mehosky far exceeded the normal requirements of a combat leader. Major Mehosky distinguished himself through his constant personal presence in exposed positions in order to encourage the construction and strengthening of outposts and fighting positions, and his driving determination to conduct an aggressive, active defense against the enemy.

Through exemplary qualities of leadership, sound application of tactics, and tireless devotion to his men, Major Mehosky knit together a highly efficient fighting team, capable of accomplishing any assigned mission.

His unit being already committed in combat in the vicinity of Mundung-ni, Korea, Major Mehosky assumed command with a sureness and deliberation that inspired confidence in all those who served under him. Major Mehosky immediately conducted a complete reorganization of his unit and fashioned to his own high standards a highly effective combat team. Due to Major Mehosky's unceasing efforts and sound application of military principles, the critical defensive position which his unit occupied was greatly improved and strengthened. With great determination Major Mehosky overcame logistical problems imposed upon his unit by its location on a high and steep hill under direct enemy observation. Thinking constantly of the welfare of his men, Major Mehosky through his imagination and initiative, established shower and recreational facilities within range but thoroughly secure from enemy fire. These facilities continued operations in spite of the winter and adverse conditions which paralyzed similar facilities in reserve areas. This alone was an important factor contributing to the continued high morale of Major Mehosky's unit.

JAMES MCKEE
CAPTAIN, INFANTRY
Adjutant

CHAPTER 43

REGIMENTAL S-2

By February, 1953, we were pulled off line and placed in regimental reserve. The conflict had now entered a true static phase because of truce negotiations going on. I guess what best characterized this phase was the almost constant movement of the regiment to positions south of the defensive line. There occurred a vacancy at regimental headquarters, a major's slot, for the intelligence officer or S-2. Colonel Dillinder brought me to regiment to fill that position and in no time I was getting used to a new line of work in a branch quite opposite infantry. Colonel Dillinder was very supportive and had a great deal of confidence in me. I appreciated the opportunity and challenge, not to mention working for my old boss again.

During this time the 160th Regiment got a new commander by the name of John H. McAleer, a West Pointer. This officer had originally been in the infantry branch, combat arms, but went into the logistics career field where there was a great need at that time. Anyway, Colonel McAleer had been on the X Corps staff, and when the opening came, he was put in to command the 160th over the objections of the division commander. Well, this didn't sit very well at all with the assistant division commander, Brigadier General Buck Rogers. Rogers could be most severe and relentless if he didn't like you. His favorite expression was "horse shit," which he'd say with emphasis as he smacked the side of his leg with his pointer when something went wrong or when he was on you. General Rogers was armored cavalry. From the first day Colonel McAleer reported for duty, General Rogers made his life miserable; he couldn't do anything right no matter what. Colonel McAleer never gave in, always kept a couple of steps ahead of the general, and always maintained the highest professionalism. I can remember a particular CPX when General Rogers came on the scene and chewed out Colonel McAleer unmercifully in front of all us junior officers. Said the general, "We don't want any damn retreads down here, Colonel. You read me? That's horse shit, Colonel, pure horse shit! What the hell are you running here anyway?" And on and on, but Colonel McAleer, to his credit, took every bit of it and held his tongue.

This went on for weeks, but the colonel just replied with a firm, "Yes sir," and looked him right in the eye every time. You see, this old bird colonel was also one tough soldier too; a gruff, tough fighter who had been around and was street smart. He had won our utmost respect and loyalty that first day, so the staff worked as hard as we could to protect him and to make sure nothing slipped, so there wouldn't be anything General Rogers could find wrong. Before long, seeing he couldn't break the man, General Rogers let up. I learned a very important lesson here that stayed with me the rest of my career. This same scenario would play again, this time against me, when I served as the S-2 with the 11th Airborne Division in Germany.

As much as we preached safety in all units and all ranks, we still had accidents. This one in particular happened in a rear area. One day one of the sergeants was cleaning a 75mm recoilless rifle, standing directly behind the gun, a no-no, when he leaned forward and somehow must have touched the trigger. We heard the explosion and were told immediately what had happened. All that remained of him was part of the lower torso.

By late summer of '53, the regiment got orders to move south to the island of Koje-do to guard the prisoner of war camp there. A year earlier had seen rioting and the takeover of several compounds by hard core communist prisoners that resulted in the capture of an American general, the commander in charge at the time. Order was restored and things were pretty quiet when we got there. Nevertheless, our mission was to make sure that what had happened would not happen again. We were determined there would be no disturbances under our watch.

Off-duty sometimes presented its own problems. Soldiers like to drink, raise hell, and generally let off steam. We had gotten reports that the entertainment shacks in town were run by "slickie boys," rip-off artists, who could get into anything, steal anything, and sell anything to make a buck. One of the things they were doing was taking bottles of alcohol, emptying their contents, and filling them with wood alcohol and selling them to soldiers! There had been some deaths attributed to this in other units. You just can't ever let your guard down, even in quiet sectors.

Major General Gaither assumed command of the 40th Division at the time Colonel McAleer had put me in for promotion to major. Mike Chester had recently been promoted and tipped me off that he had seen my paperwork sitting in the adjutant's in-box, and that no action had been taken to get it to division. The next day was the cut-off! Not knowing when the next window of opportunity would appear, I lost no time in getting my paperwork squared away and got one of the piper cub pilots to fly me up to division headquarters where I got in under the wire. As things turned out, truce negotiations had started in earnest, so that put a stop to promotions for the time being.

All in all, it was a good tour. I had served as a company commander, regimental S-2 and S-3, received my majority, then finished my time in country as the regimental executive officer.

On December 8, 1953, I received orders assigning me to the 11th Airborne Division at Fort Campbell, Kentucky. After a ship ride home of almost two weeks, I arrived in San Francisco then headed east for thirty days leave to be with my family again. What a wonderful homecoming that was, and how the kids, Diane, my oldest, and the boys, Ivan and Stan, had grown. Our newest member, baby Edward was getting bigger, too. Yvonne was as beautiful as ever.

PART XIII

THE AIRBORNE SOLDIER'S CREED

I AM AN AMERICAN SOLDIER. I AM A TROOPER IN THE 11TH AIRBORNE DIVISION OF THE UNITED STATES ARMY—PROTECTOR OF THE GREATEST NATION ON EARTH. AS A SOLDIER, I UPHOLD THE PRINCIPLES OF FREEDOM FOR WHICH MY COUNTRY STANDS. AS A TROOPER, I AM A SUPERIOR SOLDIER IN PHYSICAL FITNESS, COMBAT READINESS, MILITARY BEARING, COURTESY, CHARACTER, AND SELF DISICIPLINE. MY ACTIONS ALWAYS REFLECT MY PRIDE IN MY COUNTRY, MY FLAG AND MY UNIFORM. I TRUST IN MY GOD AND IN THE UNITED STATES OF AMERICA. I AM AN AMERICAN SOLDIER.

502d Airborne
Battle Group in Defense

— Deployment of the Recon Platoon —
(Maj) E. S. Mehosky

Enemy

Recon Platoon —
split — makes contact
with the enemy

Withdraws away
from Battle Group

Takes up firing position
on Battle Group's flank

Enemy Advance

Enemy Advance

Enemy Advance

Battle Group

A
B
C
D
E

CHAPTER 44

ANGELS AND FALCONS

Thirty days of home leave never seems long enough after an overseas tour. My family and I arrived at Fort Campbell, Kentucky, home of the 11th Airborne Division in February, 1954. I was assigned to the 511th Airborne Infantry Regiment as the regimental intelligence officer, the S-2. Colonel Patrick F. Cassidy, who served with the 101st in World War II, commanded the regiment. Major General Wayne C. Smith commanded the 11th Airborne that included two other famous regiments, the 503rd, "The Rock," and the 188th 'Winged Attack.'

The 11th Airborne Division traces its origin back to WW II, at Camp Mackall, North Carolina when it was activated on February 25, 1943 under the command of Major General Joseph M. Swing. The division distinguished itself in combat against Japanese forces on the Philippine Islands. It has been said that the most successful airborne operation in history was conducted by Colonel Orin D. Haugen's 511th Infantry Regiment when they dropped on the island of Luzon in February, 1945, to seize the Los Banos internment camp which held Allied prisoners of war. When Company B, 1st Battalion came smashing through the gates of the prison camp, they were surrounded by hundreds of jubilant inmates who said they were like angels sent from heaven. It was from this account that the 11th Airborne Division received its nickname, "The Angels."

In all my soldiering with the 11th Airborne, and even today at my age, I still get a great deal of comfort from the link between the two prominent symbols of the unit I proudly served: "The Angels" and "The Falcons." The words emblazoned beneath the 511th Regiment's crest, "Strength From Above" still stirs within.

Being airborne, you maintained your jump proficiency by making at least one parachute jump a month, sometimes more. Someone was always jumping, so there was never any problem getting a jump because you could always tag on with another unit. I can't recall ever having anything other than good jumps while at Fort Campbell.

Some of my duties required my serving as airborne control officer or landing zone officer on occasion. Close coordination was required with air force personnel from a nearby base to ensure load times and take-off times were consistently met. In those days we jumped from the C-114s, known as the "flying box-cars." This was a much better aircraft because it carried more paratroopers, had two exit jump doors, and did not have the turbulence of the older aircraft because the exit doors were at the rear of the plane.

1954 brought a big field test for the regiment known as "Exercise Follow Me." We convoyed down to Fort Rucker, Alabama and were designated to be the aggressor force against the 3rd Infantry Division. There we dressed in olive green uniforms complete with insignia and distinct helmet. We organized into a combat team assuming the role of a larger attacking force. By a series of bold, surprise attacks, we gained the initiative and put dents in the enemy's line. My intelligence section was able to get the big picture as we identified their operation plan and key installations mostly through patrol listening posts. Colonel Cassidy was extremely pleased with his intelligence section and said as much.

Following on the heels of "Follow Me" came the annual Third Army Command Inspection not long after we returned to post. Here was a situation that afforded an opportunity to excel when everything was on the line. That was when I seemed to be at my best. What we did was roll up our sleeves and put in some long hours, leaving nothing to chance. All was ready and when that day came, we sparkled. And the result? We received a superior rating in organization and operation of Regimental Intelligence, S-2! It was the highest rating of any of the major units in the division. General Smith and Colonel Cassidy both sent letters of commendation, and as Colonel Cassidy noted in his letter to all members of the regiment: "You were commended by the Third Army Commander and the Commanding General of the 11th Airborne Division for the outstanding job you accomplished as the aggressor force during exercise 'Follow Me.' Immediately upon return from that maneuver you passed the Third Army command inspection with flying colors indicating that you were always striving to make the best just a little better."

CHAPTER 45

OPERATION GYROSCOPE

Colonel Cassidy went to division to become chief of staff. One of the first things he did was bring me to serve as his G-2, intelligence officer. He liked the work I did and had a lot of confidence in me, and the only thing he told me was that I would have to shave my mustache. I was holding down a lieutenant colonel's slot.

Since March, 1955, when it was announced that the 11th Airborne Division would be going to Germany to replace the 5th Infantry Division at Augsburg as part of "Operation Gyroscope," the place took on an urgency scarcely seen before. The main reason for so much concern was the army training test that every battalion would undergo upon setting foot in Germany. Word had it that the 7th Army commander was ruthless in the standards he expected every unit to measure up to. You either passed the test at Hoenfels or suffered the consequences. When the 11th Airborne arrived in Germany and underwent the tests, seven out of the nine battalion commanders were relieved on the spot.

I was part of the advance party that left New York on November 16, 1955. We arrived with families at Frankfurt International Airport and bused down to Augsburg in one of the worst snowstorms to hit Germany in one hundred years. We got quarters in Spickel, a suburb of Augsburg at 48 Werndt Strasse, a three-story stucco that belonged to a field marshal during the war. There were two other families that lived down the street: Major Jones and Major Humphrey.

Major General Hugh P. Harris commanded the 11th Airborne. I had the opportunity to be a part of his staff when Colonel Cassidy selected me as the assistant chief of staff. By the summer, Colonel Cassidy had gone to 7th Army Headquarters in Frankfurt, and Colonel Sammie Homan replaced him.

In December, 1955, I was succeeded as the G-2 by Lieutenant Colonel Cameron Knox. I remained at headquarters during the transition, then was assigned to Oberammergau to attend the intelligence and military police school. In 1957, the army went from the triangular division to the "pentomic," creating three battle groups of five companies each in a division. It was still considered experimental since to date there was no tested doctrine as to how to deploy a battle group.

THE 502ND AIRBORNE BATTLE GROUP

The 503rd was the first to reorganize into a battle group and was designated the 1st Airborne Battle Group. From the 503rd would come a nucleus of officers and men whom I would join and, along with the 502nd Infantry Regiment, would form the 2nd Airborne Battle Group. I was assigned to the 502nd as the battle group intelligence officer in March, 1957, at Warner Kaserne in Munich. Colonel Walley Haynes was the commander. Lieutenant Colonels John McKnight and James Griffin were his deputies.

During peacetime, many would argue, the role of the S-2 Intelligence Officer is not as great as in wartime or during an exercise. It had been my experience that some of the commanders I served under were uncertain of how to use their S-2, nor understood its role, preferring instead to rely on information from their S-3 or S-4. What usually happened then was an accumulation of extra duty that ate up most of your time, things like courts martial duty, inspecting mess halls at 0500, serving on investigation boards, and inspector general duties. Now if for some unknown reason the commander didn't take a liking to you, those extra duties I mentioned increased. There was never a time in my whole career when I served on so many courts martial boards or inspected so many mess halls. There is, however always a silver lining in the worst coat one has to wear at the time.

It happened like this. Over the next fifty-two days, April-May time frame, I went to the Hoenfels Training Area with a team of fifty-six officers and two rifle companies to serve on the VII Corps Infantry Battalion Control Group during battalion tests. I was designated staff umpire in charge of the attack team. Lieutenant Colonel McKnight was in charge of the delay and withdrawal team. It was during this time that I got to know McKnight. We talked about the war and the 101st, and he told me that during the Normandy drop he was captured by the Germans and treated pretty rough.

After we returned from Hoenfels, I detected a change in the commander, a change that was not favorable. It seems that one of his executive officers had been making derogatory remarks aimed at me. Now I knew why I was getting more than my fair share of the "crap" assignments.

Does the outsider tag play a role in situations like that? Unfortunately, yes it did. And it all depended on who was in command. I was from the division staff, and prior to that, the 511th, rivals of the 503rd, so naturally there may have been a tendency to consider me or any other officer from another unit, an outsider. But to carry it to harmful extremes? Therein lay the problem. I never gave much thought to things like that, or got involved in sides. Because of the opinion he had formed, Colonel Haynes was at one point trying to relieve me. But when General Harris got wind of it, he told Haynes point blank in no uncertain terms, as I was later told by someone close to the general, "Colonel, if you relieve Mehosky, I'll relieve you!"

The plans formulated by the Department of the Army to activate a pentomic division, based on the battle group concept, generated a multitude of questions at all levels concerning tactical deployments. One of the first Department of the Army questionnaires to come down concerned how do you deploy a battle group reconnaissance platoon? This action was assigned to the 502nd commander for response, which he assigned to me. My first reaction to reading the document was overwhelming. Nevertheless, after three hard days and nights, I completed the task within the assigned deadline and turned it over to Colonel Haynes. "You did all this by yourself? Damn good job, Ed! Looks good." The colonel seemed very impressed and very pleased with the results, not hesitating to forward it to higher headquarters. The report was submitted through army channels and was well received at all echelons. In my view, this was the first written response from the field concerning tactical deployment of a unit under the new battle group concept. It was from this point, I believe, that things began to change for the better.

A week later the 502nd reported to Hoenfels to undergo a specifically designed test to find out how to deploy a battle group. In a test like that, the umpires checked each level from staff down to company to see how each communicated and if procedures were being followed. Each phase of the test was followed up by a detailed critique from the chief umpire to the battle group commander and his staff, and believe me, nothing was missed. When it came time for the critique on the S-2 intelligence play of the battle group, the chief umpire gave us a superior rating. Then he announced to Colonel Haynes, "Your intelligence, lead by Major Mehosky, was the best intelligence of any group that has ever taken an Army Training Test here." Old Colonel Haynes came out of there with flying colors because of that, and he finally acknowledged my performance and value to the unit. Here's how it happened:

Nothing had really changed when we got to the field. Colonel Haynes was still pretty much freezing me out. He still did not understand nor know how to use an intelligence officer such as myself, and consequently, had no use for S-2 intelligence, preferring instead to rely on other sections of his staff. After we established our command post at the start of the test, calls began coming in from the companies on line to inform command of enemy movement on their front. When I called to that unit for more clarification, they told me they had already given that information to the S-3. I checked with the S-3 and he said, "Yes, I already passed on that information to the commander." Sure enough, it was up there on the board at the command post right where they thought the enemy was according to the information received. The trouble was, the commander was receiving erroneous information and the umpires were noting the errors, writing as fast as their hands could move, and I was getting madder by the minute!

When the next call came, I heard the S-3 repeat, "Two enemy tanks in your front, right. I'll pass it on."

I grabbed the phone away from the major and said, "That's it! Give me that damn phone! That's information for me, Major! That's my job!" There was no mistaking my look as the major sat there, stunned. "This is Major Mehosky. Now, give me the exact coordinates of those tanks," I insisted. "O.K., I've got your location, now what direction are you facing? Give me your compass reading. From now on, I want you to report your information by coordinates and azimuth, is that clear?"

I then plotted the location of the enemy tanks and brought the commander up to date. A disaster was averted. When Colonel Haynes assembled his company commanders, he told them they were to communicate directly with the S-2, Major Mehosky, and without exception, coordinates and azimuth were to be called in. Anyway, the whole series of events was exactly the correct interplay between the staff S-2 and company commanders the umpires were looking for. After that, things went pretty smoothly, and I now had an advocate in Colonel Haynes. I firmly believe at each stage of life, everybody needs an advocate, regardless of vocation.

CHAPTER 46

'SABRE HAWK' AND 'SALAMANDER'

"If you know the terrain and can interpret it as to how an enemy might use it, then you can use it to your advantage and play the terrain game, a key element of intelligence work," I was always telling younger officers.

During the summer of 1957, the 502nd received a simultaneous mission: three rifle companies were directed to the Hoenfels Training Area to perform a tactical demonstration for General Maxwell Taylor and visiting members of Congress. The other two companies of the battle group were to participate in field training exercise "Sabre Hawk" against the 10th Special Forces at Bad Tolz. Colonel Haynes and Lieutenant Colonel McKnight would take the three companies north while Lieutenant Colonel Griffin and myself would head south with the other two companies.

Attached to us for this mission was an intelligence and reconnaissance platoon, a helicopter unit, and authorization to use agents from a counter-intelligence detachment, which happened to be located right outside Warner Kaserne.

We'd be going against the 10th Special Forces, one of the army's elite units. Organized into three battalion-size teams, one was located in Berlin, the other two in Bad Tolz. Their training was conducted in accordance with their wartime mission: to infiltrate an area and organize a resistance movement against any aggressor force in the region.

The area of operations for this exercise covered 3,000 square miles, running 115 miles east to west, and 65 miles north to south, taking in a good portion of the land lying below Munich to the foothills of the German Alps.

An agent-in-charge (AIC) was assigned to me during the initial planning stage in July. An officer or an enlisted soldier I couldn't tell, because these guys always wore civilian clothes and kept their identity secret. They liked it that way. He would be in charge of the other agents who would join us later to head the infiltration teams. We started our planning with a close look at the area of operations. Using the best topographical maps and aerial photographs, we divided the area of operations into three distinct areas: Area I, Area II, and Area III, according to natural boundaries. When a team was inserted, they would operate in their assigned area only. That was the first rule. It was forbidden to cross over into another's area.

For our operations headquarters, we selected a wooded area on a ridge near a mountain stream to the east of the three designated areas. Nearby was a clearing which looked adequate for helicopter use. The only way in or out was an old single lane logging road. Since each area would have to have an undercover team assigned, we decided the best way to do this was to pick five soldiers from each company, soldiers who had the special qualifications. We were looking for soldiers able to speak German, and experienced in jobs such as a waiter, bartender, or gas station attendant. And they would have to be able to operate various kinds of vehicles like a tractor, truck, and motorcycle. Most important of all, these soldiers would have to have the right attitude. They would be hand-picked by me and the AIC. Twenty-five soldiers were then picked from the five battle group companies. To complete this phase, three more agents were brought on board. Each would head up an eight-man infiltration team from the twenty-five soldiers who had been selected. We divided the talent as evenly as possible.

At this point each team disassociated from the other and, working independently with the AIC, began developing cover stories for the role each team member would play, and secondly, began devising a method of introducing them into their area. Everything had to be rehearsed until it was perfect and I was satisfied. Every single detail, from the clothes each team member would wear to personal documents each would carry had to be exact, nothing that could be traced. The special forces people were so well established that you didn't know if the local bartender or hotel clerk was a German or American. The cover stories were picked apart so much that we finally arrived with plausible stories that would hold up if they were picked up for any reason, a story that would give a logical reason for being in the area, and thus alleviate any suspicion. This phase of preparation was so guarded, so secretive, that even I had only a general idea of what they were doing. Each team leader was responsible for establishing a method as to how his team would communicate. Communication with my headquarters would be only two ways: either by using a civilian pay telephone or by personal visit. When I was fully satisfied the teams were ready, I gave the okay to deploy ten days before the exercise was to start. No one at any level outside our group knew this until the exercise was over. That's how tight our security was and would remain throughout.

CAPTURING AN 'A' TEAM

Word had it that no unit had ever been successful against the special forces. These phantoms had an attitude of operating with impunity. The army wanted a tougher opponent that could perhaps do something against these Green Berets, test them, make them sweat, so that's basically how we got the job. We were recognized as a pretty tough airborne unit and so considered a worthy opponent. This was good stuff and I was fired up for the challenge. I was in my element.

Colonel Griffin approached me after we had set up our tent headquarters at our designated location. "Ed, I'm going over to Bad Tolz to spend time with the commander there, an old friend. You're in charge; it's your show. I'll stop in from time to time to see how things are going." After that Colonel Griffin was in maybe twice for briefings. I got word that the two of them disguised themselves as monks and went undercover from village to village, and were having a heck of a time.

The focal point of our operations center was a huge map, scale 1:50,000. Here we plotted every piece of information that came in from our teams and our patrols. Areas were marked as to where we believed the special forces teams could most likely operate, especially areas away from the population where they could be headquartered and conduct meetings without detection. It was the high ground on which we zeroed in. I conducted situation briefings for visitors from division and corps. They were always surprised when told of the undercover agents and teams I had in these areas, and even more astonished that these infiltration teams were composed of ordinary soldiers from the 502nd who had undergone intensive training for this role.

One of the fundamentals focused upon by all in my group was this: when somebody comes in who's not living there, in the area we were operating in, someone who is an outsider and wants to organize something, he has to do something for the people to see without banding together and thus coming under the eyes of the aggressor forces occupying the country. He has to be smart. We were the aggressor force at this time in that part of the country, and we were trying to detect the special forces and root them out. The special forces, the resistance army, had hand bills everywhere-on buildings, telephone poles, and fence posts-as a way of letting the people know a resistance movement was being organized. Whenever we saw those things, we started plotting them on our situation map as to location and any name that might identify the code name of the group. Let's say our patrols found the name "Wolf" on posters, and this name kept popping up in and around the villages in one of our areas. Without hesitation, this information would be called in to headquarters and plotted. We reasoned that this area belonged exclusively to team "Wolf." Soon a pattern began to emerge indicating there were three special forces teams operating there, each with a code name, and each in a distinct operating area: Wolf was showing up more in Area I, whereas team "Fox" held Area II. That left Area III open, for up to that point, no key information had been received from that area.

We figured these resistance teams had to get the people together to train them, pass along instructions, and execute. Everything they did had to be secretive so as not to attract attention. Therefore, meetings would most likely be in areas away from the towns. Since we were operating in Bavaria at the foot of the mountains, we looked for activity on the high ground. We knew the villagers would not be the ones moving around at night because of the tight control we applied in restricting their movement. Patrols were sent out every night to wait, watch, and listen, in areas that might afford good meeting places, like back roads, woods, the high ground.

During the first twenty-four hours of the exercise, one of my infiltration teams captured the entire "A" team from Berlin right at their point of insertion! One complete special forces team was captured and put out of the exercise. These prisoners were brought bound and gagged to my headquarters where they were roughly interrogated, knocked around a little and put into a cold, mountain stream. They would be treated as if captured by a real enemy before we released them. They never expected that! One of the captured prisoners was the brother to the sergeant I had there with me, who served in my company at Fort Benning. "Damn it to hell," he cursed, "I should have known you were here! We heard you were going to be in this exercise, and I even told them you had better watch out for Major Mehosky! Now they'll find out for themselves!"

They were all pretty good sports about the treatment they were receiving, although they called us every name in the book and vowed to get even someday. The following day they were picked up and returned to Bad Tolz with their egos bruised more than anything else. The information we got from these prisoners was invaluable in that we were able to construct their organization right down to their equipment. Now they knew they were dealing with people who thought and operated like them. They also knew they could not take the exercise lightly.

SALAMANDER

Now came another crowning blow. We had been getting reports of aircraft at night at different locations in the mountains. This meant that someone was being resupplied. One evening we got word from one of the agents that one of his team members was in a bar when he observed the bartender, who he believed to be an American, talking with another fellow who just arrived. The word "salamander" was overheard and promptly reported. It was put out to all patrols, "What is salamander?" Two nights later, at a roadblock south of Chiemsee, one of my patrols stopped what appeared to be a German walking a back road at two in the morning. He spoke German, had the proper credentials, and everything appeared to be in order. Upon further inspection, though, there appeared on one of his identification cards the word, "Salamander." Another odd thing noticed was a bright, yellow stain on his jacket. He was taken prisoner and brought to headquarters where he was interrogated. It turned out that he, "Salamander," was a key operative for one of the special forces teams, and that he had been using flares for a resupply drop, hence the stain on his jacket.

The next day, I got a call from Lieutenant Colonel Griffin: "Ed, what the hell is going on? You've got the whole damn special forces down here in an uproar!"

Every patrol I sent out set up listening posts. Helicopters were sent out at different times, covering different routes and approaches, focusing primarily on the high ground. Since we knew that anyone on a ridge, for example, would freeze on the approach of a helicopter, we tried to catch them off-guard. We'd fly over to the next ridge to give the impression to whomever might be down there, that we were looking in a different area away from them, but in fact we were looking back and scanning that area with our binoculars. Every single piece of information on every sweep was reported to headquarters and plotted.

"Bulldog Green to Leader, over."

"Leader to Bulldog Green. I read you, over."

"A glint of light spotted on Ridge A10 at the following coordinates…"

And on another sweep, "Bulldog Red to Leader. A party of what looks like five hikers moving west on Ridge A10, coordinates…"

"Leader to Bulldog Red, I copy. Is there any area down there for possible resupply? Over."

"Affirmative, Leader. Two clearings adjacent to each other. Looks like they can handle choppers, maybe light aircraft, over."

Ground patrols, too, had reported aircraft activity in vicinity of Ridge A10. After two weeks, the situation map was showing a strong likelihood of an enemy base camp somewhere on Ridge A10. All the pieces were fitting together. It was time to put the plan into motion, an operation based on surprise and speed utilizing all the resources at my disposal.

We hit them at dawn. One company positioned themselves at key points at the base of the ridge, setting up roadblocks. The other company landed by helicopter at the top of the ridge, fanned out, and began a steady sweep down the ridge, flushing out anything that was alive. Soon there was a great commotion of men being rooted out of their camps, abandoning all equipment, and running furiously in all directions down the hill to escape the approaching soldiers! They were stunned and they bolted!

Down they ran until the last man was captured at the roadblocks at the base of the ridge. We chased a couple of special forces teams off their mountain stronghold, capturing in all about forty of them. These guys got the same treatment as the last bunch, maybe even a little rougher because of their arrogant attitude and their unending mouthing off, not to mention cursing I hadn't heard in years. "You wait," they kept saying, "we'll get even one day!"

I wasn't impressed. "Isolate that big mouth!" I yelled. They were tied and marched to my headquarters where the interrogation began in earnest. The bad attitudes got the worst of it as they were stripped naked, dunked in the freezing mountain stream, and roughed up a little bit. My sergeant and AIC let these guys have the full treatment, no kid gloves or anything like that, but not really hurting anyone either. They broke these guys down to where each guy talked and divulged such critical information that we were able to map out their entire organization and plan of operation to the smallest detail.

Thus ended the three-week exercise against the highly touted special forces. To my knowledge, we were the only unit to ever do anything of this magnitude against these guys, before or since.

It was at this time that serious negotiation was under way between Bad Tolz and the 502nd for me to take over command of their C Team. Back at Warner Kaserne in Munich, as I was preparing the briefing of the results of our operation for the G-3, 7th Army, Heidelberg, Colonel Griffin confided to me, "Ed, I have never seen a commander chew ass like my old friend at Bad Tolz! It got so hot that I had to leave. You sure stirred up a hornet's nest!"

I was excited about the possibility of taking over a special forces team. But, alas, my hopes were dashed when I got orders to report to the Command and General Staff College at Fort Leavenworth, Kansas. I needed this to advance in my career, but I didn't count on it arriving this early.

ACKNOWLEDGEMENT

Just prior to leaving the 502nd my men and I were honored when Coloniel Haynes applauded the success of the operation against the Special Forces, and went on to say, ...

"His special interest in the training of the reconnaissance platoon was evidenced by the enviable record achieved by the platoon. During an anti-guerrilla exercise with the 10th Special Forces near Bad Tolz in August 1957, he planned, organized and supervised the intelligence and security activities of the battle group in a professional manner that won him the unqualified respect of all who witnessed the exercise. The battle group and Major Mehosky received letters of commendation citing the imposing record that was attained in the capture of special forces personnel. The intelligence activities of the battle group, to include reporting, staying behind patrols and long range patrols, were particularly outstanding during FTX "Sabre Hawk" and elicited praise from division, corps, and army headquarters!"

PART XIV

*21ST INFANTRY DIVISION, REPUBLIC OF VIETNAM ARMED
FORCES RESPECTFULLY OFFERS LIEUTENANT COLONEL
EDWARD S. MEHOSKY A TOKEN OF OUR APPRECIATION*

CHAPTER 47

ADVISORY DUTY IN VIETNAM

Arriving home in the summer of '58, we spent the next year at Fort Leavenworth, Kansas, where I attended the Army's Command and General Staff College, graduating on June 19, 1959. Students and families were quartered in a large, old, three-story building that looked like a former barracks, known as the "Beehive." Mom and Dad came out for a visit that spring. It was their very first time traveling by airplane, and indeed the first time in their lives they had been that far west. Dad was up early every morning walking Prince, our German Shepherd, around the grounds of the old fort.

One of the things that always stayed with me from the Command and General Staff College, something that served me very well at the Pentagon and later assignments, was a short piece called, "Completed Staff Work." It went something like this:

"A study of a problem and presentation of its solution in such a form that only approval or disapproval of the completed action is necessary. To do this, you must work out the details completely, consult other staff officers, study, write, restudy, and rewrite. Next, you advise the chief what to do; you don't ask him. You present a single coordinated proposal action—do not equivocate! Do not present a long explanation or memoranda; correct solutions are usually recognizable. If you were the chief, would you sign the paper you have prepared and thus stake your professional reputation on being right? If not, take it back and work it over; it is not yet completed staff work!"

Upon graduation, I was assigned to Washington, D.C. at the Pentagon to ACSI, Assistant Chief of Staff, Intelligence, Counter-Intelligence Branch. In 1961, I was promoted to lieutenant colonel. It was during this time that I wrote and submitted two papers based on my experiences against special forces units in Germany.

That year I was sent on a special assignment to Greece to observe a special forces unit there and to look at their organization and anti-guerilla operations. I stopped in at Bad Tolz where an exercise was being conducted. This time they had an entire battalion going against the special forces just as we had done with two companies three years before. It was obvious these guys were just going through the motions—floundering around out there accomplishing nothing. At one of the briefings, one of the umpires told me that it was hopeless, that these guys couldn't do anything against these elite, elusive special forces.

From Athens I visited one of the camps at Mt. Olympus, the other on the coast. They were not happy to see me as they made it clear that they did not like anyone from the Pentagon spying on their operation. They were cool and distant toward me and made no effort to assist in any way during my visit. They looked at me as a visiting fireman. After my five days were up, I was never more eager to leave a place. I got orders for Vietnam in March, 1963.

HEADQUARTERS
MILITARY ASSISTANCE ADVISORY GROUP, VIETNAM
Saigon, Vietnam

MAGAR-AG   19 Mar 63

Dear Colonel Mehosky,

Let me be one of the first to congratulate you on your selection for assignment to MAAG Vietnam and to extend to you a most hearty expression of welcome. We're delighted to have you. Our congratulations are apropos since the Department of the Army has assured us that all personnel being assigned to MAAG Vietnam will be of the highest professional caliber available.

The role of MAAG Vietnam of assisting this country to stem the tide of communism in Southeast Asia is becoming increasingly important. Our advisors are working shoulder to shoulder with their counterparts in the field, at the planning table, or in the supporting elements in order to insure that the best possible advice and assistance can be rendered as soon as it is required. Both the Vietnamese Armed Forces and our own personnel are receiving invaluable experience in waging a counter-insurgency campaign. Our advisory mission is succeeding and every day we can see indications that the struggle for control of the country is progressing in favor of the government. The communist Viet Cong forces are being forced into a defensive role. Their elimination is only a matter of time and, of course, a lot of continued hard work. Your presence and loyal support will assist us in furthering the progress already achieved. Upon completion of your tour, we believe you will look back upon it, as the great majority of others have in the past, as a most rewarding and valuable experience.

At the present time, it is not practical to specify your exact assignment. Due to changing personnel requirements, we can only promise that your training and experience will be given due consideration at the time of your arrival. Naturally, the needs of the service must come first, but we will do whatever we can to enhance you and your career. I am sure that any job you receive will prove beneficial in almost any of your future assignments.

I am enclosing an information guide which will give you some of the pertinent details concerning Vietnam, its people, your personal needs and other matters relating to your assignment here. While this information does not present the complete picture in regard to our activities in Vietnam, it will serve to assist you in preparing for your journey to this area.

If there is any further information you desire, please do not hesitate to let us know. In the interim, best wishes, and have a good trip. We will look forward to your arrival and I hope to be on hand to greet you personally.

Sincerely,
Charles J. Timmes, Maj. Gen., USA, Chief

In preparation for my assignment there, I was sent to the U.S. Army Special Warfare School, Military Assistance Training Advisor Course at Fort Bragg, North Carolina. It was a lot of information to digest in such a short period. We learned about the Vietnamese people and their country, and the role we'd play as military advisors to their armed forces in combatting communism in that part of the world. I got a good idea of what to expect in this far away country that hadn't yet caught the attention of the American people. That would come later.

"Good morning, gentlemen. This briefing will cover intelligence and operations.

The people of Vietnam are locked in deadly conflict against an aggressor whose weapons are terror, subversion, and persuasion. This is the only country in the world today which is openly fighting communism.

The entire country is a physical battlefield in which the Vietnamese fight. As in any combat environment, the terrain affects many aspects of the military operations against the guerrilla and insurgency. The nature of this terrain restricts communication, limits maneuvers, and requires dispersion of military forces to protect critical features that are remote from each other.

The enemy in this environment is the communist guerrilla. Although he is known as the Viet Cong in the Republic of Vietnam, he is the same communist terrorist with whom the free world has fought for many years. He adheres to the principles subscribed to by Mao Tse Tung and reiterated by the Vietnamese communist leader Ho Chi Minh. The primary targets of the Viet Cong are the Diem government, the civil populace, and U.S. government assistance and aid programs. When he cannot subvert or corrupt, he terrorizes—when he enjoys successes, he multiplies like a tropical fungus, feasting on dissatisfaction where it exists or where he can create it. He selects his own battlefield, attacks when he is assured of success, avoids a stronger force, delivers a lightning blow, and fades away into the jungle or swamps. This, then, is the enemy which the Vietnamese fight—a formidable enemy, but certainly not unbeatable or not without its inherent weaknesses. Every military success against the enemy strengthens the government in the eyes of the people and the final victory will only come through the people's loyalty to, and confidence in, the present government.

That concludes my briefing. Are there any questions?"

———————————

Ft. Bragg, July 1, 1963.

Dear Yvonne and kids,

They certainly are throwing a lot at us in final preparation of our twelve month tour of duty in Vietnam. Every briefing has a homework assignment. It looks like I'll be assigned to the IV Corps area, the delta area called the Ca Mau

Peninsula, the extreme southern part of the country, but I won't know for sure until I arrive. I'm learning some Vietnamese words and a heck of a lot about the climate there, which I'll tell you about later. I'm looking forward to the three weeks with you and the kids before I fly out. I'll be counting the days.

Love always,

Ed

There were approximately 1,100 U.S. military personnel in Vietnam in August, 1963 when I arrived. My initial introduction to the country was Saigon, the capital of South Vietnam and an old, colonial French city. One of the first things I did after processing in and getting quarters was to try the exotic food about which I had heard so much. A group of us went to this floating restaurant on the river, a place reputed to be one of the best in town. There on the dock we encountered a young beggar who was so badly deformed that he crawled around like a spider, going from one person to the next, begging for money. That evening during orientation, I felt sick as a dog, and between frequent toilet visits, managed to check into the emergency room. There they confirmed I had a bad case of amoebic dysentery and gave me pills to knock it out.

From Saigon, I was flown by helicopter south to IV Corps Headquarters at Can Tho, on the Bassac River, a large village and capital of the province. There were 200 advisors in IV Corps to cover the entire Ca Mau Peninsula. My job was senior military advisor to the civilian defense troops on the peninsula. My boss was Colonel Samie Homan, whom I worked for previously with the 11th Airborne. During the next couple of weeks I toured the entire IV Corps area, the low, flat area encompassing all the land south of Saigon known as the Ca Mau Peninsula. I saw a land devoted to rice production; a land of thousands of miles of waterways and few bridges; a land where most of the transportation was by boat, and where most of the population lived in villages along the rivers and canals. Their villages were built on stilts because of the severe flooding during the wet season. The middle of a wet season was usually accompanied by such severe flooding that the entire landscape looked like a vast sea of water. It was during such flooding there occurred an outbreak of typhoid fever because of human waste getting into the drinking water supply.

There were very few roads there. The roads that existed, especially further south, are so flat and straight that anyone could spot something coming for miles. Since there were no bridges, trucks and jeeps had to be ferried across and were always subject to ambush. Attacks on convoys were frequent, and that was another reason we got around by helicopter.

The dry season, when it was the hottest, was November through April. During this time the water receded, the fields became parched, and the Viet Cong became more active. I went to the tip of the peninsula, about 150 miles south of Can Tho, where there was a civil guard camp run by a Catholic priest. They were getting hit every week, so I thought I would see what I could do. I went on a couple of patrols, but the enemy always seemed to be ahead of us. I gave suggestions for security and fortifying their camp and after two days, left. One of the reasons the place was always under attack was because the Viet Cong did not like the influence this priest was having on the local population. The entire place looked like scrub brush, having been defoliated by chemicals.

My old boss, Colonel Dillinder, was at the Pentagon at this time. He was the liaison officer to Congress, served as a trouble-shooter for inquires and complaints, and provided escort functions for Congressional fact-finding visits. I met with him on one such visit at Can Tho. They flew back to Saigon after a half-day visit. It was good to see him again after nine years.

At the civil guard villages I visited, manpower strength was at most a company of guards, more often a squad. Each province had a civil guard force that operated under the province chief. The problem, though, was that these soldiers were always getting ambushed. That was probably the biggest problem I encountered, and the most frustrating! It was like pulling teeth trying to get them to alter their patterns instead of being so predictable. When they received word of a Viet Cong attack in their vicinity, the civil guard would come down the same road every time, not deviating in anything, and every time they got attacked, they suffered greatly. As hard as I tried, they wouldn't change their ways. You could predict an ambush, and it was the same way with the Vietnamese Army. Their truck convoys traveling the main roads got ambushed time and time again. The enemy had these roads zeroed in and knew the best places for ambush. The "good guys" never reconnoitered the roads; the "bad guys" set the trap. What the enemy did was disable the first and last vehicle on the road so as to block the convoy in, then with small arms fire catch everything in the middle in a crossfire. They were small, quick, hard-hitting groups, and after a short duration, they disappeared into the surrounding country. That's how the Viet Cong operated.

There was so much corruption in the country that the good equipment wasn't getting down to the civil guard level, instead being diverted for profit somewhere. The province chiefs I met were military personnel of various ranks who had the power and control of their provinces. Their constant complaint to me was they were not getting enough new equipment. We had advisory teams in each province consisting of a lieutenant in charge, a sergeant, a radio operator, and a driver. It was their job to advise the province chief on any military action to be conducted and to keep in daily contact with headquarters.

Can Tho, during my six months there, never came under attack, but the nearest attack to us was a special forces detachment up the road that was hit a couple of times.

Can Tho had two good eating places. One was a Chinese restaurant and the other a corner noodle shop. You could get a bowl of noodles, fried crab claws, crab mushroom soup, which was out of this world, and beer with ice. It was wonderful stuff. They had a special sauce made from dried, decayed fish drippings which was quite tasty. We always carried side arms wherever we went. I never sat with my back to the door or near a window, but made damn sure I could see all entrances. There was no pattern to my activities and I wasn't predictable.

From Can Tho, I was assigned to the 21st Vietnamese Division as part of the division advisory team at Bac Lieu, a village on the coast of the South China Sea. The commander there, Colonel Cushman (later general), had asked for me. The pace at Bac Lieu was faster than at Can Tho. This was another large village, but one secured by Vietnamese troops. There were contingency plans on hand as to how the town would be defended if attacked. Outside our compound was a security detachment. I would serve as the assistant division advisor at Bac Lieu until my tour expired seven months later. I was in charge of running the compound. I supervised day to day operations, which included the mess hall. I met with a sergeant who was a steward for the general's mess at the Pentagon. He was a "diamond in the rough" in the world of army cooks. We developed an understanding as to what I wanted. He ran my mess hall like a four star restaurant and it soon became the best mess in Vietnam. Word spread far and wide about how good the food and service were and everyone was dropping in whenever they got the chance. It seems everybody wanted to visit Bac Lieu, especially for those tasty, A-1 steaks you could cut with a fork. Never, anywhere, had I had a steak of that quality. The cooks were trained to give the red carpet treatment. My sergeant in charge of the mess hall had great connections in Saigon and was a master at wheeling and dealing. He was, without a doubt, one of the best I ever worked with. He was a master chef and an artist in sauces, seasonings, spices, and tenderizing.

I saw to it that our compound was well supplied and clean. Local village women were assigned to cleaning teams and carefully screened by division and our interpreter before they were allowed to clean our area.

Close coordination with division headquarters occupied a lot of my day. They were located just across the street in a walled estate, now a compound. It was a French Colonial structure in a somewhat state of disrepair, yet gave you a sense of its grandeur of former times.

Near the coast south of us was a swampy area where Viet Cong were located. I was detailed to go there to advise and assist the troops in their action against the VC. Once deployed, it was a sharp, brief affair whereby we eliminated their nest. Nineteen VC were killed in this action and six wounded and taken prisoner. Their communication center was located and destroyed along with a significant amount of weaponry ranging from assault rifles, the AK-47, mortars, grenades, and land mines. How many escaped into the far reaches of the swamp was unknown.

A most memorable occasion was the Sunday morning symposium where we got together for some good food, cold beer, and volleyball. I lost so much weight that my clothes were too big. I was down to my old playing weight.

After a year in Vietnam, I out-processed at Can Tho, flew to Saigon for further out-processing, and flew out of Saigon for home.

CHAPTER 48

BATTALION COMMAND

After completing my tour of duty in Vietnam, the summer of '64, we were off to the U.S. Army Training Center, Armor, at Fort Knox, Kentucky. I was assigned to the 4th Training Brigade where I took command of the 16th Battalion in September. My job was to provide basic combat training to new recruits, who, upon completion of this training, would be sent on to advanced training in preparation for the most trying experience of their lives—duty in Vietnam. I felt a deep responsibility for these men. My goal, therefore, was to instill in the cadre that same spirit of commitment to provide the very best training and supervision possible to prepare these men for Vietnam. It has always been my conviction that basic training is the primary building block for effective tactical training. It is these basic skills, which once instilled, will allow the soldier to adapt more readily and prepare him for combat. It is my belief the officers and NCOs of my battalion provided these soldiers such training. I have always wondered how those we trained had fared. Did they reflect on their basic training? I'd like to think we made a difference and they were better soldiers because of the training they received at Ft. Knox.

We had several cases of spinal meningitis break out in the fall of '64. Implemented to the lowest level were measures such as the "double arm length rule" where no soldier could be any closer to another soldier than double arm's length anywhere, anytime—mess hall, formation, gymnasium. Soldiers were taught to sneeze on the back of their hand instead of the palm. Once a week the barracks were scrubbed with disinfectants, especially damp areas in the toilets and showers. The result of all this was keeping the casualty rate low, so low, in fact, that the best record among the battalions was achieved: no deaths and fewer hospitalizations.

Every time a new batch of recruits reported in, they looked like a rag-tag bunch of soldiers passing my headquarters on the way to their barracks. What I implemented was to send cadre personnel to the in-processing station to primarily conduct some introductory training of these raw recruits. Then when they marched to their barracks they at least knew how to salute, stand at attention, and march to cadence.

After their first formation of the training day, for the first hour they practiced "school of the soldier" which focused on proper stance, posture, military bearing, facing movements, and the manual of arms. It was an area of training that was indispensable in creating the proper military attitude and bearing. The results showed and the brigade commander had the "school of the soldier" concept implemented brigade-wide. I suppose the hardest thing to get them to learn in bayonet practice was to make a proper thrust with the bayonet and butt strokes, doing it with vigor and determination, not the half-hearted motions I encountered. My instructors knew it was a sore spot of mine and knew that if I spotted this I would be after them and correct the problem. I expected them to carry out this training as I would, and with enthusiasm. It is in bayonet practice where reality hits home and the civilian turned soldier realizes he is being trained to kill the enemy.

In June of 1965, during the outbreak of the crisis in the Dominican Republic, it became necessary for the Commander, the Atlantic Command, Norfolk, Virginia, to request augmentation from various branches of the service in order to establish joint command and control capability for an indefinite period. On short notice and with little chance for preparation, I was selected to represent my command in Norfolk. During the month of June, I took over assigned watch standing duties in the war room.

At the end of my assignment in April, 1966, at a farewell presentation, my wife and I were serenaded by the brigade chorus and toasted. It was indeed a heartfelt moment.

My boss, Colonel Carlyle P. Woelfer, Commander, 4th Training Brigade, whom I hold in the highest esteem, paid the 16th Battalion a great complement when he said: "Nowhere have so many men been led and trained by so few as in this brigade where our assigned strength regularly has been between 6000 and 9000 men and battalions have six companies totaling more than 1500 men." Then he went on to say, "One of the strong points of this brigade has been the establishment of many training records based on commanders such as yourself who selflessly worked to improve our training, standards, facilities and duty performance."

Colonel Woelfer concluded by saying, "By your example, you have helped our younger officers, non-commissioned officers, and many thousands of basic trainees become better soldiers. The duties of the battalion commander in a basic training brigade of this size are many and arduous. You have demonstrated that special ability to command large numbers of troops most successfully."

Colonel Woelfer was replaced by Colonel A.D. Guffanti, a down-to-earth commander, pleasant, and like Woefler, approachable. Guffanti, in many ways reminded me of Colonel Sink. It was Colonel Guffanti who recommended me for promotion to full colonel. Yet, according to what the Pentagon told me, I figured my next assignment would be my retirement post.

CHAPTER 49

"THE ROCK", EAGLE, AND "SILK PURSE"

My next assignment was the Alternate National Military Command Center, Joint Chiefs of Staff (JCS), at Fort Ritchie, Maryland. I began my new job as the operations staff officer, Operations Team # 3, on April 8, 1966. I worked under Colonel Bisset and Colonel Vandebogart. Although we lived at Fort Ritchie, a small post tucked away in the Cococtin Mountains above Thurmont, Maryland, we worked in a vast, underground communications center known as "The Rock." I advised the Joint Chiefs on plans and operations of "hot spot" areas around the world.

Then, clear out of the blue, the unexpected happened. I was promoted to full colonel on February 23, 1967! I think I was one of the last to obtain that rank without a college degree. To this day, I believe two people were most influential in my being promoted: Colonel Guffanti, my boss at Fort Knox, and my old boss from the 11th Airborne, the 511th Infantry Regiment, Colonel Patrick Cassidy, who was then a major general.

MILDENHALL AND STUTTGART

We would be going overseas again, this time to Mildenhall, England as a team leader, with the Alternate Airborne Command, known as "Silk Purse," of the United States European Command. Unlike "The Rock" which was underground, this command center was in the sky on board a Boeing 735.

This was one of the best assignments for us so far, because Yvonne's relatives were in England. All in all, it was one of the best tours of my career. How often Yvonne and I thought of one day living in England I can't say, but we loved the place and could have made it our last assignment and retired right there. We were there from early 1968 until early 1970.

The rest of 1970 and half of 1971, I was assigned to the European Command headquarters, at Patch Barracks, Stuttgart, West Germany. My job here was as a team chief in charge of the operations center, another command and control position. I was in constant contact with the commander of the European command. If anything came in that was "hot," I was to call him immediately, and if I was on the late shift, to call him at his quarters regardless of time. Since Berlin was hot at the time, well, I was in constant contact with the general at all hours. The second "hot potato" was the Jordanian Crises of '71.

It was in 1971 that I found out my next tour of duty would be in South Korea as Inspector General for 8th Army. The thought of retirement was also on my mind, but as fate might very well have it, we were soon overcome by events, and the decision to retire was sealed.

My youngest son Edward, living with us and a high school senior, was involved in a terrible automobile accident on the way to the prom. He was horribly injured and his girlfriend killed when they were run off the road and hit a concrete abutment. Edward's situation was critical. Early one morning, while trying to catch some sleep after returning from the hospital, I dreamed a sword was descending from above heading straight for young Edward lying there in his hospital bed, when suddenly a great shield came forth and knocked the sword harmlessly out of the way. I bolted upright and awoke, sweating like mad, and then quickly woke my wife to tell her Edward was out of danger and everything would be all right. Young Edward was holding his own, but would need more extensive care. He was put on a plane to be medically evacuated to Walter Reed Army Hospital in Washington, D.C., my wife and I accompanying him. It was to be one of the longest summers of our lives. The family was at the hospital the day after we arrived. With God's help and the loving support of the family, Edward was able to heal from his terrible injuries and go on to finish a fine career in the Air Force as crew chief for a C-130, and later, with the Department of Defense.

That summer was a time of momentous decision. At a family gathering we discussed the Korea assignment and retirement.

Toward the end of July, I went to the Pentagon to retire from the Army. Interestingly enough, it is not far from Fort Myer and the old Arlington

Cantonement area where I started my military career thirty-one years earlier. I was relieved from assignment and duty and placed on the retired list as of August 1, 1971. August was the same month I enlisted back in 1940.

Thus it came to a close, as does this chapter and narrative, of a humble military career that spanned three decades and three wars by a soldier who did his duty for his country as best he knew how and with no regrets, just the story of a soldier.

Looking across the years, it doesn't seem that long ago, and yet, it has been sixty years since I reported to Arlington as a raw recruit. But they are fleeting thoughts for they are not as clear as they once were. For the longest time I never talked much about the war. Today I think of the present and wonder how the army will fare in future conflicts of the next century which are sure to come. Everything has changed so much from the five armies I knew during my time. My mind is still sharp, and though the pounding my legs and back took from those parachute jumps has been rapidly catching up with me, I still get around pretty well. My overall health is good. I have a lot to be thankful for. And now, it is a new millennium.

Sometimes, early in the morning, before my wife is up and I'm alone at the kitchen table looking out at the new day, I often catch a glimpse of a time and an event, a face from long ago. I pause, and with a deep sigh, I remember how it all began.

Edward Mehosky during a break at OCS, Ft. Benning, GA, 1943.

Edward Mehosky and his son, Ivan, North East, MD, 1999.

POSTSCRIPT

Upon retirement, Yvonne and I settled in Centreville, Virginia. I dabbled in real estate, but that wasn't really for me. An offer to teach military science and run the ROTC program at a school in Ohio never materialized.

All the children are now married, and we are loving and enjoying the grandchildren. As of this writing, we have ten grandchildren and ten great-grandchildren. Over the years we attended some reunions, made numerous trips to Reading, and managed to get back overseas, this time visiting family and relatives in Germany and England. In 1993, we moved south to Solomons Island, Maryland, and then, in 1996, we moved next to my youngest son and his wife in St. Leonard, Maryland where we currently reside. We enjoy visits to Ocean City and Atlantic City from time to time, and have managed to take a number of cruises, our favorites being the Western Caribbean and the Panama Canal.

In 1994, I was honored to represent the 101st Airborne Division as a guest of the French government to commemorate the 50th Anniversary of the June 6, 1944, D-Day invasion of Normandy, France. My wife and I will never forget that wonderful experience and the gracious reception we received on behalf of the French people. It was a moving and emotional moment that brought back a lot feelings as though it were only yesterday. Then, at various ceremonies and walking to different sites, fleeting instances rolled through my mind of all we did there fifty years ago, and all we left behind.

THE END

Colonel Edward Mehosky closes out his 31-year military career at EUCOM Headquarters, Patch Barracks, Stuttgart, Germany, 1971.